Intent to Deceive

Intent to Deceive

*Denying the Genocide
of the Tutsi*

Linda Melvern

VERSO
London • New York

First published by Verso 2020
© Linda Melvern 2020
Maps © Phillip Green 2020

1 3 5 7 9 10 8 6 4 2

Verso
UK: 6 Meard Street, London W1F 0EG
US: 20 Jay Street, Suite 1010, Brooklyn, NY 11201
versobooks.com

Verso is the imprint of New Left Books

ISBN-13: 978-1-78873-328-1
ISBN-13: 978-1-78873-330-4 (UK EBK)
ISBN-13: 978-1-78873-331-1 (US EBK)

British Library Cataloguing in Publication Data
A catalogue record for this book is available from the British Library

Library of Congress Cataloging-in-Publication Data
A catalog record for this book is available from the Library of Congress

Typeset in Sabon by MJ & N Gavan, Truro, Cornwall
Printed and bound by CPI Group (UK) Ltd, Croydon CR0 4YY

Contents

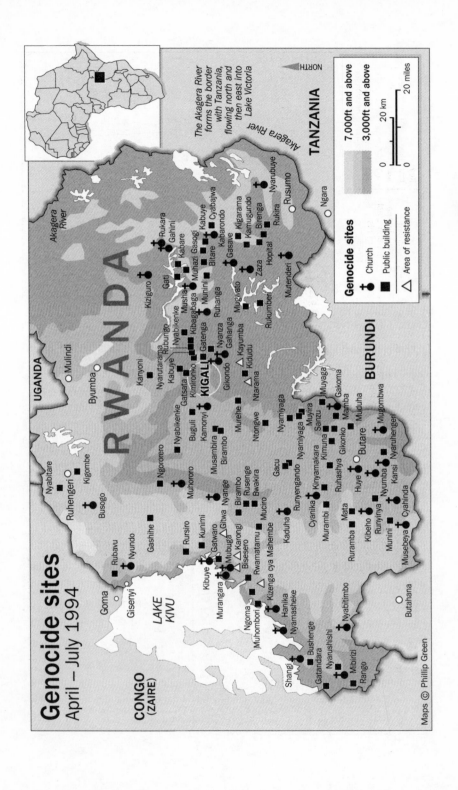

Genocide sites
April – July 1994

CONGO
(ZAIRE)

UGANDA

Goma
Giseny
Rubavu
Nyundo
Gashihe
Rursiro
Kunimi
Gatwaro
Kibuye
Murangara
Mubuga △Gitwa
△Karongi
Bisesero
Ngoma
Muhombori
Hanika
Nyamasheke
Shangi
Bushenge
Gatandara
Nyarushishi
Rango
Mibirizi

LAKE
KIVU

Nyabitare
Ruhengeri
Kigombe
Busogo
Ngororero
Munororo
Musambira
Birambo
Nyange
Birambo
Rusenge
Bwakira
Rwamatamu
Kizenga cya Mahembe
Muciro
Gacu
Kaduha
Nyabitimbo

Mulindi

Byumba

Kanyoni
Kabuye
Gatsata
Kimironko
KIGALI
Nyabikenke
Buguli
Kamonyi
Murehe
Ntongwe
Nyamiyaga
Muyira
Sanzu
Runyengando
Cyanika
Nyamiyaga
Kinyamakara
Kimuna
Muduha
Murambi
Mata
Ruramba
Kibeho
Runyinya
Munini
Musebeya
Cyahinda

RWANDA

Akagera
River

Kiziguro
Rukara
Gahini
Gati
Kabare
Musha
Muhazi Gasogi
Kabuye
Bitare
Cyabajwa
Kigarama
Kabarondo
Gasave
Munini
Ruhanga
Gasave
Zaza
Mugwato
Rukumberi
Hopital
Mutenderi

Nyarutarama
Rubungo
Nyabikenke
Kibagabaga
Gatenga
Nyanza
Gahanga
Kayumba
Gikondo
Ntarama △Kidutu
Kayumba

Nyaruje

Muyaga
Gakoma
Mamba
Muduha

Runyamiyaga

Ruhashya
Gikonko
Huye
Butare
Mugombwa
Nyamba
Nyaruhengeri
Kansi

BURUNDI

Butahana

Nyarubuye
Rusumo
Ngara

TANZANIA

The Akagera River
forms the border
with Tanzania,
flowing north and
then east into
Lake Victoria

Akagera River

NORTH

7,000ft and above
3,000ft and above

0   20 km
0   20 miles

Genocide sites

✝ Church
● Public building
■
△ Area of resistance

Maps © Phillip Green

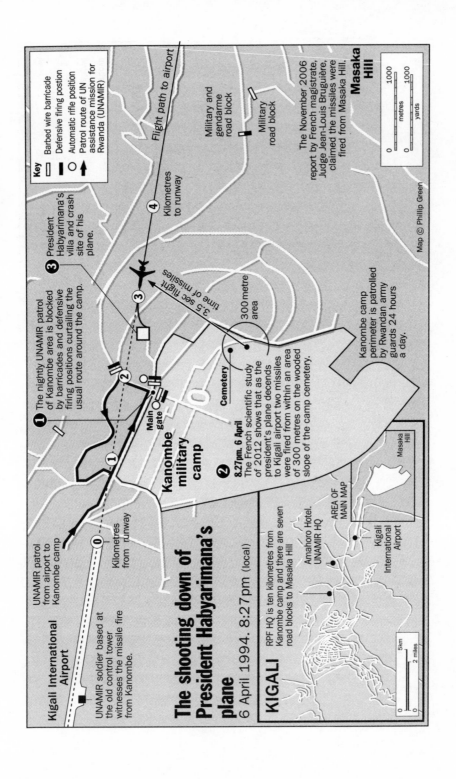

The shooting down of President Habyarimana's plane

6 April 1994. 8:27pm (local)

Kigali International Airport

UNAMIR patrol from airport to Kanombe camp

Kilometres from runway

UNAMIR soldier based at the old control tower witnesses the missile fire from Kanombe.

❶ The nightly UNAMIR patrol of Kanombe area is blocked by barricades and defensive firing positions curtailing the usual route around the camp.

❸ President Habyarimana's villa and crash site of his plane.

Flight path to airport

Kilometres to runway

Key
- Barbed wire barricade
- Defensive firing position
- ○ Automatic rifle position
- ➜ Patrol route of UN assistance mission for Rwanda (UNAMIR)

3.5 sec flight time of missiles

Main gate

Kanombe military camp

❷ **8:27pm. 6 April**
The French scientific study of 2012 shows that as the president's plane descends to Kigali airport two missiles were fired from within an area of 300 metres on the wooded slope of the camp cemetery.

300 metre area

Cemetery

Kanombe camp perimeter is patrolled by Rwandan army guards 24 hours a day.

Military and gendarme road block

Military road block

Masaka Hill

The November 2006 report by French magistrate, Judge Jean-Louis Bruguière, claimed the missiles were fired from Masaka Hill.

0 1000 metres
0 1000 yards

Map © Phillip Green

KIGALI
RPF HQ is ten kilometres from Kanombe camp and there are seven road blocks to Masaka Hill.

Amahoro Hotel. UNAMIR HQ

AREA OF MAIN MAP

Masaka Hill

Kigali International Airport

0 5km
0 2 miles

Introduction

It is twenty-five years since the genocide of the Tutsi of Rwanda in 1994, when in the course of three terrible months more than 1 million people were murdered in one of the most horrific crimes of modern history. The genocide was committed in the name of a racist ideology known as Hutu Power and, in a planned and political operation, the intention of the perpetrators was the elimination of a minority people.

The basic facts of the genocide of the Tutsi, documented and detailed in international inquiries, by journalists and contemporary historians, might seem incontrovertible. This has not prevented a pernicious campaign of propaganda that exists to undermine the established facts and minimise what occurred. This is genocide denial, and in its aid facts are reversed, disinformation and fake news promulgated, and phoney science given credence.

This book tells the story of the denial campaign waged by the Hutu Power movement and designed to knowingly deceive public opinion. With contempt for factual evidence the perpetrators of this genocide have tried to alter the story, diminishing the death toll, claiming the killing was in self-defence, and blaming the victims. They have talked of 'mutual violence' and tried to explain the huge number of dead as the result of 'inter-ethnic war'. They have claimed that the killing of Tutsi was a response to the fear and chaos of war and that there was no central planning for any of the massacres. The génocidaires continue to maintain that the mass murder of Tutsi resulted from a 'spontaneous uprising' by an angry population. They argue there was no genocide of the Tutsi. With no planning or preparation, they argue the intent to destroy a human group was lacking, and so with no intent, the 1948 Genocide Convention does not apply.

The idea of a spontaneous slaughter is not borne out by direct witnesses, by survivors or by the collective research of internationally recognised experts.

There is nothing spontaneous about genocide. The father of the 1948 Genocide Convention, a Polish lawyer, Raphael Lemkin, described the crime as the result of a coordinated plan of action, and not a sudden and abominable aberration. Genocide arises from a conspiracy against people who are chosen as victims because they are members of a target group. The destruction of a human group, in whole or in part, requires effective propaganda to spread a racist ideology that defines the victim as being outside human existence. It requires a dependence on military security and a certainty that outside interference will be at a minimum.

The génocidaires of Rwanda were masters of deceit. These skilled propagandists created a powerful weapon, the hate radio RTLM, the voice of genocide, providing a steady stream of fake news. The génocidaires used sophisticated information management. With disinformation they camouflaged their coup d'état, pretended the elimination of the political opposition was unexpected 'political violence', and claimed at the outset to have been 'powerless' in the face of a series of catastrophic events.

In a masterstroke of public relations, the génocidaires placed the United Nations at the centre of their plans. They used their membership of the Security Council to promote genocide denial. The blueprint for their denial campaign was found in UN documents, in the diplomatic language of cables and letters, and in archives abandoned in Rwandan embassies abroad. As the death toll increased through April 1994, Rwanda's diplomats explained how there were 'victims on all sides'. The génocidaires turned the Security Council into a global forum to give voice to a genocidal regime whose sole policy was the extermination of a part of the population.

~

Denial is an integral part of genocide. One of the pre-eminent scholars of the crime, US professor Gregory Stanton, describes it as a process in ten stages. The crime begins with the classification of the population, proceeds to the symbolisation of those classifications, and includes discrimination against a targeted group, the dehumanisation of the pariah group. The crime requires organisation, the polarisation of the population, preparation by killers, the persecution of the victims, and the extermination of the victims. The denial of the crime is a part of the process. Denial ensures the continuation of the crime once it is initiated. It incites new killing. It denies the dignity of the deceased and mocks those who survived. In all cases, the final stage of genocide is the denial it ever happened.

The perpetrators of genocide rarely show remorse. Instead, they use deceit to deny the crime, to try to prove that events have been misinterpreted. In the case of Rwanda, there were numerous supporters who rallied to the Hutu Power cause. Like those who tried to prove the gassings exaggerated in the Nazi concentration camps, they too were determined to minimise, obscure and diminish what happened. In the trials of the génocidaires at the International Criminal Tribunal for Rwanda (ICTR), there has been no shortage of scholars, regional experts, journalists and military officers to appear in court in their defence.

While the public face of Hutu Power has been the brutal militia in the DRC, the Forces Démocratiques pour la Libération du Rwanda (FDLR), a direct descendant of the army responsible for the 1994 genocide, a covert campaign has sought to inflict reputational damage using information warfare. Both parts of the Hutu Power movement, military and civilian, rely on the same racist ideology that underpinned the genocide, that 'the Hutu' constituted the majority, a distinct, homogeneous political category, and that political parties and therefore governments needed to reflect perceived Hutu–Tutsi divisions.

In the aftermath of the genocide of the Tutsi, the plans for a campaign of genocide denial devised in the refugee camps in the DRC were found in documents abandoned by the génocidaires, along with evidence of efforts to counter the 'false UN claims of genocide'. A collection of documents from the National Archives of Rwanda revealed the disinformation strategies used at the UN and diplomatic instructions to further that denial issued by Hutu Power's so-called Interim Government.

The pernicious influence of Hutu Power lives on in rumour, stereotype, lies and propaganda. The movement's campaign of genocide denial has confused many, recruited some, and shielded others. With the use of seemingly sound research methods, the génocidaires pose a threat, especially to those who might not be aware of the historical facts. The pain caused to survivors is incalculable because the purpose is to destroy truth and memory – the final stage of the genocide process.

1

Prime Suspects

On 19 February 1995, Colonel Théoneste Bagosora boarded a Cameroon Airlines flight in Kinshasa, Zaire, bound for Douala, the largest city in Cameroon. A frequent visitor, he had come to meet the remnants of the leadership of Hutu Power, a genocidal movement forced out of Rwanda whose former dignitaries now lived with their families in quiet residential districts in southwest Douala and in the capital city, Yaoundé, in expensive villas and apartments funded by loot stolen from Rwandan state coffers.[1]

These were wanted men, many of whom were prime suspects for the genocide of the Tutsi of Rwanda that took place from 6 April to 18 July 1994. They were army officers, former government ministers, lawyers, officials, politicians, civil authorities, propagandists and mass killers. An investigation at the crime scene had uncovered proof of their criminal conspiracy. This included damning documentation that proved the physical liquidation of the Tutsi people was a carefully planned political strategy, designed well in advance.

Their motive was to monopolise power in Rwanda, while the means was a youth militia trained to kill at speed. Here was concrete evidence of 'massive breaches in 1948 Genocide Convention', which had achieved the fastest murder rate of human beings recorded, exceeding that established by the Nazis during the Holocaust.[2] Hutu Power was responsible for the largest known child slaughter to date; the majority of the more than 1 million victims were aged between zero and fourteen years old, thus destroying any future of the Tutsi group.

The French expert Gérard Prunier in his 1998 account believed these criminals turned Rwanda into a sadomasochistic inferno.[3]

By 1995, the perpetrators had fled the crime scene. Those who planned, financed, instigated, ordered, committed or otherwise aided and abetted the extermination of Tutsi were gone by the end of the year, now dispersed across various countries. Among those who retreated was a significant group of genocide suspects who settled in Cameroon and, in doing so, did not bother to hide their identities.

When Bagosora, the so-called mastermind of this great crime, landed at Douala International Airport on 19 February, he was recognised by a young Rwandan physician on the same flight who watched as one of the world's most wanted men sailed through immigration controls.[4] The doctor, who was visiting Cameroon for an international AIDS conference, quickly noticed a number of genocide suspects living in Yaoundé during his short stay and informed the Cameroon Foreign Ministry during a hastily arranged meeting, yet no one seemed to care. As the weeks passed, Rwandan fugitives further integrated into newfound communities while their children settled at local schools. They invested in small businesses; they opened shops and created transport companies. They tried to keep a low profile.

Their anonymity did not last. On 25 July 1995, a Yaoundé biweekly newspaper, *La Nouvelle Expression*, named forty-four Rwandan 'genocide suspects' hiding out in Cameroon. The list served as a who's who of the most powerful figures of the Hutu Power movement, with a catalogue of criminal charges including genocide and crimes against humanity, murder, extermination, rape, persecution and other inhumane acts.[5] The newspaper then accused Paul Biya, president of Cameroon, of harbouring international criminals.

At the top of the list was Bagosora, who had assumed de facto control of Rwanda's military and political affairs as the genocide began, and is wanted by authorities in Belgium for the 7 April 1994 murder of ten peacekeepers of Belgian nationality who had been serving with the UN Assistance Mission for Rwanda (UNAMIR). Another notable suspect on the paper's list was Major Protais Mpiranya, former commander of the French-trained Presidential Guard Battalion, wanted for elimination of the political opposition starting in the early hours of 7 April.[6]

In addition, the newspaper named Hutu Power lawyer Jean-Bosco Barayagwiza, creator of the Coalition pour la Défense de la République (CDR), an overtly crypto-fascist gang of middle-class professionals that resembled the Ku Klux Klan. The chief ideologue of Hutu Power, Ferdinand Nahimana, was also listed as being in Cameroon. A professor of history, Nahimana was responsible for the notorious hate radio station Radio-Télévision Libre des Mille Collines (RTLM), which broadcast propaganda portraying Tutsi as subhuman vermin. The 'Goebbels of Rwanda', Nahimana was a proven expert in fake news and disinformation, using the airwaves to spread fear and terror among the population.[7] Meanwhile, his professional career afforded academic legitimacy to his argument that the Tutsi were a different 'race' from elsewhere in Africa. National unity between these 'two races' was just a myth.[8]

La Nouvelle Expression issued a warning: these fugitives remained politically active, having recently rebranded their image in an attempt to distance themselves from Hutu Power. They had created a new political party, the Rassemblement pour le Rétour des Réfugiés et la Démocratie au Rwanda (RDR), purporting to be a legitimate organisation. Their use of the word 'democracy' increased, and meanwhile they portrayed themselves as 'victims' in a 'Rwandan drama', describing the killing of civilians in 1994 as a 'spontaneous uprising', its death toll exaggerated. A story about 'genocide' had managed to fool the 'pro-Tutsi' Western media, they argued.

While in Cameroon, Bagosora found time to write and disseminate his own version of the denial. A photocopied book of some thirty typed pages cheaply bound in plastic was distributed throughout the Hutu Power network and diplomatic community. The author stated his desire to ensure that the 'international community' knew the 'distant origins' of Rwandan events, that they understood the different phases of the 'conflict between Hutu and Tutsi', that peace was only achievable under rule by the Hutu, the country's 'majority people'. 'The Tutsi are the masters of deceit,' he wrote, 'even going as far as comparing themselves with the Jews of Europe to gain the sympathy of this powerful lobby. But the Tutsi have never had a country of their own. With their arrogance and pride they are trying to impose their supremacy in the region.'

Meanwhile, Bagosora described the Hutu as 'modest, candid, loyal, independent and impulsive', the unwitting victims of Tutsi perfidy. He warned the international community to watch out for these 'inveterate liars' with their false information. The Tutsi, he explained, were from Ethiopia and should have sought peaceful coexistence with those who welcomed them to Rwanda; instead, with their pride and arrogance, they were trying to impose their 'supremacy' in the region. His account of early April 1994, when Hutu Power seized control, was notable for its disinformation and false alibis. Indeed, Bagosora's version of history – that a 'spontaneous uprising' caused 'excessive massacres' – later formed the basis of his defence during his legal trial.[9]

Hutu Power had promised utopian national salvation. Yet, in August 1994, a description of post-genocide Rwanda was relayed to Washington from US Assistant Secretary of State for Democracy, Human Rights and Labor John Shattuck, who wrote of a 'country devoid of human life, depopulated by machete ... the equivalent of a neutron bomb'.[10] 'All power is Hutu Power,' the gangs of youths had chanted in the weeks leading up to the event while they terrorised the streets on motorbikes and in military jeeps, drinking beer, hurling vulgarities at Tutsi, waving machetes. 'Power, power,' they shouted. 'Oh, let us exterminate them.' When the time came, they did.[11]

The task of apprehending the principal perpetrators of the 1994 Tutsi genocide fell to the UN Security Council. Having spectacularly failed to prevent genocide in Rwanda, the Council membership was especially keen to fulfil at least one part of the 1948 Genocide Convention by punishing those responsible; but the initial approach was cautious.[12] An Independent Commission of Experts was established on 1 July 1994, in order to accrue evidence, resulting in reports confirming that massive violations of the 1948 Genocide Convention had occurred.[13] Here was documentary evidence of a plan for genocide against the Tutsi, with an astonishing level of organisation, political resolve and a clear determination to try to wipe out the minority. The extermination of Tutsi was explicitly motivated by 'ethnic hatred', it reported, fuelled by racist propaganda disseminated widely in order to further dehumanise the people. A camp was discovered where Hutu Power indoctrination of the unemployed youth had taken place, where the militia trained in mass murder. Experts described the massacres as having been 'concerted, planned, systematic and methodical', the extermination clearly premeditated.[14] The methods for killing large numbers of Tutsi civilians had been tried and tested in the previous three years, and had followed a familiar pattern throughout.

It was recommended by the Commission of Experts that the Security Council take all necessary and effective action to ensure that those responsible for the 1994 Tutsi genocide were brought to justice.[15] The Security Council responded by creating the International Criminal Tribunal for Rwanda (ICTR) on 8 November 1994, the second such tribunal in history after the International Criminal Tribunal for the former Yugoslavia (ICTY, established 25 May 1993).

It was a huge experiment. The New Zealand ambassador, Colin Keating, president of the Security Council at the time of the genocide in April 1994, recalled: 'For a lot of the permanent members of the Security Council, there was a sense of guilt or responsibility about the failure to stop the genocide. New Zealand seized ownership of the issue and drove the process.'[16] David Scheffer, the first United States ambassador-at-large for war crimes issues, later wrote of his hopes for 'a powerful Nuremberg-like signal sent to the people of Rwanda'. International support for the tribunal was not purely a function of high-minded idealism.[17]

There were doubts, however, that such a tribunal could ever be organised. The first anniversary of the start of the genocide took

place on 7 April 1995, and along came public speeches promis-
ing the arrest of the perpetrators, yet there were no arrests. Not
one legal action against any Rwandan fugitive in any country in
the world, under any jurisdiction, had taken place. One prosecutor worked alone in an otherwise empty office in Kigali.[18] The
ICTR faced logistical and financial issues. For reasons that remain
unclear, the staffing of the prosecutor's office – the recruitment,
hiring and deployment of personnel – encountered significant
delays. This was an embarrassment for the Security Council,
accused of a parody of justice for Rwanda, with no power
or muscle.[19]

The task of putting the perpetrators on trial was huge, with an
initial list of four hundred category-one suspects produced by the
ICTR in January 1995. These were the main perpetrators: those
who planned the killing and were in command positions before
and during the genocide; those who incited or directed others to
take part; those in positions of power both locally and nation-
ally, who sought to gain personal advantage.[20] These suspects had
scattered across Cameroon, Kenya, France, Belgium and Canada,
while others had arrived in the UK and the Netherlands and
gained refugee status in countries with little previous knowledge
of Rwandan politics.[21] The London-based human rights group
African Rights, known for its remarkable early work documenting the terrible reality of the genocide of the Tutsi with testimonies
and eyewitness accounts, accused countries of harbouring known
killers.[22] African Rights knew the names of suspects, and accused
the United Nations of not taking seriously the pursuit of genocide
fugitives despite extensive evidence from witnesses and survivors,
not least the mass graves that littered Rwanda.

In early 1995, the US brought the issue of the scandalous, continuing freedom of Rwandan genocide fugitives to the Security
Council and proposed that all member states should be called
upon to arrest and detain those suspected of genocide, recalling
the 1948 Genocide Convention. The US wanted the resolution
to be legally binding in order to provide UN member states with
the authorisation to detain suspects immediately if found on
their territory. In addition, it was argued that the ICTR should

have time to prepare cases and issue formal indictments, with the overall aim of global cooperation in tracking down the suspects through coordination with the ICTR's chief prosecutor, Richard Goldstone.

The French objected, however. Their UN ambassador, Jean-Bernard Mérimée, told the Security Council he could not approve of any 'detention' resolution invoking the enforcement provision of the UN Charter.[23] A US ambassador, David Scheffer, later remarked, 'One of our closest allies appeared determined to act as an accomplice in facilitating the génocidaires' freedom.'[24]

Regardless, when the French made what the US called an 'anemic proposal', the US went ahead and voted for it. Resolution 978, on 27 February 1995, carried a 'request' to states. Non-binding in nature, it provided for the detention of international fugitives to be in accordance with national laws. France initially argued for the Council to issue a Presidential Statement, which carries much less weight than a resolution, to 'remind' states of their duties. French policy on the detention issue was made clear in July 1994 when they told the Council their judiciary had no authority to arrest Rwandan suspects on French soil, because French law had not adopted the 1948 Genocide Convention.

The US State Department determined France to be a 'key player' on the issue of Rwanda. In a declassified cable dated 12 July 1994, it was speculated that France 'may have the most complete information of any Western government on war crimes in Rwanda and access to witnesses, evidence and even perpetrators'.[25] France had been an ally of 'Hutu nationalism', and long-term cordial relations existed between Hutu Power fanatics at senior level and French military officers and diplomats. In the Security Council the French were skittish over the detention of genocide suspects; the US believed this was because France was a safe haven for Hutu Power fugitives.[26] The sanctuary accorded to Hutu Power in Cameroon was due solely to that country's close relationship with France. As a Francophone nation, Cameroon had benefited from French investment into French-speaking African nations and former colonies, primarily through military and financial aid.[27]

Attempts to apprehend Rwandan fugitives faltered. The US managed to identify four Rwandan suspects in Cameroon, and subsequently sent their names in a cable, dated 13 April 1995, from the State Department to the US embassy in Yaoundé. US ambassador Harriet Winsar Isom urged the government in Cameroon to apprehend the fugitives. At the same time, she reminded the government of the need for international justice, and for clear signals to those who committed genocide and other atrocities that they would not escape.[28] In accordance with instructions, she told the government of Cameroon that not arresting these four suspects breached UN Security Council resolution 978.

It was a toothless resolution; the French version simply urged member states to arrest and detain anyone present in their territory 'against whom sufficient evidence existed that they were responsible for genocide and other systematic, widespread and flagrant violations of international humanitarian law committed in Rwanda in 1994'. A minimal response from Cameroon resulted. While the authorities refused the applications for asylum submitted by the four named fugitives, they were otherwise left in peace.

As the second anniversary of the genocide of the Tutsi approached, there was debate among the US mission to the UN in New York about the possibility of sanctions against Cameroon for harbouring international criminals. This increased embarrassment for the Cameroonian president Paul Biya, who was preparing to host the thirty-third heads of state summit of the Organisation of African Unity (OAU) that summer. In response, Biya asked to see the evidence the Belgian judicial authorities possessed on Bagosora's crimes. He also sought assurances in response to an extradition request from Rwanda that they would not execute Bagosora without a fair trial.

It was surprising, nonetheless, that on Sunday, 10 March 1996, gendarmes in Cameroon detained Bagosora trying to cash American Express travellers' cheques previously stolen from the Rwandan Treasury. Furthermore, two weeks after taking Bagosora into custody, gendarmes detained eleven Rwandans in Yaoundé in a dawn raid, a secret operation that involved the personal support of the justice minister, Douala Moutomé, and was carried out by one hundred carefully chosen officers. Seven fugitives managed to escape.[29]

The eleven Rwandan detainees were taken to Kondengui, a top-security prison in Yaoundé, where they were reunited with Bagosora. From the prison, the group immediately set about a press campaign. Within days, an exclusive newspaper interview had achieved maximum publicity. The *Cameroon Tribune* ran a banner headline on the front page of the newspaper on 8 April 1996, timed to coincide with the second commemoration of the genocide, 'The twelve Rwandans detained in Yaoundé speak out'. There was an astonishing photograph alongside the headline, a shot of twelve smiling, overweight middle-aged men. Bagosora wore a white tracksuit, not concealing his paunch, standing slightly in front of the others. He stared straight ahead, hands behind his back. In a row behind stood the others, most of them in shorts and short-sleeved summer shirts, sunglasses and sandals. They appeared in a spacious courtyard, sequestered from the deprivations of local prisoners.[30] In the interview, the detainees explained the Rwandan situation was complicated and not properly understood. There had been 'inter-ethnic' killings, and they were in prison as a result of false accusations.

This was followed, in May, by an article that appeared in a pro-government journal, *Africa International,* that gave the prisoners further support. In it, they were portrayed as 'refugees' who were imprisoned for dubious reasons. They were 'Hutu intellectuals' who occupied high government office, and had been 'demonised in the eyes of international public opinion'. There was an attempt, they claimed, to criminalise the entire Hutu political and intellectual elite.[31]

In the confusion, there were conflicting claims concerning the twelve Rwandan detainees held in Yaoundé. The Belgian government wanted to put Théoneste Bagosora on trial in Brussels and a judicial investigation was well under way into his role in the murders of ten UN peacekeepers of Belgian nationality. At the same time, there was a request for the extradition of all twelve from the government in Rwanda, brought personally to Cameroon by the foreign minister, Anastase Gasana. His visit coincided with that of Judge Richard Goldstone, the new chief prosecutor of the ICTR, who came to Cameroon to claim international jurisdiction. In July 1996, in deference to the ICTR, Belgium dropped its request for the extradition of Bagosora.

The continuing delay in taking any suspects into international custody was of increasing concern at the ICTR. Among the newly appointed international judges, the Swedish Lennart Aspegren thought these delays served to weaken international justice. In an unprecedented move, in June 1996 he travelled to Yaoundé with a group of ICTR legal officers. With the help of officials in the Cameroon Ministry of Justice, they gained access to four of the detainees, and Judge Aspegren convened a special session of the ICTR in the office of the governor of the prison, during which he ordered the continued detention on remand of four of them: André Ntagerura, the former minister of transport and communication; Colonel Anatole Nsengiyumva, a former head of military intelligence; Théoneste Bagosora; and Ferdinand Nahimana.[32]

Aspegren then formally arrested Bagosora and Nahimana. He also requested that the Cameroon government comply with an order for the transfer of Bagosora to stand trial at the ICTR. In October 1996, the first registrar of the ICTR, Andronico Adede, a Kenyan lawyer, went to Cameroon to ask for the transfer of Bagosora into international custody. He waited in vain for three days for an audience with Cameroon's justice minister.[33] President Paul Biya finally signed extradition papers the following year and Bagosora, Nahimana, André Ntagerura and Colonel Anatole Nsengiyumva were flown in handcuffs to Arusha, Tanzania, on 23 January 1997 and locked inside a UN detention facility. The eight remaining Rwandans in Yaoundé were released a month later, yet were held nearly a year on international arrest warrants issued by Rwanda. Almost immediately after the release, Jean-Bosco Barayagwiza was rearrested and detained following an urgent message from the prosecutor at the ICTR, Louise Arbour.

It was in the dusty backwater of the Tanzanian town of Arusha that the ICTR made its home and that the suspects waited for their trials to begin.[34] Here, they were provided with teams of lawyers and investigators paid for from the public purse in order to mount a vigorous defence. Some of the detainees took time away from these legal matters and wrote books and articles, continuing their public relations campaign to try to change the 'negative press coverage'. They continued to argue that a genocide story was encouraged by the United Nations, and that victims existed 'on all sides' in Rwanda; they advised against apportioning blame because this made reconciliation impossible.

Here, their denial campaign entered a new phase.

2

Propaganda Wars

From the moment the leadership of Hutu Power seized control of the state, it had determined to distort the reality of events to the outside world. The UN was central to these plans. By some terrible irony, in January 1994, three months before the mass extermination of Tutsi began, the UN General Assembly had elected Rwanda to one of the fifteen non-permanent seats on the UN Security Council, despite the numerous reports of human rights violations taking place there. As a result, three months later, when in April Hutu Power hastily installed its genocidal Interim Government, its presence in the Security Council assured it the international legitimacy it craved. Throughout the genocide, all UN member states and official bodies recognised this Hutu Power government and this allowed Hutu Power the opportunity to spread its fake news in the hallways of the UN and in meetings of the Security Council. It was here that Hutu Power pulled off its greatest coup, a propaganda masterstroke bringing genocide denial to the heart of the UN. We can only speculate on the reports sent back to Kigali by Rwanda's UN ambassador, Jean-Damascène Bizimana, who sat in all the Council's daily informal and secret discussions. He fled New York afterwards, taking his documents with him. By all accounts he was a dutiful and a constant presence. Bizimana would have noted the weariness in the Council with African civil wars, and the overriding interest among the Council in the wars of former Yugoslavia. He must have calculated the fears of peacekeeping casualties in the wake of the catastrophic attempts at nation building in Somalia, an idea enthusiastically supported by the US until eighteen of its soldiers were murdered. It would not have escaped him how little his colleagues in the Council really knew about Rwanda and the Secretariat's dismal failure to prepare options for action.[1] He must have noted the little time reserved for Rwanda.

On Good Friday, 1 April 1994, the United Nations Secretariat closed for the Easter holidays. The presidency of the Council, a position that changed on the first day of every month by alphabetical rotation, fell to New Zealand, whose ambassador was a young diplomat and lawyer, Colin Keating. On Saturday, 2 April, Keating received a telephone call at home to tell him Serb forces in Bosnia had begun a massive military attack on Goražde, one of six designated UN protected areas, and UN commanders requested NATO close air support. The scepticism about the ability of UN peacekeepers to deter attacks against civilians in these Council-designated so-called safe areas was well founded. The European civil war dominated Council time and attention, and forty-eight hours earlier the Council had extended the mandate for the United Nations Protection Force (UNPROFOR) in former Yugoslavia and approved an additional 3,500 troops, bringing the force to 38,000, the largest UN mission anywhere.[2]

Low on the Council agenda was the small peacekeeping mission created for Rwanda, the UN Assistance Mission for Rwanda (UNAMIR), at peak military strength of 2,548, that was monitoring a peace agreement that had ended a three-year civil war. At the outset, there had been high hopes that this mission would salvage the battered reputation of UN peacekeeping. Its task seemed unambiguous. This was classic peacekeeping. A handshake between two former enemies and a joint visit to New York by representatives of the protagonists, the Rwandan government and the Rwandan Patriotic Front (RPF), was accompanied by a joint request for UN help. The UN mission was needed to monitor the application of the Arusha Accords, a landmark peace agreement credited as one of the best in Africa.

The UNAMIR mandate was due for discussion and renewal in the Council on Tuesday, 5 April, and so during the Easter holiday weekend Keating dipped into some historical papers about Rwanda and the civil war that had begun on 1 October 1990, when a rebel force, the Rwandan Patriotic Army (RPA), crossed into Rwanda over the northern border with Uganda. The RPA was the armed wing of a political movement dedicated to the return home of an estimated 900,000 Rwandan refugees, the stateless and exiled families who had fled murderous anti-Tutsi purges that began in 1959. Denied the right of return, they comprised the continent's largest refugee crisis and, over thirty years, the United Nations High Commissioner for Refugees (UNHCR) registered Rwandan refugees in Uganda, Burundi, Zaire and Tanzania.

The small rebel force comprising the children of these exiles that crossed the northern border with an estimated 4,000 soldiers and 120 officers had big ambitions. With its political wing, the RPF, the movement was widely perceived as Tutsi but nonetheless it included a number of prominent Hutu opponents of then President Juvénal Habyarimana. The RPF wanted a new Rwanda and demanded an end to the ethnic divide and an end to a government system that required compulsory identity cards with an ethnic designation. It wanted an end to the institutionalised ethnic quotas, used to restrict the presence of Tutsi in education and employment that served to reinforce a racist ideology that two distinct ethnic groups existed. It wanted an end to the misuse of public offices and funds, and an end to the twenty-year murderous and corrupt power of a northern Hutu clique within the presidential family known as the Akazu.

The RPA was unique. It was a guerrilla army created in a neighbouring state, within the ranks of the Ugandan army. When the RPA launched its military offensive from Uganda, it included several thousand troops from the National Resistance Army (NRA) of Uganda. The young Rwandans had enlisted from refugee camps in order to obtain military training and they now deserted and crossed into Rwanda taking their weapons and supplies, ripped the Ugandan military insignia from their uniforms and, together with medical doctors, scouts and messengers, finally declared their true purpose – a return home by force.

The resulting civil war between the RPA and the Rwandan Government Army (RGF) of President Habyarimana was a disaster. The RGF did manage initially to defeat the RPA but only because of substantial help from France, including the dispatch of French forces. With French help, Rwanda's army rapidly increased in size and in the next two years grew in all ranks from 5,000 to 28,000 and, thanks to France, Egypt and South Africa, was equipped with modern weaponry. Rwanda, one of the poorest of the world's countries, became the third-largest importer of weapons on the African continent, partly by using money siphoned from loans from the IMF.

After an initial defeat, within weeks, the RPA had regrouped and rearmed, and a former Ugandan major and Rwandan refugee, Major General Paul Kagame, took command and reorganised the forces into mobile guerrilla groups, creating a flexible force structure that contributed to the RPA success against government forces. With continued help from the Ugandan military, the RPA was transformed into a 15,000-strong disciplined light infantry army that relied on resupply by foot. The army also had extraordinary endurance levels and was highly motivated. While the government in Kigali built up its military strength, the RPA continued to mount attacks from territory it held inside Rwanda and along the Ugandan border.

In February 1993, the RPA launched a massive offensive with 8,000 troops, the biggest military operation ever on Rwandan soil, and drove back the government army. The continuing massacre of Tutsi civilians by elements of the RGF was the reason given for the military offensive. The invasion created a wave of terrified people fleeing south, adding to the misery of those already displaced by civil war. One million people were now homeless – one-seventh of Rwanda's population. Families were driven to live in huge camps where children were dying of starvation and dysentery, dependent on food aid for their survival. An exodus from fertile land, and fears that because of drought the next harvest could be down by 40 per cent, were accompanied by predictions of widespread famine. There was growing violence in society, with an increase in weapons in civilian hands.

The fighting in February 1993 between the RPA and government forces ended once again with a last-ditch military intervention by the French. The offensive had given the RPA significant military advantage on the ground, which then aided ongoing peace negotiations. According to a UK declassified cable, the RPF asked for a guarantee of an end to the 'genocide' of the Tutsi and wanted the replacement of local officials where killings of Tutsi had happened. They were horrified at what was happening in Rwanda but did not want to lose all that had been achieved in the peace talks, resulting in the Arusha Accords.[3]

The Arusha Accords were signed in August 1993. They provided for the demobilisation of both armies, the repatriation of an estimated 1 million refugees, and democratic elections to create a power-sharing government. The once all-powerful presidency was to become largely ceremonial. The French military forces would leave, the armies of the RPF and the Rwandan army would integrate, and there would be disarmament and demobilisation. A battalion of RPF soldiers would be stationed in Kigali. All this was to be achieved in the space of twenty-two months, the agreement to be monitored by a UN peacekeeping force.

That Easter weekend in New York, the more Keating read about Rwanda, the worse he realised the situation was. The reports provided by the UN Secretariat were of poor quality, offering little analysis on the implication of events, and UN officials seemed overly eager to present good news. It was far too simple to categorise this as a civil war – rather, ethnic violence was a central feature of Rwandan politics. As a result, the reports provided by officials in the UN Secretariat significantly underestimated the ethnic complexity of the situation. 'I was surprised to learn that the previous instability had involved mass murder of Tutsi civilians that seemed to verge on genocide,' Keating wrote later.[4]

When he looked back twenty years later, Keating described how the officials in the UN Secretariat portrayed the Arusha Accords as an 'unvarnished success story that would put an end to a highly destructive civil war'. The agreement was presented 'as though it were gold', Keating said.[5] However, the ambassadors in the Security Council failed to do due diligence about the quality of the advice given. More careful consideration should have been paid to the terms of the Arusha Accords, as well as to the needs and realities on the ground. Keating said that the situation was more dangerous and complex than was ever presented to the members of the Council.

Crucially, missing from the background information provided by the UN Secretariat was a series of landmark human rights reports. In August 1993, an investigation into allegations of grave and massive violations of the right to life in Rwanda was under-taken by the Special Rapporteur on extrajudicial, summary or arbitrary executions for the Commission on Human Rights, Bacre Waly Ndiaye.[6] The report explored the use of propaganda by the Rwandan government to create a situation in which 'all Tutsi inside the country were collectively labelled accomplices with the RPF'. It described a Hutu elite that, in order to cling to power, was fuelling ethnic hatred. On civilian massacres, Ndiaye wrote: 'Such outbreaks were planned and prepared, with targets being identi-fied in speeches by representatives of the authorities, broadcasts on Rwanda radio, and leaflets ... [and] the persons perpetrating the massacres were under organised leadership'. Local govern-ment officials were found to have played a leading role in most cases. Although advised against using the word 'genocide' by superiors in the Secretariat in Geneva, he went ahead anyway.[7] He reported that the 1948 Genocide Convention was applicable to describe killings that were taking place in Rwanda. For all the attention this report received at the time, Ndiaye later said he might as well have thrown it into the sea. It was published just as the Arusha Accords were signed, and from then on all efforts were concentrated on a rushed and desperate effort to implement the new deal.

In addition to this brief, six more crucial human rights reports were not mentioned.[8] These documented the impunity that accompanied massacres of Tutsi carried out in 1959, in 1963, in 1973, in 1991 and in 1992. In each case no one was brought to justice. For example, in January 1993, an international coalition of Western human rights groups went to Rwanda to investigate human rights abuses.[9] Among the observers was William Schabas, a Canadian lawyer from the International Centre for Human Rights and Democratic Development, who argued strongly for the word 'genocide' to be used. However, in the end Human Rights Watch, part of the investigating commission, resisted the use of the word in the final report and it was omitted. The conclusion of the international coalition was that those who held power in Rwanda had organised the killing of some 2,000 Tutsi. 'If we had known what we now know', Keating said of the UN mission, 'I am sure we would have all come to the conclusion that a Chapter VI mandate and 2,600 soldiers was simply not good enough for the job.'

Another fault line appeared on 21 October 1993, with the assassination of the president of neighbouring Burundi, Melchior Ndadaye. His death ended a five-month-old experiment in democratic power-sharing. Ndadaye had symbolised historic unity, a Hutu elected in a country traditionally ruled by Tutsi, and Burundi had made startling progress towards a multiparty democratic form of government, holding the most successful elections since independence in July 1962.

The assassination was believed to have been part of an abortive coup by a Tutsi-dominated army, and it generated a month of mass killings of civilians with an estimated death toll of 150,000–200,000 people from both Hutu and Tutsi groups. There were refugee camps created in southern Rwanda for the estimated 350,000 people who fled Burundi during the violence. In Kigali, the announcers on RTLM in news bulletins and in phone-ins continually blamed the assassination in the neighbouring state on progressive politics and on the 'reconciliation' with Tutsi. The station's journalists told listeners the assassination was part of a plot aimed at the elimination of all Hutu. The Tutsi intended to dominate the entire region to create a 'Tutsi-land'.

The Security Council launched UNAMIR with much reluctance. By now, the Arusha Accords were seriously delayed and violence in Rwanda was on the increase. A CIA background paper, since partly declassified, blamed delays on President Habyarimana, who had procrastinated and stalled, and manipulated the political parties to cause delay.[10] Once established, the US then lobbied for UNAMIR to close. The administration of President Bill Clinton was keen to show Congress it could get tough at the UN, and UNAMIR appeared the ideal choice for closure. The Clinton administration saw an escalation in the cost of UN peacekeeping, and the US was liable for one-third of the total UN peacekeeping bill. This was the eighteenth UN mission in five years.

In return for Washington's unwilling support of UNAMIR, the Council agreed a short mandate that would need renewal by the Council every few months. Keating said this meant the US had the ultimate negotiating leverage when it came to the size of the force, what the force would do, and its future.[11] Keating believed the US and France reached a secret deal, and France, in order to obtain US support for UNAMIR, agreed to keep the mission on a short leash.[12] France was keener than others on UNAMIR. It wanted to salvage its interests in Rwanda by promoting a negotiated settlement on terms favourable to its ally, the Hutu regime of President Habyarimana. The French hoped that the UN troops might be a buffer against the RPA, perceived as an army intent on a Tutsi takeover of the region. They therefore campaigned for the UN to freeze the military situation before the RPA advanced any further.

France further guaranteed Rwanda that her position as a permanent member of the Security Council insured that their concerns would be taken into account in the mandate and deployment of any UN force. On 5 April 1993, France argued for a six-month extension of the mandate but, in the end, the only basis upon which both the US and the UK agreed to extend UNAMIR's mandate was to give it a short lease of life. In Security Council resolution 909, voted on 5 April, UNAMIR was given only six weeks. Unless the peace agreement was back on track by then, UNAMIR would pull out. The US ambassador, Madeleine Albright, explained that the US was prepared to help only those who helped themselves, and perhaps the Rwandan people were not serious about peace.

Keating said later, 'We only dimly perceived the steady deterio-
ration. The deeper and more dangerous problem of a monumental
threat to human life was ignored.'[13] With better information, the
Council might have proceeded quite differently, he said. Instead, it
proceeded on the assumption that the various parties in Rwanda
really wanted peace. Keating added, 'But now we know that the
opposite was the case. The hard-line Hutu did not want peace and
they had access to a privileged insider's view of the discussions in
the Council.'

By the time the UN peacekeepers arrived in Rwanda at the end
of 1993, it was probably too late for peacekeeping. The Hutu
Power extremists had their own plans, beginning a policy of denigration of the Arusha Accords, encouraging violence against Tutsi
and their murder, seeking a slide back into conflict. The extremists around Habyarimana saw the power-sharing concessions in
the Accords as a sellout. Habyarimana, who had held power on
behalf of the Akazu, the northern mafia, for twenty years, had
been forced into political multiparty recognition and political
reforms, and power-sharing with the RPF, but was looking for a
way out.

It had not taken Lieutenant General Roméo Dallaire, the
Canadian force commander of UNAMIR, long to understand the
situation was highly explosive, and he was increasingly aware
that a well-established and politically powerful clique wanted to
scuttle the Arusha Accords. Meanwhile, the country continued
to descend into chaos. There were frequent killings and political assassinations, disintegrating security with nightly grenade
attacks, and political and 'ethnic killings'. Dallaire was insulted
over the airwaves of the Hutu Power radio station, RTLM,
accused of burying his head over the killing of civilians and of
supporting the RPF. Any notion of a settlement with the RPF
was denigrated over the airwaves. In the Hutu Power journal,
Kangura, a news item in January 1994 claimed UN peacekeepers
had been sent to Rwanda in order to help the RPA to conquer
the country by force.[14] *Kangura* told readers the Arusha Accords
amounted to a Tutsi plot.

Dallaire received anonymous warnings that Hutu Power extremists within the inner circle of President Habyarimana were formulating a plan to subvert the agreement, and they considered that the 'old man Habyarimana' had finally 'sold out the farm' to the Tutsi RPF. There were rumours of a fallback plan to defeat the RPF and wipe out the political opposition. At the same time, the Hutu Power militia, financed illegally, geared up for a major escalation, while the propaganda increased over the airwaves about the 'evil' nature of the RPF and its internal accomplices whose real intention was to return all Hutu to slavery. Dallaire was also informed that Hutu Power was consolidating its strength in the army, with the support of senior military figures, the French-trained elite unit commanders, the Presidential Guard, some of the country's préfets, most of the local authorities, the extremist Coalition pour la Défense de la République (CDR), a large section of the RGF, plus an estimated 20,000 militia.[15]

The international pressure to get the peace agreement back on track continued. The president of neighbouring Tanzania, Ali Hassan Mwinyi, facilitated talks between the Rwandan government and the RPF from the outset, and feared the creation of a much larger refugee crisis. At this eleventh hour, Mwinyi persuaded President Habyarimana to attend a meeting in Dar es Salaam scheduled to discuss the crisis in Burundi. The meeting, held on Wednesday, 6 April, took place in the afternoon in a suite at the Kilimanjaro Hotel with President Mwinyi in the chair. Also present were President Yoweri Museveni from Uganda; the vice president of Kenya, George Saitoti; President Cyprien Ntaryamira of Burundi; and Salim Ahmed Salim, the secretary-general of the Organisation of African Unity (OAU).

It was an uncomfortable meeting for Habyarimana. He was told that the delay in implementing the peace agreement was threatening the entire region and a renewed civil war would mean international isolation and empty bank accounts. Habyarimana was apparently shaken and agreed with them that power-sharing was inevitable, telling them he had already alerted opposition politicians to prepare for the swearing in of a power-sharing government. He signed a hurried joint statement before boarding his

Falcon jet for the flight home. As his aircraft came into land at Kigali International Airport at 8:23 it crashed in the garden of the presidential villa, killing everybody on board.

The news that a suspicious plane crash had killed the president of Rwanda reached New York by 4:30 p.m. on Wednesday, 6 April. Immediately, Ambassador Keating sensed an awful tragedy was about to unfold. 'And it literarily did before our eyes,' Keating said later. That first night French diplomats provided more details, reporting to the Council that the presidential plane had been shot down by a 'rocket attack' while it was in the process of landing and then caught fire. Keating started to prepare the text for a presidential statement to offer condolences to be issued by the Council.

The following day, Thursday, 7 April, it was confirmed by early evening that the presidential jet had been brought down by missile fire. Following that, there was nothing but bad news and given the speed of events, Secretariat officials gave the Council an oral briefing. There was considerable loss of civilian life in Kigali, including the assassination of various government leaders. Ten UNAMIR peacekeepers from Belgium were sent to protect the Rwandan prime minister, Agathe Uwilingiyimana, who was preparing to make a radio appeal for calm but she was brutally murdered by soldiers from the Rwandan army. Following that attack, most of the members of her cabinet, and her five children, became targets. At the same time, a group of UNAMIR peacekeepers were held captive at the airport, prevented from reaching the site where the wreckage of the presidential plane was located.

In the daily report from UNAMIR for Thursday, 7 April, the situation was described as chaos.[16] There had been heavy firing throughout the day that continued throughout the night. UNAMIR received hundreds of calls for assistance but movement had been prevented by numerous roadblocks. The headquarters of UNAMIR attempted to maintain contact with as many agencies as possible but telephone lines to certain areas were cut early that morning. Channels on the UNAMIR radio network were saturated, while their camps were becoming inundated by civilians terrified by actions described in the UNAMIR daily report as 'ethnic cleansing'. The Presidential Guard was conducting targeted assassinations of opposition political leaders and civilians known to support the RPF.

The force commander of UNAMIR reported how at midday on Thursday, 7 April, the commander of the RPA, Major General Paul Kagame, sent a message to UNAMIR headquarters in Kigali that he was dispatching a battalion to Kigali from his northern headquarters in Mulindi to assist government forces in keeping their renegade soldiers from killing innocent people. Lieutenant General Dallaire advised him that new forces in Kigali were not helpful. At 1 p.m. Kagame told Dallaire that he had learned that the houses of RPF supporters were surrounded, and Kagame told Dallaire that he had a duty to protect his own people.

At 3:06 that afternoon a UNAMIR message log records that the RPA implored UNAMIR to save threatened people; and at 4:40 p.m. a company size of RPF soldiers left their barracks in Kigali and engaged Presidential Guards who had goaded them, bringing Tutsi to their front gates and killing them in full view of the RPF. Later in the evening of 7 April, Dallaire found the bodies of ten UN peacekeepers in a hospital morgue. They were the Belgian soldiers sent to protect the prime minister early that morning.

In their northern sector, the RPF prepared for an imminent offensive operation, and at midday on Friday, 8 April, Kagame told Dallaire that one RPF battalion was moving towards Kigali to keep the 'renegade forces from killing innocent people'.[17] That day a new government was announced alongside a new president, Dr Théodore Sindikubwabo, an elderly member of the Mouvement Révolutionnaire National pour le Développement (MRND), the party through which Habyarimana had controlled the country. In a broadcast on Radio Rwanda, the national station, he read the names of the ministers in a new cabinet, describing it as a coalition established in accordance with the 1991 constitution. These figures were sworn into office on Saturday, 9 April, and were named the Interim Government.

Later that Saturday the French ambassador, Jean-Philippe Marlaud, called the Belgian ambassador, Johan Swinnen, to tell him about the new government. Swinnen immediately realised that all the ministers came from the Hutu Power wings of the political parties, yet Marlaud claimed that he thought the existence of this government would prevent a coup d'état.[18] In a later inquiry conducted by the French National Assembly, both Marlaud and the deputy defence attaché at the French embassy, Lieutenant Colonel Jean-Jacques Maurin, admitted that they tried to persuade Colonel Théoneste Bagosora, the chef de cabinet in the Ministry of Defence, to take control of the situation. It later transpired that the membership of the Interim Government had been decided at the embassy of France. It was immediately disavowed as illegitimate by the RPF.

Early in the morning of Saturday, 9 April, and without any warning to UNAMIR, three French aircraft landed at Kigali airport containing French troops ordered to effect the withdrawal of French and other foreign nationals. Dallaire told New York the French had taken control of the airport and only French aircraft were allowed to land.[19] French troops were seen escorting members of the presidential family to the airport using vehicles belonging to the Presidential Guard. Later on, clearance was given by the RGF for the UN to use the airport when it was announced that Belgian troops were expected to arrive and help with the rescue of foreign nationals. The US was also pulling out its citizens from Kigali, but by road.

The Council in New York was facing a major difficulty, Keating realised. For in its midst was the representative of the new Interim Government. At an informal meeting on Saturday, 9 April, its Ambassador Jean-Damascène Bizimana had asked to speak and sought to focus the discussion on the actions of the RPA, while ignoring evidence emerging about mass human rights abuses in territory held by the RGF.

The Interim Government wasted no time in providing the outside world with its own version of events. On the day after he was sworn in, the new prime minister, economist Jean Kambanda had cabled the country's seventeen embassies to give instructions on how to explain what had happened. He attached a four-page memorandum signed by the new foreign minister, Jérôme

Bicamumpaka. The document explained how the assassination of the president had caused surprise and stupor. The subsequent civilian deaths had resulted from the actions of unruly soldiers who reacted spontaneously and attacked people they held responsible for the assassination – including the prime minister. There had been 'general insecurity', but a military crisis committee had asked the political parties to form a new government and this government was now 'giving hope to the people'. At the same time, the UN mission was trying to achieve a ceasefire, but the RPA had 'opened hostilities' at a time when the country was in turmoil.

The Bicamumpaka memorandum, providing the Hutu Power version of events, was now spread in the corridors and hallways of the UN and it amounted to a blueprint for the campaign of genocidal denial to come. Bizimana repeatedly referred to the 'activities of the army of the Rwandan Patriotic Front (RPF)' and dismissed as propaganda the news of killings in territory held by the Rwandan Government Forces. In the Security Council, Bizimana had the right to participate in procedural decisions, to block the consensus on critical points and present significant obstacles to Council action. Given the Council's principle of consensus, Hutu Power blocked for several weeks a concerted position as the Rwandan ambassador was able to filibuster discussion on Council positions in the informal sessions.[20]

In June 1994 the presence of Bizimana in the Council was the subject of discreet discussions among the ambassadors of New Zealand, France, the US and UK. There were fears of a 'public relations debacle' in September when Rwanda was due to assume the presidency of the Council. The French sought a compromise allowing Bizimana to keep his seat at the table – avoiding the embarrassment of an empty chair – but persuaded him not to partake in their discussions and to defer the presidency. Bizimana was approached but this secret deal hit a snag and his response was to increase his participation in their discussions.[21]

And so, for as long as the the genocide of the Tutsi lasted, a Hutu Power representative remained in the Council chamber. The Council provided Hutu Power a global voice and Hutu Power made the most of its Council seat to promote the 'legitimacy' of its genocidal government and allowed the génocidaires an international forum to promote genocide denial.

The Security Council's negligence and inexcusable apathy over Rwanda was never more apparent than in allowing a representative of a genocidal government to remain at the horseshoe table. No one bothered to explain why the hastily created Interim Government, betraying every principle for which the UN stood, was legitimised in this way. In the course of three months, this government implemented a policy to eliminate the minority Tutsi. In a terrible irony and typical of a constant distortion of reality, they called their government in Kinyarwanda the Gouvernement y'Abatabazi, or the Government of Saviours.

3

The Ultimate Villain

There were no secluded death camps in Rwanda; the killing took place in broad daylight. The roadblocks were an effective and efficient part of the killing mechanism, and a few of them were in place in the capital, Kigali, by Wednesday, 6 April, before the presidential plane crashed; piles of old tyres and branches had been left by the roadside for this purpose. The roadblocks soon multiplied, located at strategic places devised by local government officials or military officers. The intention was that no Tutsi be allowed to escape. On one road into Kigali, there was a barricade every one hundred metres. In the months to come, the roadblock network on major and minor roads extended across large swathes of the country.

At each roadblock, there was usually a combination of people including local militia and the military, both the army and the gendarmerie. It was estimated that when the genocide of the Tutsi began, an estimated 6,350 military and paramilitary forces were stationed in Kigali. A night watchman, coerced to join a roadblock, was later a prosecution witness at the International Criminal Tribunal for Rwanda (ICTR) where the perpetrators of the genocide of the Tutsi were on trial. His responsibilities were to search any vehicle to see if anyone was hiding inside. Those Tutsi found hiding had to stand to one side and were killed later. The soldiers shot young Tutsi who tried to escape.

The killing was generally undertaken by the militia known as the Interahamwe, gangs of unemployed youth trained to kill at

speed and indoctrinated in the Hutu Power ideology. They murdered women, children and the elderly, mostly with agricultural
tools. The soldiers told the night watchman to use his machete
for this task.[1] The killing at roadblocks happened generally with
these tools, including the machete, stockpiled for this purpose.
The resupplies of ammunition for the roadblocks came from
Rwandan army stocks, and when they ran out there were calls
for more ammunition broadcast over the airwaves of the radio,
RTLM. Some Hutu were also killed at roadblocks, and this was
generally because of suspicions that they were opponents of Hutu
Power, were educated or spoke French, or were suspected of
helping Tutsi.

The roadblocks varied enormously, although the prevalent atti-
tude towards Tutsi victims was ritual humiliation. At first, there was
rigorous checking of the mandatory identity cards that showed the
ethnic designation – Hutu, Tutsi or Twa. After a while, it was too
troublesome to look at identity cards, and anyone who 'looked like
a Tutsi' was killed. At some of the roadblocks, there were neat piles
of cut up pieces of bodies at the side of the road. Others were organised with corpses stacked neatly alongside. Some roadblocks were
chaotic with drunkenness, drug abuse and sadistic cruelty. Dying
women were left to one side and often suffered multiple rapes.

When citizens saw the involvement of local authorities at the
roadblocks, they assumed the sanction came from the highest
level.[2] 'I did not know that what we were doing was wrong,' said
one participant. In the early hours of Thursday, 7 April, the gates
were opened at the main prison in Kigali, known as 1930, for the
year of its construction by Belgium. Among the hundreds of prisoners set free were some of the country's most violent criminals.
They joined the ranks of the Interahamwe on the roadblocks.

The evidence of the genocide of the Tutsi was for all to see.
In the morning of Saturday, 9 April, a French journalist for *Le
Monde*, Jean Hélène, and a Swiss freelancer writing for *Libération*,
Jean-Philippe Ceppi, arrived in Kigali travelling by road from the
south.[3] Ceppi described, 'What we see very rapidly is all these
corpses everywhere in the streets and barricades. The corpses
were being eaten by dogs.' The two journalists visited a morgue

at the hospital, the Centre Hospitalier Universitaire de Kigali, so full of bodies the doors could not close, and there were hundreds more bodies outside in the courtyard. The staff from Médecins Sans Frontières (MSF) told the two journalists the Rwandan army had gone into the operation block and massacred patients under the eyes of doctors because they were Tutsi.[4] The MSF medical team left the hospital that day saying it had been turned into a place of extermination.

Ceppi met the chief delegate of the International Committee of the Red Cross (ICRC), Philippe Gaillard, on Saturday afternoon in the grounds of a large Catholic mission on the top of a hill in the poor residential area of Gikondo. Hundreds of Tutsi who had sought sanctuary in the church had been killed that morning, cut to pieces by the Interahamwe. Gaillard and a team were looking for survivors. This was the first large-scale killing of Tutsi discovered by peacekeepers from UNAMIR. The sadistic brutality of the killers was duly noted by unarmed Polish UN Military Observers present at the scene, held against a wall by Interahamwe and forced to watch.[5]

The victims suffered terrible wounds to the genitalia. A three-month-old baby was terribly wounded, the mother raped and killed. Some children had their legs or feet cut off, and their throats cut. Most of the victims had bled to death. The UN Military Observers who had witnessed the killing said it was carried out by Interahamwe under the direction of the Presidential Guard. These soldiers came to the church to seal any exits before allowing in the militia.

In Gikondo on Saturday afternoon, Gaillard told Ceppi that a genocide of the Tutsi was under way and given its speed it would soon be over. The next day Gaillard estimated that 10,000 Tutsis had been killed in the capital city in the last three days. Ceppi published a story on Monday, 11 April, in which he wrote about the genocide of the Tutsi.

The medical teams of MSF joined together with the ICRC and set up a field hospital, taking over a former convent that for three months brought what Philippe Gaillard later called 'a drop of humanity in an ocean of blood'.[6] He negotiated the terms of the operation with the Interim Government and with the préfet of Kigali, Lieutenant Colonel Tharcisse Renzaho, who gave the medical teams the authorisations but also maintained control of when to let vehicles through. According to Jean Kambanda, the prime minister in the Interim Government, in his later confession to the crime of genocide, Gaillard was the only person who ever talked with him about the intensity of the massacres.

Every morning teams went out in ambulances to search through piles of bodies to bring the wounded to the field hospital. There was a liaison officer, a Rwandan army officer they knew as Colonel François who helped negotiations with the Rwandan army and the militias. At the roadblocks the militia told them there was no point looking after the wounded because 'we are killing all the Tutsi, so your work will not amount to much'.

In the Security Council, Ambassador Jean-Damascène Bizimana lost no time putting across the Interim Government's new message, this time to insist that the Rwandan Patriotic Front (RPF) had begun 'these hostilities' and reignited the civil war. He assured the Council that the Interim Government was assessing political conditions and the new cabinet 'took a number of measures aimed at restoring security for people and property all over the nation'. Bizimana told the Council his government had given the people renewed hope and there had been a 'marked decrease in murder and looting'.[7]

In New York, the advocates of shutting down UNAMIR before the crisis now pressed their case with vigour, for there was no longer any peace to keep. Given the murder of ten of its troops serving with UNAMIR, the Belgian government announced it was pulling out its 450-strong contingent, the backbone of the force, and on 13 April, the UN secretary-general, Boutros Boutros-Ghali, suggested that UNAMIR pull out altogether.

Prudence Bushnell, who was responsible for the Rwanda portfolio as deputy assistant secretary of state in the Bureau of African Affairs of the US State Department, recalled, 'Boy oh boy, did the shooting down of the [presidential] plane and the withdrawal of the Belgians give us the excuse we needed to pull the plug. It was an unfortunate period in my government's history. I regret it greatly, as I think all of us do.'⁸ The US, she said, had found every excuse to make the mandate for the UN mission for Rwanda as limited in time and manpower as possible. In the Council on 13 April, Karl Inderfurth, an ambassador from the US mission, told them peacekeeping was not appropriate for Rwanda.

On 13 April, the RPF sent a letter to the president of the Council signed by its representative at the UN in New York, Claude Dusaidi. It announced that 'a crime of genocide had been committed' in the presence of a UN force. While foreign nationals were rescued, no concrete action had been taken to protect the Rwandan people. Dusaidi informed Keating that the Rwandan Patriotic Army (RPA) intended to 'neutralise' elements of the Rwandan army that were responsible for massacres. No use would be served by calling for a ceasefire because that would only enable criminals to continue committing atrocities. There needed to be an international tribunal to put those responsible on trial. The letter was not discussed in the Council. Due to procedural rules, Dusaidi was not allowed to address the Council, and had to make do with sitting outside the Council chamber, waiting for news.⁹ In Washington, in a conversation with an official in the State Department, the RPF raised the issue of civilian slaughter and expressed concern at the minimal level of Western denunciation of the killing.¹⁰

The Security Council had other priorities. It focused first on the extraction from Rwanda of foreign nationals, and troops from France, Belgium and Italy were flown to Rwanda for that purpose. The next step was to analyse the situation in terms of the renewed civil war, to focus on trying to achieve a ceasefire between the RGF and the RPA. Two weeks after the genocide of the Tutsi began, in a report on 20 April, the UN secretary-general, Boutros Boutros-Ghali, reflected the views of the Interim Government and blamed 'unruly' members of the Presidential Guard. He insisted that the most urgent task was a ceasefire and that both sides were equally responsible for killing.

The secretary-general remained determined to pursue a ceasefire, and three weeks after the genocide began, on 29 April, he continued to blame the massacres on uncontrolled military personnel and groups of civilians taking advantage of the breakdown

of law and order. There was continual reference to the Arusha
Accords as the only basis for peace. The Nigerian ambassador,
Ibrahim Gambari, recalled some years later, 'We kept supporting
Arusha, all of us, even when it was collapsing before our eyes. We
kept talking about Arusha, kept talking about a ceasefire, long
after it was clear that genocide was going on in Rwanda.'[11]

On the ground Lieutenant General Roméo Dallaire was
instructed to talk to both sides. But the RPF refused to have anything to do with the Interim Government, whom it dismissed as
'a clique of killers'. The RPF declared that it would not talk about
a ceasefire until the Interim Government had called a halt to the
massacres. The Interim Government for its part asserted that the
main obstacle to peace was the advance of the RPA into Kigali.
No progress towards a ceasefire was possible. Meanwhile, huge
numbers of people were dying because of massacres, not war. The
areas most affected by large-scale killing had seen no battles at all.

In the midst of the stalemate the Council decided on 21 April to
draw down its force to a symbolic level. This retreat ensured that
the Tutsi population was alone, with no protection from anyone.
Within hours of the vote which, in the words of UK Ambassador
David Hannay, left a 'token force to appease public opinion', the
genocide spread south.[12]

A week later the UN ambassador for the Czech Republic,
Karel Kovanda, submitted a draft Presidential Statement that
used language from the 1948 Genocide Convention about how
the systematic killing of any ethnic group constitutes an act of
genocide. The statement made the point that genocide could not
be justified, under any circumstances, either by civil war or by
past history. The statement called on the Interim Government to
rein in all elements of the Rwandan Government Forces and the
Presidential Guard who were responsible for the brutalities. It
called on the Interim Government to investigate all acts of genocide. The strongest objections to the contents of the statement
came from Ambassador Bizimana, accusing Kovanda of blaming
only one side in 'the tragedy' because of the 'intoxication' of international public opinion by the RPF. Bizimana said massacres had
taken place in the zones occupied by the RPF.

The next day, in an eight-hour discussion, the Security Council debated whether or not to include the word 'genocide' in a Presidential Statement. Bizimana made a major contribution to the discussion. In a cable to London that night, since declassified, the UK ambassador, David Hannay, wrote, 'As the evening progressed the Rwandan ambassador's continued insistence on seeking deletion of the language on genocide and on the RGF responsibility for the bulk of the attacks on civilians.' Hannay considered that Bizimana 'rather soured the atmosphere of the negotiations'. For Hannay, the discussions that night were 'tortuous' and 'demonstrated for the first time' the extent to which the Rwandan ambassador in the Council was becoming a problem. He tried until the very last moment, Hannay wrote, 'to slant the text in the Interim Government's favour'. This was a factor that would no doubt complicate discussion of any further Council action on Rwanda.[13]

Bizimana's archive went missing when he fled Rwanda's UN mission offices in New York, but the diplomatic letters and cables between the Interim Government in Kigali and the Rwandan embassy in Brussels were revealing. Here was an account written by Ambassador Bizimana to the Interim Government detailing his efforts on their behalf in the Council. It covers twelve detailed pages and was copied to the ambassador in Brussels, François Ngarukiyintwali, and sent by fax on 5 June from the Rwandan mission in New York.[14]

Bizimana boasted of attempts in May to dissuade the Council from imposing an arms embargo when he had argued that Rwanda needed weapons for 'self-defence'. He described how he urged senior UN Secretariat officials of the necessity of a ceasefire and claimed how 'profoundly attached' the Interim Government was to the Arusha Accords. Bizimana offered advice and urged the Interim Government to establish a press office to handle relations with the outside world. He stressed the importance of finding witnesses who could tell of 'RPF atrocities'. Throughout the debates Bizimana had sought to focus the discussion on RPF actions, and ignore what was happening in the territory held by the Rwandan government.

~

Diplomatic efforts elsewhere involved a visit to Paris by the foreign minister in the Interim Government, Jérôme Bicamumpaka, along with Jean-Bosco Barayagwiza, the leader of the Hutu Power party, the Coalition pour la Défense de la République (CDR).[15] In a meeting with Jean-Marc Simon, a senior director in the office of the minister of cooperation, on 26 April, Bicamumpaka blamed Uganda for the entire mess, claimed Uganda used the RPF as a proxy to invade Rwanda, and advised France to send a strong signal to Uganda that it would not tolerate its ambitions.[16] French officials declared the trip private but on 27 April, according to human rights groups, they met the French foreign minister, Alain Juppé, and Bruno Delaye, head of the Africa Unit in the Élysée.[17] Diplomatic support for the Interim Government came three days later when the French ambassador joined with Rwanda in Security Council discussions to deny the government forces were responsible for massacres, with both states resisting the use of the word genocide to describe what was happening.[18]

The great Hutu Power diplomatic coup came later, however, on Monday, 16 May, when the foreign minister in the Interim Government addressed the Security Council. In a shameful episode in UN history, Bicamumpaka brought genocide denial directly into the Security Council chamber. In front of the whole world he officially denied genocide was happening, even as the number of victims rose by the thousands. He spoke one falsehood after another, spouting the racist ideology of the movement, claiming the 'hatred on display' was forged over four centuries of cruel and ruthless domination of the Hutu majority, the mental enslavement of an entire people. The events in the country were 'complex and difficult to grasp'. He warned ambassadors not to be naive and blame either the Rwandan army or the Interim Government for the massacres. He told the Council the assassination of President Habyarimana was part of a prepared plan by the RPF to take power, coordinated with Ugandan authorities. The large-scale massacres of Hutu civilians had taken place in an 'inter-ethnic war' of unbelievable cruelty. He blamed the entire crisis on the RPF for a sudden and ruthless bid for power. He said, 'The resumption of hostilities by the RPF, along with large-scale massacres of Hutu civilians ... unleashed repressed hatreds and a festering desire for revenge ... It is said some RPF fighters eat the hearts of men they have killed in order to become invincible.'[19]

No one was persuaded by the speech. Keating, the New Zealand ambassador, described Bicamumpaka as odious, the mouthpiece of a faction who provided a shameful distortion of the truth. Karel Kovanda, the ambassador of the Czech Republic, agreed. 'All reports indicate that these atrocities have been committed by Hutu cut-throats ... against their Tutsi neighbors,' he said. In the Council, Kovanda listed massacre sites and gave an estimated death toll for each one.[20] The UK ambassador, David Hannay, described the speech from Rwanda's foreign minister as offensive. In a cable to the Foreign Office in London Hannay described how the performance almost defied description and it illustrated vividly how 'unsuitable their position as a member of the Council is'.[21]

Nevertheless, for the last three months not one government had called for the expulsion of the representative of Rwanda's Interim Government from the chamber. From the beginning of the genocide until its end, all UN governments and official bodies continued to recognise as legitimate the Interim Government, knowing its one overriding policy was the extermination of a part of the population. Not one government called on the perpetrators to stop the genocide. The génocidaires remained safe in the knowledge that outside interference was never likely.

Not until 15 July, when the RPF had brought the genocide of the Tutsi to an end, did the international diplomatic community expel Rwandans from the Council chamber, prompted by the US government's own decision to call for the closure of the Rwandan embassy in Washington, DC, and expel Rwandan diplomats from the US because they represented a 'genocidal regime'.

As the genocide of the Tutsi was getting under way at dawn on Thursday, 7 April, a rumour heard at the roadblocks near the Ministry of Defence and spread by Rwandan gendarmes alleged UN peacekeepers from Belgium had played a part in the assassination of the president. The rumour soon found its way to the morning news bulletins of RTLM, and the radio was the first to

broadcast that the president's aircraft was shot down by missiles. The news from RTLM told how Belgian troops affiliated
with UNAMIR downed the plane. Belgium had actively assisted
the RPA.[22]

The rumour appeared elsewhere, thousands of miles away in
Brussels, in a press release issued by Papias Ngaboyamahina, who
was part of an RTLM support group in Belgium. Issued within
hours of the assassination and dated 7 April, the press release
claimed that the weapons used to down the presidential jet came
from Belgium and that Belgian soldiers serving with UNAMIR
were responsible for the attack. The press release was issued in the
name of an organisation, the Crisis Committee in the Rwandan
Community in Brussels, and claimed a plot existed between the
RPF and the Belgian government intended to bring the RPF to
power.[23] A letter from this same organisation and along the same
lines went to the UN secretary-general, Boutros Boutros-Ghali, that
same day. It demanded an immediate withdrawal from Rwanda
of Belgian troops.[24] Also on 7 April, in an informal meeting of
the Security Council the Rwandan ambassador, Jean-Damascène
Bizimana, told the Council that any inquiry into the presidential
assassination should not rule out UNAMIR, as peacekeepers had
been responsible for the security at the airport. Karel Kovanda
recalled how Bizimana 'made no bones about his opinion that the
assassination of President Habyarimana was an act of terrorism,
with the RPF the ultimate villain'.

In Washington, three days after the assassination, Rwanda's
ambassador to the US, Aloys Uwimana, telephoned the State
Department in the early evening. He speculated the Belgians
might have shot down the plane. He explained the subsequent
killings were an understandable reaction to the assassination of
the president.[25]

The story spread and the prime minister of Belgium, Jean-
Luc Dehaene, was obliged to issue a denial and on 12 April, in
a television interview, said the allegation was a fantasy. A press
communiqué from the government described the accusation as
fanciful. Nonetheless, the génocidaires persisted. A letter from
the new Rwandan president, Théodore Sindikubwabo, sent

to Boutros-Ghali pointed out that the Belgian contingent of UNAMIR was responsible for the security of the airport and that the assassination could not have happened without this inexplicable security failure.

This was followed by a set of instructions issued on 15 April by the minister of foreign affairs, Jérôme Bicamumpaka, addressed to all embassies abroad and sent by fax from the Rwandan embassy in neighbouring Burundi. The fax announced an inquiry into the assassination to shed light on the responsibility of the UN peacekeepers of Belgian nationality suspected by 'public opinion in Rwanda' of having been involved in the assassination plot. The minister instructed ambassadors to spread this information in the defence of the national interest and to establish the truth.[26]

The Rwandan ambassador in Brussels, François Ngarukiyintwali, was summoned to the Belgian foreign ministry, where he was given a dressing down by the secretary-general, Frans Roelants. The ambassador was shocked at the menace and the discourtesy of the Belgian official, particularly someone of his rank, his age and experience. The Belgian official told the ambassador that in Paris the previous day, a man who 'purported to be the Rwandan Foreign Minister' had repeated the same lies told by Rwandan ambassadors in Kinshasa and New York. These lies blamed Belgian soldiers for shooting down the presidential plane. This was a 'campaign of lies', and the Belgian authorities were losing patience.[27]

Another summons was issued to the Rwandan ambassador on 11 May, when the Belgian government demanded an official statement from the Rwandan government to deny accusations that implicated Belgium in the assassination. The director of African affairs in the ministry, Wilfried Jaenen, told the ambassador he knew the Rwandan government was behind these claims and had sent instructions to their ambassadors to spread the word. The Rwandan ambassador denied receiving any such instruction.[28]

In June, the Rwandan ambassador in Brussels informed the Interim Government that relations with Belgium were at an all-time low and risked getting worse. He advised the government to hold back on claims about the assassination until an official inquiry took place. The Belgian foreign minister, Willy Claes, would have nothing to do with the Interim Government because of the grave accusations against Belgium and a continuing anti-Belgium campaign of denigration waged over the airwaves of the hate radio, RTLM. Claes described the members of the Interim Government as 'extremists and terrorists'.

Of the existence of a plot to murder UN peacekeepers from Belgium to ensure UNAMIR would pull out, there was no doubt. A later inquiry into these events by the Belgian Senate showed that an extensive anti-Belgian campaign waged over the airwaves on RTLM had started in January 1994, and Belgian military intelligence described how the radio station 'stigmatised' both the Belgian contingent and UNAMIR.[29] The day after the murder of the ten peacekeepers, their deaths were blamed by the Belgian military attaché in Nairobi on 'inflammatory, anti-Belgian broadcasts on the hate radio station, RTLM'. It had broadcast rumours that the president's plane had been shot down by Belgians.[30]

Some months earlier, in December 1993, predictions that Belgian UN peacekeepers would be murdered had been made to the Belgian journalist and expert on the Great Lakes region, Colette Braeckman. Braeckman, who was in Kigali on the night of the presidential assassination, heard that the wife of one of the three French crew members on the presidential Falcon jet who telephoned the French embassy for information was told that Belgians were responsible for the attack on the plane. It was an accusation levelled at the ten Belgian peacekeepers by their killers as they hopelessly fought for their lives in a six-hour battle in a military camp in central Kigali on the morning of 7 April.

The génocidaires claimed that these were unexpected events and in the first few days of the crisis they were overwhelmed. They blamed external forces for the ensuing violence. Yet there is evidence that points from the very outset on 6 April to a calm resolve. This was certainly the impression of Dallaire. Within hours of the missile fire, he described seeing Presidential Guards and elite units everywhere. The Rwandan government army headquarters was fully mobilised. 'They knew what the hell was going on,' said Dallaire.[31]

The idea of a coup d'état was later dismissed by the commander of the Belgian contingent of UNAMIR, Colonel Luc Marchal, who said that on the night of Wednesday, 6 April, it was too quiet. He seemed to misunderstand that this was not a case where the military displaced the administrative authority or overpowered the civilian authority, they rather co-opted or secured the collaboration of the administrative authorities where Hutu Power had widespread influence. The US probably knew this. Joyce Leader, the US embassy's deputy chief of mission in Kigali, had a conversation with a 'well-placed Rwandan army colonel' on 12 April. He told her that a secret military-civilian organisation was ordering the atrocities and the president's death was the provocation needed to put a long-standing plan into effect.[32] The moderates were not strong enough to prevent a Hutu Power takeover and in any case received no help.

Most government analysts in the US believed the assassination of Juvénal Habyarimana was plotted by his own allies. He had edged too close to reforms that would threaten the power of the Akazu, the inner circle of Hutu extremists from the north who occupied many of the most important positions in the military, political, economic and administrative sectors of Rwandan society. It was a conclusion reached early on. On 8 April, the Daily Activity Report from the State Department in Washington read, 'To recap: "rogue Hutu elements of the Rwandan military – possibly the elite presidential guard – were reportedly responsible yesterday for shooting down the plane."'[33] The State Department received credible but unconfirmed reports that Hutu elements in the military opposed to the Arusha Accords killed Habyarimana to eliminate the RPF and sympathetic Hutu, one cable revealed.[34]

Although there are interesting snippets in declassified US cables, much information on these events remains unavailable. One of the most informative partly declassified cables came from Ambassador Pamela Harriman in the US embassy in Paris, who on 28 April told Washington that for ten days she had held meetings about the increasingly high civilian death toll in Rwanda, talking with Médecins Sans Frontières (MSF) and officials at the French

Foreign Ministry and from the office of President Mitterrand in the Élysée Palace.[35]

There was a hypothesis, Harriman wrote, made up by some Hutu hard-liners, that Belgian soldiers in UNAMIR were somehow involved in the assassination of the president or directly aided RPF soldiers to enter the general airport area so they could fire on the plane. Harriman then speculated that if such assistance was given, then these may have been the white mercenaries who had been sighted fighting with the Rwandan Government Forces.[36] One of her contacts, whose name remains obscured in the document, told her that the charges of the involvement of the RPF in the assassination were not credible given that the missile attack had taken place from a site near the president's residence which was secured by forces loyal to Habyarimana. Harriman was told that the death of the president was the signal for pre-planned ethnic massacres to begin.

Harriman told Washington about the wife of Habyarimana, Agathe Kanziga, who was flown to Paris by the French military from Kigali and now lived in Paris. Harriman wrote that based on information from Rwandans who knew this woman, since the assassination of her husband, the power in Rwanda of her Hutu extremist entourage had grown dramatically. Harriman was told that Agathe and members of her family were extremely hard-line and encouraged some of the most radical Hutu who argued the time had come to end for ever the Tutsi presence in Rwanda.

In May 1994 a classified US Defense Intelligence Agency (DIA) report, while still heavily redacted, revealed in a crisis overview, 'It is believed that the plane crash that killed the Rwandan and Burundian presidents and their entourage was actually an assassination conducted by Hutu military hardliners.' The DIA described how, almost immediately afterwards, the Presidential Guard began the systematic execution of prominent Tutsi and anyone else sympathetic to reconciliation. 'Multiple sources indicate that the violence by the Presidential Guard and various youth militias was not spontaneous but was directed by high-level officials within the Interim Government.'[37]

Toby T. Gati, the US assistant secretary of state for intelligence and research (1993–1997), wrote in an informational memorandum for the US Department of State that Hutu extremists in the military feared being ousted by President Habyarimana and shot down his plane to keep him from implementing the Arusha Accords. Gati thought the RPF had threatened to use a provision in the peace agreement to impeach him for human rights abuses.[38]

An unclassified assessment by analysts in the State Department reported that there were 'credible but unconfirmed reports that Hutu elements in the military opposed to the Arusha Accords killed Habyarimana in order to block the accords and eliminate the Tutsi-dominated RPF and sympathetic Hutu'.[39]

For UNAMIR, it proved impossible to access the crash site until May. The plane had come down in the garden of the presidential villa, just under the flight path. An hour after the crash, at 9:35 p.m., an armed UNAMIR patrol sent to investigate the crash was stopped, disarmed and held at the airport by Rwandan Government Forces. At the airport, the UN Military Observers stationed there were confined to a room. In the course of the next hours Dallaire twice asked the chef de cabinet, Colonel Théoneste Bagosora, for the military to allow UNAMIR access to the crash site.[40] To no avail.

At 2:45 a.m. on Thursday, 7 April, a few hours after the assassination, while Dallaire was at Rwandan army headquarters, he was confronted by the head of the French military mission in Rwanda and another French officer at RGF headquarters. They told Dallaire they had instructions from Paris to ensure a qualified crash investigation was conducted. Dallaire assured them it would be. They pressed further and offered a military technical team currently six hours away in Bangui, an offer Dallaire refused.

No scientific or forensic investigation into the missile fire on the presidential jet took place for the next seventeen years, and the wreckage remains to this day where it fell. The downing of the plane continued to be a useful enigma; it left room for the génocidaires to manipulate history and present their own alternative facts. It was a propaganda coup and became their most successful item of fake news.

~

The confusion created in the first seventy-two hours, with false stories spread at the UN and by Rwandan ambassadors abroad, allowed the génocidaires enough cover to implement their plans and achieve their coup d'état in the name of Hutu Power. The network of roadblocks created in Kigali was the first visible sign of the mechanics of the genocide of the Tutsi, of the plans in place, a visible part of an overall strategy that was designed to ensure that for Tutsi there was no escape.

4

Public Relations

It was in the Hotel des Diplomates, the hotel in Kigali that served for three months as the headquarters of Hutu Power, that Colonel Théoneste Bagosora and Lieutenant General Roméo Dallaire had one last meeting towards the end of June. Once more Bagosora raged at the top of his voice, calling Dallaire a sympathiser of the Rwandan Patriotic Front (RPF), and berating his UN troops for failing in their mission. Bagosora promised if he ever saw Dallaire again he would kill him.[1]

The hotel had been in the government zone, the city cut in half by the three-month civil war. It was to the Hotel des Diplomates that the senior officers of the UN Assistance Mission for Rwanda (UNAMIR) had come to try to obtain ceasefires for rescue missions, and it was where the peacekeepers met the leaders of the Interahamwe to patiently negotiate safe routes and argue for the clearance of roadblocks. Dallaire met with the leadership of the Interahamwe in this hotel, eighteen young killers who neatly signed their names on an attendance list and gave the position each held in the organisation at either local or national level. They included the head of its Judicial Committee, Bernard Maniragaba, and national treasurer Dieudonné Niyitegeka.[2] Some meetings at the Hotel des Diplomates between the peacekeepers and the génocidaires were recorded on video.

On May 16, Bernard Kouchner, a well-known French humanitarian and former French minister of health, came to the hotel to negotiate the rescue of a group of orphans he hoped to take back to France. Several members of the press accompanied him, and he said he was acting on his own initiative but had the blessing of the UN secretary-general, Boutros Boutros-Ghali. Kouchner wanted to create a 'humanitarian corridor', and he met Bagosora at the Hotel des Diplomates to enlist his help. He told Bagosora what a wonderful public relations coup the rescue of orphans would be for the Interim Government and how it would alter its deteriorating international image.[3] When Kouchner met Dallaire, he told him the rescue of orphans was in his own interests, as Dallaire was 'seen in a very bad light in Paris'.[4] It seemed no more than part of a propaganda exercise, for the plan was to fly the children to Paris with their triumphant arrival timed for the morning news bulletins.

There were several orphanages in Kigali. One of them was in Nyamirambo, a densely populated district in the southeast of the city controlled by the Interahamwe. One afternoon a Canadian doctor working with Médecins Sans Frontières (MSF), James Orbinski, and a UNAMIR officer from Canada, Major Luc Racine, with the protection of an armoured personnel carrier, got through twenty-three roadblocks to reach the orphanage. They found the children partially malnourished; some had machete wounds or were suffering from malaria or pneumonia. Orbinski described them huddled together in small clusters, afraid to go anywhere near the walls or gate. Surrounded by militia, the children were slowly being killed, butchered five at a time, and sometimes more, depending on the mood of the killers. The militia threw bodies and severed limbs over the orphanage wall so that the living would know what they faced.[5] The local Rwandan Government Forces commander told Orbinski that the children were Tutsi inyenzi (cockroaches) and were to be 'crushed like insects'.

Kouchner failed in his mission. At the last moment, the Interahamwe insisted that only militia members could accompany orphans directly to the steps of the aircraft. It was most likely an attempt by the militia to hide behind the children and UN peacekeepers in order to leave the capital and reinforce the para-commando battalion in the military camp of Kanombe adjacent to the airport. The camp was under a sustained attack by the Rwandan Patriotic Army (RPA). Five days later the RPA took control of the airport.

Bagosora, who had been enthusiastic about the rescue of orphans, had another version of events. He blamed Dallaire for the delayed orphan rescue, and said that the UN commander had deliberately stalled in order to make the Interim Government look bad.

In the course of his visit to Kigali, Kouchner had told Dallaire that the French public was in a state of shock over Rwanda and was demanding action. A dramatic press campaign was under way in France organised by MSF, the agency having decided to speak out about the genocide. 'We had a special responsibility, because France has a special responsibility', said Jean-François Alesandrini, director of communications of MSF-France. Jean-Hervé Bradol, an MSF doctor who had just returned from Kigali, appeared on the French nightly news bulletin (TFI) on 16 May. The huge death toll was not the result of civil war, he explained. The killers were trying to present the catastrophe in Rwanda as the result of tribes slaughtering each other. This was an insult to the victims. Bradol explained that a deliberate, systematic and well-planned extermination was under way. 'France has a particularly serious role', he said, and informed viewers that France had funded, trained and armed those carrying out the slaughter, something they kept quiet. It was scandalous that no French authority had explicitly condemned those responsible or called on the killers to stop the slaughter since French officials knew these killers.

After the television interview, as Alesandrini later described, there was a call to the MSF offices from the French Foreign Ministry. 'What are you playing at? What is going on? We can't have ourselves insulted in front of 15 million people by some idiot humanitarian who turns up and calls himself a doctor.'[6]

Two days later, in a full page in *Le Monde*, MSF-France published an open letter to President François Mitterrand: 'France, that bastion of human rights, has such a serious responsibility in the shameful events that have unfolded in Rwanda since 6 April'. It repeated the accusation that France had supported and armed the faction carrying out the killing. That day, Bradol told the Paris newspaper *Libération* that MSF was a 'humanitarian alibi' for politicians to hide behind and avoid decision-making. This was genocide and yet governments expected them to continue their work regardless.

'Since the start of the conflict there had been a sort of silence in France,' reported Philippe Biberson, president of MSF-France. The humanitarian organisation changed all that, and their campaign to draw attention to the realities of Rwanda was unique in its history. Invited to meet Bruno Delaye, the head of the Africa unit, who reported directly to President Mitterrand and the foreign minister, Dominique de Villepin, Bradol and Biberson listened while the two politicians justified their policies. Bradol did not want to argue. 'You have friends in Kigali and these friends are exterminating Tutsi. Can you tell them to stop?' Bradol said, and later claimed that Delaye had made the excuse that he could not get them on the telephone.

In New York, MSF organised a briefing for Ambassador Colin Keating from Jean-Pierre Luxen, who had spoken directly with Rony Zachariah, the coordinator of an MSF-Belgium team who had just fled a hospital in Butare. On Friday, 22 April, Zachariah recounted, soldiers wearing the uniform of the Rwandan Government Forces rounded up all the local staff of the hospital and killed them, saying they would return for the patients the following day, which they did. MSF believed a clear policy of genocide existed and there was a need for secure perimeters at places where people were sheltering. If the killing did not stop, within a few weeks there would be no Tutsi left in the south of the country.[7] Keating wrote to his capital on 26 April, 'At present none of the big players on the Council are particularly seized of the problem and seem unlikely to become so unless public opinion or media attention develop.'[8]

A few days earlier, on 21 April, the UN Security Council voted to reduce UNAMIR ranks. Those remaining, including unarmed military observers, known as MILOBS. The Security Council had mandated 270 to remain, the only figure the US would agree to, Ambassador Colin Keating later revealed at an international conference in The Hague in 2014. 'I know because I was the one who was negotiating with them.'⁹ That was their bottom line, Keating said of the US position, and he reluctantly acquiesced. He knew that Lieutenant General Dallaire and the deputy force commander, Bridagier General Henry Kwami Anyidoho and his Ghanaian troops would stay anyway. This was important if the US was going to shift from total opposition to offering help. In the end, there were just 450 volunteers who remained in Kigali.

This small corps was trying to protect thousands of desperate people sheltering in churches, orphanages and clinics. The MILOBS created a 'Humanitarian Action Cell', and a map on the wall showed where people were sheltering. It was a hopeless task. By 12 May, the International Committee of the Red Cross (ICRC) had detailed information on ninety-one such sites with an estimate of displaced people at 756,747, of whom 416,000 were trapped in the zone controlled by the Rwandan Government Forces (RGF). A detailed map was created, showing each site where people were trapped and starving, and sent to New York.¹⁰

On those occasions when UN peacekeepers and military observers managed to get through the roadblocks around Kigali, sometimes all they could do was bring a few medical supplies and some food. Orbinski was astonished that the UN was obliged to limit rescue attempts for lack of petrol. Morale was low. Dallaire wrote of 'the acrid odours of death and starvation, to eat expired tinned rations and to cope with the resultant diarrhoea without toilet paper or running water' (*sic*).

On 17 May, the Council reversed its decision and mandated 5,500 reinforcements for UNAMIR, but nothing came. The resolution was a sham. There were no troops available. Those UN governments who offered troops did so without airlift or equipment or, like the US, offered equipment but wanted money. Governments even offered unsuitable equipment: the UK gestured with a consignment of broken-down flatbed trucks. Some countries offered equipment for UNAMIR on terms so difficult that extensive negotiation was required. It was Bernard Kouchner, during another visit to Kigali on 16 June, who broke the news to Dallaire that the French military was coming back in to 'sort out the Rwandan government territory and create a safe area'.

Dallaire thought that if the French had really wanted to end genocide and support the aims of the UN they should have reinforced
UNAMIR; he thought the real intention was to split Rwanda in
two, like Cyprus. From now on, and with immediate effect, the
concerns of UNAMIR slipped down the Security Council agenda.
From mid-June the focus was on the French military mission and
what it could achieve as the French sought Council legitimacy for
their initiative, called Turquoise. It was apparently designed to
protect those populations threatened with extermination. President
François Mitterrand said there was not a moment to lose. On 14
June, he received Philippe Biberson and Jean-Hervé Bradol at the
Élysée Palace. The president told them, 'We've had enough. We are
going in. We will try to sort things out and save people.' On this
occasion, Mitterrand had clearly changed his tune. He told them
he thought the Interim Government a bunch of assassins. Bradol
wrote afterwards, 'These people were becoming much less attrac-
tive company now.' France started to realise that it would have a
major international political problem on its plate.[11]

Dallaire's official reaction was delivered in a twenty-four-page
cable to headquarters on 20 July in which he described the French
plan as a 'covert attempt to restore the other side'.[12] The commander of UNAMIR believed that the French hoped to prevent
the RPA destroying the RGF and bringing the membership of the
Interim Government to justice. His RPF liaison officer told him the
French would protect the criminal elements they in fact created
and which they had all along been supporting. Major General
Paul Kagame, the commander of the RPA, told Dallaire that this
was another mistake by outsiders, typical of the West's attempts
to solve problems in foreign lands. Kagame predicted correctly
the humanitarian problems that faced Rwanda would worsen and
spill over the border. The French aggression would only escalate
tensions and the conflict.

There was jubilation in Kigali at the news announcement on
RTLM of the imminent arrival of French troops. It improved the
morale of the RGF, who were losing the war in the face of the RPA
that had by now taken control of six out of the ten *préfectures*.
The news broadcast on RTLM was that the French were coming to

replace the useless UN mission. The Interim Government stepped up its propaganda campaign against UNAMIR in general and its force commander in particular. The Rwandan foreign minister, Jérôme Bicamumpaka, issued a nine-page rant against Dallaire, accusing him of smuggling weapons into Kigali to help the RPA seize power.[13] There were instructions broadcast on air to 'kill Dallaire', offering a reward for his corpse.

The French had wanted their June mission to Rwanda to appear to be an international effort. There were strenuous efforts by French diplomats to obtain military contributions from European allies and African states. The British were reluctant to offer anything, suspecting the French were going back in to protect their ally. The French remained adamant about the humanitarian and international nature of their intentions, although only Senegal and Chad offered a few hundred soldiers each. The British ambassador, David Hannay, thought the idea 'crazy' but the views of the British would be made known privately to the French and because of her bilateral relationship with France the British eventually expressed approval in the Council. The US thought it a disastrous policy and diplomats concluded that the French were aiming to maximise influence in Francophone Africa and had a 'desire to be perceived as a great power'.[14] The US agreed to vote in the Security Council to give UN authority to the mission as long as the French bore the financial burden.[15]

A spokesperson for the French government, Nicolas Sarkozy, explained: 'We are not a middle power … we are a great power … if France does not react, Sarajevo falls; and finally Rwanda.' The UK ambassador in Paris, Sir Christopher Mallaby, was more sceptical. In a cable to London he wrote, 'The French have been stung by the continued criticism of their policy in Rwanda and clearly felt the need to take action of some sort.' The ambassador was dismissive and said of the French, 'They will probably try to work out the practicalities as they go along.'[16]

The UN secretary-general, Boutros Boutros-Ghali, was enthusiastic from the outset. He wrote to the Security Council on 19 June about a 'French-commanded multinational force to assure the security and protection of displaced persons and civilians at risk'.

France was granted a Chapter VII mandate to allow for the use of force, needed to protect French troops. French soldiers would not be 'shackled by the kind of restrictions that had turned UN soldiers into helpless bystanders'. The French had given assurances the troops would stay in Rwanda for a limited period of no more than sixty days. By then UNAMIR II, mandated by the Council on 17 May, would be operational. The French troops would not be wearing blue berets, and mission 'coordination' rested with the UN secretary-general.

The decision by Boutros-Ghali to lobby for the return of the French military to a conflict that France had done so much to fuel seemed to some to be unspeakable. While Secretariat officials believed the French intervention a near-certain disaster, Boutros-Ghali had been persuaded of its merits by Alain Juppé, the French foreign minister.[17] Boutros-Ghali later gave instructions to UN officials to be openly supportive of the French idea.[18] In the face of criticism, Boutros-Ghali argued that he had no choice in his support of France. While the US refused to pay its UN debt France had offered to provide troops and pick up the bill. As the vote in the Security Council approached, the UK ambassador, Sir David Hannay, was increasingly critical of the secretary-general. 'The French, with the assistance of Boutros-Ghali, will be going into high gear to massage the resistance and isolate those, such as New Zealand and Canada, who have the strongest objections.' It was astonishing, he cabled London, 'that the Secretary-General should be turning a deaf ear to the misgivings of his Force Commander'.[19]

Hannay raised this issue at a meeting with Boutros-Ghali and told him he had made a mistake in giving his support to the French operation. He complained that the French were unable to explain why they did not simply contribute their resources to UNAMIR.[20]

On the ground, Dallaire was shocked that Boutros Boutros-Ghali had condoned the French initiative without taking into account either the UNAMIR mandate or the modus operandi in Rwanda. Dallaire wrote later, 'I would never have guessed at the time the extent to which the Interim Government, the RGF, Boutros-Ghali, France and even the RPF were already working together behind my back to secure a French intervention ... under the guise of humanitarian relief.'[21] The French quickly obtained a Security Council endorsement for the mission known as Opération Turquoise, mandated in resolution 929 and voted on 22 June, all voted in favour, although five countries abstained in the vote – Brazil, China, New Zealand, Nigeria and Pakistan.

On Monday, 4 July 1994, as dawn broke, the forces of the RPA took Kigali, and the remaining Rwandan Government Forces abandoned their positions and fled north. Meanwhile, the Presidential Guard that had held the RPA at the Kacyiru roundabout scurried to the Hutu Power stronghold of the northern town Ruhengeri. As the government soldiers fled, they fired mortars indiscriminately, and one of them hit the casualty ward at the makeshift ICRC hospital, killing seven patients.

The city fell silent. The génocidaires had held power since the coup on the night of 6 April but were now forced to make a hurried exit. In Camp Kigali, the army barracks close to the Hotel des Diplomates, military officers burned incriminating archives, and dozens of files and ring binders were packed into suitcases, cardboard boxes and whatever was at hand. Taken into exile was a bus full of documents removed from the Ministry of Defence. Nevertheless, in their haste, the génocidaires left a mass of evidence in government ministries. Documents discovered afterwards in the offices of the Banque Nationale du Rwanda (BNR) in Kigali amounted to a paper trail of the purchases of the tools for genocide and military hardware. There were invoices, bank statements, arms contracts, faxes and telexes to show how some finance came from loans from international funding that paid for the genocidal project, including the Interahamwe militia, to buy beer, clothing and food for their families and to buy weapons and vast quantities of machetes.

The archives of the security services, the Service Central de Renseignements (SCR), attached to the office of the president, were found to be intact, including detailed and substantial files on 44,000 citizens. This archive revealed the full horror of a quota system used to restrict the participation of Tutsi in public life and discriminate against them. Here were the reports of the state employees who had conducted investigations to find out if people were 'pure Hutu' or whether they were secretly Tutsi and faking their identity.

Rwanda's state records, its national archive, containing millions of pages of documents, photographs and sound recordings, had largely survived the civil war, including paperwork neatly filed in the Kigali offices of President Juvénal Habyarimana.

In July 1994, as the Hutu Power movement abandoned the country, they drove the population into exile. Broadcasts over RTLM incited the people to flee, instilling fear and terror of the advancing RPA troops. The last Hutu Power strongholds in Rwanda fell over the next two weeks: first, the northern town of Ruhengeri on 14 July, and then Gisenyi three days later. Over the course of the next five days 1 million people crossed into the North Kivu province of Zaire. The UN department in the British Foreign Office estimated this was the fastest and largest refugee flow in history. It was later described as a 'politically-ordered evacuation' that was targeted at the Hutu population.

For the flight north, the administrative authorities in each commune had induced their population to leave, and there were reports of those refusing being killed by militia. Two million Rwandans eventually fled the country, among them the perpetrators of genocide, the militia and local authorities. The first influx arrived at the Tanzanian border in April, when 170,000 people crossed over, eventually swelling to more than 500,000. Others made their way into South Kivu and Burundi. This figure would have been greater if hundreds of thousands of people had not remained internally displaced in what was called a 'humanitarian protection zone' established in July by French troops in southwest Rwanda, a sanctuary for Hutu Power. It contained 1.7 million displaced people. In these massive refugee flows, the French military facilitated the escape of the genocidal leadership and its militia, doing nothing to disarm them.

The creation by French troops of the zone, announced on 1 July, was a departure from the original mandate but gained the full support of the UN secretary-general, who argued that with a tide of refugees fleeing the RPF advance it was France's only option. The zone would protect people fleeing 'the fighting'. In fact, the force protected the fleeing génocidaires. The French zone occupied an area comprising some 20 per cent of the country and was considered illegal under international law, particularly when French commanders announced that they would exclude the RPA.

As the people fled, they looted and ransacked, taking cattle and chickens, destroying hospitals and schools, loading furniture onto trucks and dismantling whole factories. An estimated 610 trucks and 1,380 cars belonging to the Rwandan state were stolen, while purloined stocks of coffee were offloaded for US$300,000.

The exodus to North Kivu created huge camps, established on hard lava plains. Here the weak, the sick and children lay dying without access to care. A subsequent cholera outbreak set another world record.[22] There were 600 deaths a day, and almost overnight the French troops became gravediggers. Within the first month of the exodus, 50,000 refugees in Zaire died as a result of cholera, dysentery, dehydration.[23] Goma is on the northern tip of Lake Kivu and is the capital of North Kivu Province. The Rwandan city of Gisenyi, the former heartland of Hutu Power, was less than two kilometres across the border. It was from here that the the prime minister of the defeated Interim Government, Jean Kambanda, announced, 'We have lost the military battle, but the war is by no means over because we have the people behind us.'

In the camps, local officials and militia took control of the population and imposed a tax on everyone, organising the sale of food aid and channelling the profits into military rearming. The Interahamwe militia sheltered among the population, and genocidal officials murdered anyone who talked of home.[24]

The staff of MSF-France walked out of the camps, stating publicly that they were disgusted by the diversion of humanitarian aid by the same people who orchestrated the genocide and the use of refugees as hostages.

It was in Goma in August 1994 that a journalist spotted Colonel Théoneste Bagosora and conducted an on-camera interview with him for a TV documentary broadcast in France later that month. Bagosora was unkempt and wore civilian clothes. He was far removed from the arrogant officer who only weeks earlier had given Lieutenant General Dallaire a dressing down in the lobby of the Hotel des Diplomates. This was Bagosora's first on-camera interview in exile, before he began his jaunts to Cameroon and Kinshasa. It was after his trip to the Seychelles when, in breach of a UN embargo some months earlier, he had purchased eighty tons of weapons, using a transfer of US$1.3 million allegedly sent through the French bank BNP Paribas, with consignments delivered to Goma.[25] The camera panned around Bagosora to show the pathetic remnants of a shattered army sleeping in the streets.

The interview with Bagosora was by Swiss journalist Philippe Dahinden, an expert on Rwanda who weeks before had addressed the United Nations Human Rights Commission special session in Geneva where he called for the arrest and prosecution of RTLM announcers and promoters and urged for action to defeat the genocidal forces.[26] Dahinden, now in Goma, chanced upon Bagosora, and with no hesitation began the interview by telling him how well versed he was in Bagosora's murderous activities in death squads pre-genocide. Dahinden said he had an informer who had given him the details. For several seconds Bagosora stared at Dahinden. They never existed, he snapped. They were an invention of the RPF. 'There were *RPF* death squads,' Bagosora said. Dahinden persisted. Bagosora sneered and said, 'You are beginning to really annoy me.' His jowls trembled with rage. 'You will die one day,' Bagosora said and sauntered off.[27]

The camps eventually spread over a network of 100 kilometres of roads, all refugees fed and sheltered by the aid agencies. Within the camp the militia had grown to an estimated 30,000 people as the Hutu Power leadership began to recruit boys, some as young as ten years old, for militia training. Some 4,000 murders took place in Goma in the first month of the exodus. Killings, threats, extortions, rape and brutality were common.

The fleeing military contingents had crossed the border into Zaire (DRC) in an orderly fashion, with weapons intact. They had moved in units with artillery, mortars and at least four anti-aircraft guns and anti-tank weapons intact. The arms deals, concluded in exile with flights into Goma airport, allowed the forces to rearm.²⁸ Deliveries of weapons came directly from the French military.²⁹

Thanks to their safe retreat, the high command of the RGF gathered together for a week of meetings in Goma starting on 2 September.³⁰ A detailed typed account of the discussions held by these twenty-eight officers and their commander, Major General Augustin Bizimungu, was later found in an archive abandoned in three buses in a refugee camp.³¹ In their meetings, the defeated officers agreed that the RPF had caused the entire catastrophe, by having invaded in 1990. They complained of their 'demonisation' by the UN and the international media. There were false reports about 'genocide of the Tutsi' and there needed to be some balance, some positive press coverage. This had been a civil war, and what they needed was a concerted media campaign to counteract the 'falsehoods'.

The army's propaganda commission reported the successful production of thousands of leaflets about their forthcoming 'liberation struggle', and how they would soon be on the verge of retaking the country. They decided to increase the ideological education given to all ranks. They decided their Commission of Politics and Exterior Relations should deploy emissaries to foreign countries to explain their plight and shift international public opinion; they needed to use the Western press to get their message across.

Elsewhere, in Bukavu, South Kivu, ministers in the exiled Interim Government were also busy with plans for the future. In abandoned archives was a fascinating account of a visit to Paris in September 1994 written by the exiled foreign minister of the Interim Government, Jérôme Bicamumpaka, who had addressed the UN Security Council in May. Now in exile, he was desperate to drum up financial and political support for the Interim Government, and his account of the visit to Paris was written as a letter to the exiled president Théodore Sindikubwabo. There was nothing but bad news. Only one French official had agreed to meet him, and two others met him informally. Their warning was that given the current reputation of the Interim Government, he should keep as low a profile as possible.³²

Bicamumpaka described how French officials had told him the most urgent task was to compile dossiers to show that the RPF had committed genocide. They needed names of the RPF 'death-squad' members. They needed to show how Lieutenant General Dallaire, the force commander of UNAMIR, was to blame for the catastrophe. The Security Council's expert report on Rwanda was due in November and this information had to be available before then. One further piece of advice the anonymous French official gave Bicamumpaka was the necessity of a new communications strategy. They should launch a press campaign in the international media. They needed to find people skilled at strategic communication and opinion-making, people not compromised in the massacres. The French official assured him that the position of the exiled Interim Government was 'comparable to the French government in exile in London during World War II'.[33]

5

Crime Scene

The early attempts to find justice for the victims of the genocide of the Tutsi were disastrous. There were no teams of forensic scientists at massacre sites sent by the International Criminal Tribunal for Rwanda (ICTR), no meticulous search for criminal evidence, no careful study of government archives. In the tribunal's Office of the Prosecutor, established in Kigali, there was no overall strategy. No one knew where to start. No central index of documents was established, no index of interviews and other evidence.[1]

With no witness protection unit, Hutu Power remained a threat. Survivors became too scared to talk to anyone, ICTR staff received regular threats, and not enough security personnel were hired to accompany investigators into the field. In June 1996, for example, thirty-six potential witnesses were murdered to ensure their silence. Meanwhile, at the Office of the Prosecutor in Kigali established at the Amahoro Hotel the front gate was often left wide open and the front desk was frequently unattended.[2]

In October 1996 the genocide had already been over for two years and not one trial had started when the newly appointed chief prosecutor of the ICTR, Louise Arbour, made her first visit to the Office of the Prosecutor in Kigali. She was astonished at what she found. The staff had removed the doors of their offices and mounted them on crates to make desks. They used wooden boxes for chairs.[3] A frequent complaint was a lack of pens and pencils. Telephone calls were regularly interrupted, while monthly telephone bills remained unpaid. There were no functioning photocopiers, and the only computers were provided by the UN Assistance Mission for Rwanda (UNAMIR II). The investigators lacked vehicles to go to massacre sites.

After listening to disgruntled staff, Arbour collected letters and testimonials and took them to the United Nations Secretariat in New York, resulting in an internal audit by the inspector general, Karl T. Paschke, undersecretary-general for Internal Oversight Services. In November 1996, Paschke travelled with a team of investigators to Arusha and Kigali to conduct interviews and examine records.

The Paschke report arrived in February 1997. It immediately resulted in two resignations: the tribunal's Kenyan chief admin-istrator, Andronico Adede, and the deputy prosecutor, Honoré Rakotomanana of Madagascar.[4] Paschke had concluded that since its inception, not a single administrative area at the ICTR func-tioned effectively. There was no accounting system established. The tribunal used finance officers to transport several hundred thousand US dollars across Tanzania, from Dar es Salaam to Arusha and Kigali, because dollars were not available from banks in Arusha. Paschke noted that the payment of salaries in cash was risky, costly and inefficient. Financial records and reports were incomplete and unreliable.

The single most important failure was within the Office of the Prosecutor, where no prosecution strategy existed. The investi-gative teams set their own plans and strategies and day-to-day guidance was lacking. Instead of targeting high-ranking officials, investigators sought out middle-level bureaucrats. The office urgently needed a deputy prosecutor with experience of direct-ing significant investigations. It needed experienced investigators, and intelligence analysts with strategic experience who knew how leads were developed and prioritised.[5] The legal officers assigned to the investigation teams had little or no experience in criminal investigations and yet were expected to advise on how to collect evidence as well as draft indictments.

Paschke concluded all indictments needed review. 'It would seem axiomatic', he wrote, 'that the most important criminal trials since the Nuremberg would require a high degree of expertise in criminal law ... and significant relevant experience.'

The recruitment problem was acute. With no regular appropriation of money from the UN and staff offered only three-month contracts, there was trouble attracting suitable candidates. Some positions took more than a year to fill, and some staff were hired with no interview process. At the time of the Paschke visit to Kigali, the budget provided for one hundred direct-hire criminal investigators, but only thirty-five were on staff. These investigators were borrowed largely from the Dutch police, who had started to return home; and when staff left there was no follow-up on their cases. There was secondment of some staff for up to six months only. The investigators from various police forces from UN member states had no experience of investigating a crime of such magnitude.

Two years from the date of the creation of the tribunal, Paschke noted, so many problems faced the Office of the Prosecutor that they undermined its mission. He laid the blame entirely with the UN Office of Legal Affairs. 'If the UN means to keep its promises to the Rwandan victims of genocide ... then the Secretariat must assist the Secretary-General in the tasks of ensuring that the body established to bring justice ... becomes fully functional.'

The UN Office of Legal Affairs in New York, while intimately involved with the tribunal for former Yugoslavia, had virtually ignored the tribunal for Rwanda.[6] From the earliest days, the first chief prosecutor, Richard Goldstone, had suspected the ICTR was going to be the poor cousin to the International Criminal Tribunal for the former Yugoslavia (ICTY) established in The Hague.[7] His successor, Louise Arbour, found a marked difference between the two. In The Hague, the offices spread over three floors with scores of lawyers, investigators, forensic experts and administrators. Some of the world's best legal minds worked at verifying and organising the evidence that concerned three Balkan wars over five years. Evidence collected was carefully stored in a steel-lined vault in the building's basement and neatly filed in acid-free containers.[8] This included raw evidence from field workers and material collected from graves. There was personal testimony, descriptions of mortar and sniper attacks, and hundreds of hours of taped interviews with victims and perpetrators.

The ICTY benefitted from the most comprehensive fact-finding operation in UN history, the work of a commission established in 1992 by the Security Council in resolution 780 to investigate war crimes. For two years, thirty-five field investigations took place and an extensive database was established. The eventual report exceeded 3,300 pages.[9] Over a period of two years, more than 140 lawyers and law students worked at the database, producing 80,000 documents and 300 hours of videotapes. The funding came from states' voluntary contributions, together with personnel, private sources of funding, and ultimately the support of DePaul University in the US, which enabled the establishment of a database in Chicago.[10]

There was nothing remotely similar for Rwanda. In Kigali, the evidence unit relied on information provided by a variety of sources, including human rights groups. A first detailed account of massacres came from African Rights, a small NGO in London; its publication, *Death, Despair and Defiance*, first appeared in September 1994 and was updated in 1995. In detailed, graphic and upsetting interviews, the unbearable witness testimony collected by two activists provided an account of the preparations and named the principal killers.

The Special Rapporteur of the UN Commission on Human Rights, René Degni-Ségui, eventually gathered together the names of fifty-five people who he considered to be chiefly responsible for the genocide and against whom there was sufficient evidence to prosecute for these crimes. Documents were collected from the crime scene by the UN Independent Commission of Experts that reported to the Security Council in December 1994, establishing overwhelming proof of genocide. The tribunal also requested documents from journalists.[11] Documents found in the *préfecture* offices, in the Ministry of Defence in Kigali, and some of the documents taken into exile by the génocidaires and abandoned in refugee camps, were returned to the capital.

By 2004, ten years after the creation of the ICTR, 35,000 items had been collected and 5,000 interview transcripts had been made. When the Commander for Investigation in the Office of the Prosecutor, Maxwell Nkole, testified in the trial of Colonel Théoneste Bagosora in June that year, he said the largest collection of documents in their possession came from Belgian civilian and military investigators. They were the first on the crime scene coming from Belgium to investigate the murders of ten UNAMIR soldiers of Belgian nationality on 7 April 1994 and the circumstances surrounding the assassination of President Juvénal Habyarimana, for which the génocidaires had blamed Belgian soldiers.

There remains a widespread belief that there was a lack of documentary evidence because Hutu Power leaders had taken much of the paper evidence with them when they fled. As a result, the ICTR had largely relied on eyewitness evidence. Unlike the Nuremberg Tribunal, which received reams of documents, the ICTR had the reputation of having relied on a 'fact-finding fog of inconsistent, vague and sometimes incoherent testimony'.[12]

In fact, there was a large amount of documentary evidence. Most of the National Archives of Rwanda survived the civil war. It was a prodigious amount of paper and a legacy of Belgian colonial rule, the remnants of a vast bureaucracy created by the colonisers. The system required multiple copies of every decision in every institution of state, and daily reports written to the office of the president on the decisions made in all government offices. The archives included documents, sound recordings and photographs, classified secret and confidential intelligence reports, government memoranda, letters, faxes, invoices and diplomatic cables. The archive included the transcripts of interrogations and of listening devices and telephone intercepts. Written in business French, these were perfectly typed records of state.

Included in the legacy of Belgian colonial rule was the classification of the entire population, and when in 1933 teams of Belgian bureaucrats toured the country to determine the ethnicity of everyone as Hutu, Tutsi or Twa, careful written records were kept. Every Rwandan was measured: height, the length of the nose, the shape of the eyes and so on. The National Archives included a collection from the office of Belgian Colonel Guy Logiest, the 'special military resident' in Kigali, whose military-led administration in

1959 first put into practice a pro-Hutu policy by appointing more than 300 Hutu chiefs and subchiefs to replace Tutsi incumbents. The effect of forty years of Belgian colonial administration on the territory known as Ruanda-Urundi was key to understanding what happened in 1994.[13]

The National Archives exposed the true nature of the twenty-year rule of President Habyarimana, a man who portrayed himself as modest and religious, someone who cared only for the development of his country. In fact, Habyarimana and his cronies, mostly his wife, Agathe Kanziga, and her relatives, treated the country and its peasant population as a fiefdom, motivated by greed and racial hatred. On taking office in a military coup in 1973 Habyarimana promised to ease ethnic tension, but instead increased discrimination against Tutsi and reinforced the policy called 'ethnic équilibre' that was introduced by his predecessor, President Grégoire Kayibanda. Habyarimana further reduced the participation of Tutsi in society.

The policy of ethnic quotas ensured that the army and diplomatic service, with rare exceptions, were overwhelmingly Hutu, as were education and employment. With the use of a government census that apparently and erroneously proved that Tutsi constituted 9 per cent of the population, the government decreed the same Tutsi representation in each sector of Rwandan life. Vigilante groups visited schools to reduce the number of Tutsi pupils who exceeded the quota. Comités de Salut Public were established that checked and verified each person's ethnicity, clearly marked on everyone's mandatory identification card.

The enforcement of the system involved investigations into the 'true ethnicity' of state employees. For instance, a file with the names of all the professors at the National University of Rwanda listed the 'verifications' carried out to see if they were 'Hutu of pure blood'. After interviews in the local *communes*, agents from the domestic intelligence service, the Service Central de Renseignements (SCR), reported that six of the professors had Tutsi mothers. Two professors had apparently falsified their ethnicity, and their cases were submitted to the Minister of the Interior to 'regularise their situation'.[14]

Within the same well-guarded compound as the colonial house of the president's office was a series of anonymous single-storey buildings and it was here that these secret files were created. These were offices of the SCR, with metal bars and net curtains at the windows, hidden from view and a short distance from a plush presidential office in central Kigali. There were interrogation rooms and cells for prisoners at the back of the building, hot as ovens in the sun.

The archive of the SCR revealed Rwanda to have been one of the most monitored countries on earth. The files of this intelligence service had been moved to a basement room in a building on the other side of Kigali. They revealed twenty-four-hour surveillance reports, and records of intercepted telephone calls and listening devices in hotels and embassies. The archive of the SCR contained intercepted mail and family photographs, transcribed interrogations, and the updated addresses of Rwandans living abroad.

The domestic intelligence service had compiled the names of every Tutsi teacher, lawyer, clerk or official. The names of those judged politically subversive, those who 'distanced themselves from the regime' or those who could not be trusted as unquestioning supporters were listed. After October 1990, when the Rwandan Patriotic Army (RPA) came across the border from Uganda, the categorisation for Tutsi changed to 'enemy' or 'collaborator of the RPF'. The SCR began to compile lists of Tutsi in each commune, those who left to join the RPA and those likely to do so. The intelligence service controlled by Hutu from the north believed even southern Hutu to be their opponents because people from the south, according to the extremists, had closer links to Tutsi through intermarriage, and were branded 'the enemy within'.

A fundamental task of the SCR was to ensure the anti-Tutsi discriminatory system operated effectively, and the first document in every file first established ethnicity with lists of maternal and paternal relatives going back five or six generations. The SCR was based on a Belgian system created in 1960 and first called the Sûreté Belge du Ruanda-Urundi.[15] It was an intelligence service attached to the office of the president, and it employed mainly civilian staff. On sensitive investigations, the SCR agents kept the president informed. For instance, when a prominent opposition politician claimed to be Hutu, triumphant SCR agents presented Habyarimana with a copy of a 1948 *commune* record that showed this man's family, including his brother, registered as Tutsi. The agents concluded the man was 'probably a Tutsi who was passing himself off as a Hutu'.

Most importantly, contained in the president's papers were files on *auto-défense civile*. This was the murderous method used by the perpetrators of massacres of Tutsi to ensure public participation in the killing on as broad a basis as possible, by co-opting everyone. This system first emerged in 1963 in response to an armed and unsuccessful invasion by Tutsi refugees. It entailed an intense programme of propaganda spread by local authorities to persuade Hutu peasants that for their own safety the region needed to be 'cleansed' of Tutsi, who posed a mortal danger. The system involved roadblocks manned by civilians with weapons provided by the military. When it was first used, in four southern *préfectures*, the préfet called meetings with *bourgmestres* in order to explain the policy of *auto-défense civile* and to give necessary orders on how to combat the enemy.[16] The radio in Kigali repeatedly broadcast emergency warnings that a Tutsi plot was under way to enslave Hutu. The system resulted in the murder of 5,000 Tutsi by the local population.

The methods used to kill large numbers of Tutsi civilians involved propaganda and civilian participation in the killing, and in later massacres in 1972 and 1973 the participation of the military was more noticeable. The perpetrators in 1994 used the same *auto-défense civile*, including roadblocks to prevent escape and the distribution of weapons to local administrators.[17] In the president's paper, a history of *auto-défense civile*, neatly filed, showed how in 1991, *préfectures* established security committees and each reported directly to the president on the progress and efficiency of the *auto-défense civile*.[18]

However, despite the weight of this evidence, the National Archives of Rwanda and the offices of the SCR seemed of little consequence to ICTR investigators who were uninterested in the older documents. The temporal jurisdiction of the ICTR, on the insistence of the French government in UN Security Council negotiations, was restricted to 1994, from 1 January until 31 December. The defence lawyers for the génocidaires made strenuous objections to evidence outside the jurisdiction and claimed that whatever happened in previous years had nothing to do with what happened in 1994.

Further evidence existed elsewhere in the capital. The vaults in the Banque Nationale du Rwanda (BNR) held the documentary proof of the preparations for the 1994 genocide of the Tutsi.[19] For two years, the files and ledgers lay undisturbed until August 1996, when two experts arrived. 'We found cellars full,' recalled Pierre Galand. Galand was a former director of Oxfam-Belgium and a Belgian senator, and his colleague, Professor Michel Chossudovsky, was a Canadian economist and expert in international development and finance. Rwanda's post-genocide government had received a demand to repay the international loans incurred by the country since 1990 and had commissioned an investigation into this massive indebtedness.

The support for their work within the Rwandan government came from the minister of finance in the new post-genocide government, Jean Birara, a former governor of the BNR.[20] He believed from his close proximity to the Hutu elite that the genocide of the Tutsi was more than two years in the making. Birara had taken the risky step in 1993 of secretly informing Western ambassadors of a US\$12 million arms deal concluded with a French company at a time when Rwanda faced an economic abyss.[21] In the early weeks of 1994, Birara had seen lists of potential victims in circulation, and he believed the militia in April numbered 50,000 youth.[22]

Working in the bank vaults, Galand and Chossudovsky collected enough evidence to show that the debt built up between 1990 and 1994 had principally financed weaponry for the armed forces and the creation of a civilian militia. They described how the perpetrators financed the 'young delinquents, products of an impoverished society, enrolled in their thousands in a civilian militia responsible for massacres and genocide'.[23]

In the invoices, bank statements, faxes, telexes and ledgers, and in column after column of state expenditure, they discovered how the génocidaires paid for the training and indoctrination of the unemployed youth, siphoning money from other accounts, the funding revealed in confidential correspondence with the Ministry of Defence. Galand found invoices for large quantities of beer for recruits, accounts that showed that money for boots and clothes came from the military budget, and food stocks intended for famine relief were sold to make funds available.[24]

The militia in Kigali used hospital vehicles and filled them with petrol at the expense of the Ministry of Health, a frequent procedure. The vehicles imported for public transport were diverted to provide transport for the militia and consumer goods sold on the local market, the profit recycled towards the militia. The former head of customs at the airport revealed members of the presidential family had their own hangar and ran a parallel customs system and imported anything from fridges to BMW motorcars.

The experts found receipts and invoices for the mass importation of machetes from China by four companies in 1993, none of these companies associated with agriculture. The invoices revealed a total US$725,669 spent on 581,000 machetes, and other invoices for the same companies for quantities of lethal instruments ultimately used in the killing, including hoes, axes, hammers, razor blades, screwdrivers, pickaxes, scythes, sickles, spades and nails. According to bank records, US$4.6 million was spent on this agricultural equipment in 1993 alone.

A significant importer of machetes was the multimillionaire Félicien Kabuga, a genocide suspect who remains at large, one of the most wanted fugitives in the world with a US$5 million reward on his head from the US Rewards for Justice Program. Kabuga also paid large sums to establish the hate radio RTLM. His indictment at the ICTR described a 'strategy devised by fellow extremists, [which] included several components, carefully worked out by the various prominent figures who shared the Hutu Power ideology'. Kabuga had a 'catalytic role in the political violence'.[25]

The experts found the invoices for arms expenditures and found evidence of payments for ammunition, grenades and landmines. There was a high number of low-intensity weapons, cheap to buy and easier to stockpile. The main arms suppliers during the 1990–1994 period were France, Belgium, South Africa, Egypt and the People's Republic of China. These weapons contributed to the huge numbers of victims in the genocide, and to the speed of the killing.

Midway through their work, Galand and Chossudovsky put important documents on one side in a vault locked for safekeeping. These included documents they believed useful for future prosecutions; they then left Rwanda to fulfil professional commitments in Brussels. But when they returned to the bank some weeks later, they found the vault empty, their collection missing. They tried to replace the missing documents by looking for carbon copies in the Ministry of Defence and Ministry of Finance.

This was not the only time evidence disappeared. Sometimes the files they needed went missing or files were spirited away from them so quickly that those seizing them left a literal trail of paper on the floor, or they would arrive at the right place and the documents had vanished days before. They soon worked out that the disappearances were systematic. Galand believed Hutu Power moles were all over the new administration.[26] He suspected there were people working at the BNR whose intention was to prevent full discovery. The Rwandans who had fled abroad and were implicated in the genocide were trying to protect themselves and were paying bank staff to get rid of certain records. Both Galand and Chossudovsky urgently appealed to senior officials in the UN Development Programme to help the new Rwandan government to protect the archives, but they did not receive an adequate response.

In the three-year period studied by these experts, one of the poorest countries in the world became the third largest importer of weapons on the African continent. The army increased from 5,000 to 40,000 across all ranks. While President Juvénal Habyarimana assured everyone that military purchases were legitimate to defend the country from the RPA, the total military budget was itemised by experts at US$83 million, and probably higher. Evidence existed of military equipment disguised as civilian goods.

Clear warnings to the World Bank were found in the documents of the BNR. Rwanda was the subject of a Structural Adjustment Programme (SAP) under an agreement signed in October 1990. In their eventual report in November 1996, Galand and Chossudovsky pointed out that the austerity measures imposed on the country had no effect on military spending, but education, health and infrastructure were all subject to funding cuts. There was famine, and a dramatic increase in unemployment. The incidence of severe child malnutrition increased dramatically, as did the number of recorded cases of malaria.[27] In a damning conclusion, the experts showed how money to pay for the genocide preparations came from quick disbursing loans from Western donors who entered into agreements with the regime stipulating that funds must be used not for military or paramilitary purposes but for necessary goods such as food and equipment.

The experts concluded that the money to pay for the genocide came from loans granted to the regime in June 1991, from the International Development Association (IDA), the African Development Fund (AFD), the European Development Fund and bilateral donors including Austria, Switzerland, Germany, the United States, Belgium and Canada.

The World Bank president, Lewis Preston, wrote a letter in April 1992 and raised his objections with Habyarimana about the militarisation of Rwanda. It came one month after the Rwandan Ministry of Defence concluded a further US$6 million deal with Egypt that benefited from a guarantee from French bank Crédit Lyonnais. The first deal in October 1990 for US$5.889 million was followed by another in December for US$3.511 million. By April 1991, the Rwandan government had spent US$10.861 million on Egyptian weapons. In June 1992, a further US$1.3 million was given to Egypt. A November deal included 25,000 rounds of ammunition, and in February 1993, 3,000 automatic rifles, AKM guns and 100,000 rounds of ammunition, and thousands of landmines and grenades. The largest arms deal in March

1992 was for US$6 million for light weapons and small arms and included 450 Kalashnikov rifles, 2,000 rocket-propelled grenades, 16,000 mortar shells and more than 3 million rounds of small-arms ammunition.

Galand believed that the international financial institutions owed reparations to the people of Rwanda as a result of their negligence. Five missions were sent by the World Bank to follow and supervise the Structural Adjustment Programme between June 1991 and October 1993. Only in December 1993 did the World Bank suspend payment of a tranche of money because 'certain objectives were not met'.[28]

And did this damning evidence make its way to the international courts? Investigators from the ICTR interviewed Galand several times about the discoveries in the BNR. On each occasion, while the investigators changed, the questions remained the same. Galand said no one asked him to testify about his evidence, and no response was forthcoming to his request that he appear before a judge to tell what he knew. He is unsure whether the ICTR ever obtained a copy of their report. The ICTR rejected the photocopies he provided of some of the most crucial documents because they were not original copies.[29]

6

Denial

At the centre of the denial of the genocide of the Tutsi was the idea that far from any planning, the killings of civilians in April–July 1994 resulted from a 'spontaneous uprising'. This position was most eloquently outlined in the Security Council even as the crime took place, and was written into diplomatic telegrams, letters and cables. It later emerged in the courtrooms of the International Criminal Tribunal for Rwanda (ICTR), where the perpetrators were eventually put on trial.

The attempts to devise a collective defence strategy among the fugitive leaders of Hutu Power, to agree a common discourse, a narrative upon which they could all agree, began in exile in the refugee camps. They met with Luc de Temmerman, a Flemish commercial lawyer who worked for the family of President Juvénal Habyarimana for a number of years and sought power of attorney from members of the former regime now on the run.

In July 1996, just after the ICTR issued its first indictments, de Temmerman held a meeting in a hotel in Nairobi with a group of wanted fugitives, offering his services to supervise their defence. The meeting was financed by a political organisation that was created in the Mugunga refugee camp in Zaire (DRC), the Rassemblement pour le Retour des Réfugiés et la Démocratie au Rwanda (RDR).[1] Its members, particularly at the senior level, included genocide suspects and Hutu Power ideologues, ministers, diplomats and senior civil servants. De Temmerman announced to the gathering that he would argue the innocence or guilt not of their own individual cases but of the 'Hutu cause'.[2]

At another meeting with fugitives in the Mugunga refugee camp, de Temmerman expressed regret that among the 'Hutu leadership' were people who affirmed that there had been genocide conducted by the Hutu. 'Unless we change such attitudes we will fall into a trap and it would be impossible for him to plead not guilty on our behalf', a typed report recorded that was later found among abandoned documents. The Flemish lawyer asked how he could possibly defend anyone not prepared to defend himself. 'All Hutu had to understand', he told them, 'if the genocide was confirmed, then it was the end of them as a people.'[3] They needed to get the message across that there were victims on all sides in Rwanda and steps were needed to avoid apportioning blame for what happened.

A US lawyer at the ICTR, Michael Karnavas, was appointed to defend the first case to reach court, and he recalls how de Temmerman cautioned him about the trial. He told Karnavas he was not representing his defendant but 'the cause'. Karnavas was told in no uncertain terms that genocide had not occurred – that the idea of a genocide was merely Tutsi propaganda. Furthermore, if genocide had taken place, the Tutsis were responsible for exterminating the Hutu – something that they could prove by exhuming the mass graves.

Karnavas then went on to claim that de Temmerman told him that all he needed to do was to compare the body size and facial characteristics of the dead. 'When I refused to cooperate,' Karnavas recalled, 'he openly accused me of being an agent of the Rwandan government, a Tutsi spy who was sabotaging the trial of Jean-Paul Akayesu and of course "the cause".'[4] Karnavas left the tribunal. However, in the end, de Temmerman's collective defence strategy never did materialise. The defendants awaiting trial and their lawyers concluded that it might hamper their individual cases.

While de Temmerman stepped back, his line of defence was a continuing feature in the trials and a fixture in court.[5] The first trial at the ICTR was that of a *bourgmestre*, a local mayor, Jean-Paul Akayesu, a teacher and schools inspector who was sentenced to a life term in July 1998. For his appeal, Akayesu called on a Canadian lawyer, John Philpot,[6] who shared his own ideas about events, believing the tribunal to be a product of US imperialism.

Philpot argued that Uganda was at the root cause of everything, and had used the RPF to plot against, and seize, a Hutu country. Philpot claimed how after the assassination of President Juvénal Habyarimana, 'within two hours the RPF had been activated' and then people had defended themselves in response. 'There was a total societal breakdown. It was a war for political power. Excesses were committed on all sides,' he said in an interview in 1997.[7] For Philpot, the Hutu were on the losing side in a civil war and were currently suffering arbitrary and unjustified punishment. No proof existed of a plan.

Justice Navi Pillay addressed the issue of planning in her summary of the judgement during Akayesu's trial. To the doubters and deniers, Pillay explained there was no single meeting, no dusty document discovered in a vault, traced one day as the definitive first step in the genocide master plan. There was not one single-minded and well-defined plot that had been clear-cut from the beginning and followed through until the end. She noted, however, as the story unfolded through 1991 and 1992, there existed 'a pattern the world community had missed'. The radical and military officials were working together, she noted, testing various killing techniques. Their experiments taught them that they could massacre large numbers of people quickly and efficiently and, based on early reactions, they could get away with it.

Jean-Paul Akayesu was guilty of all nine counts on the charge sheet including genocide, direct and public incitement to commit genocide and crimes against humanity – extermination, murder, torture, rape and other inhumane acts. His life sentence was confirmed on appeal.

Judge Pillay became an expert in the circumstances of the genocide of the Tutsi. She sat as a judge in several landmark cases, including that of Jean Kambanda, the prime minister in the Interim Government, sentenced to life imprisonment in May 1998. Kambanda was the first person to enter a plea of guilty for genocide, the first head of a government held accountable for the crime, as defined in the 1948 Genocide Convention.

It took another six years for the case of Colonel Théoneste Bagosora to come to court on 2 April 2002. Here was 'Colonel

Apocalypse', said to be the genocide's principal architect.[8] Many news outlets portrayed him as a monster, an epithet he was determined to overturn.

In his defence, Bagosora said he never asked anyone to kill anyone. A European-trained army officer, he was a professional soldier who attended the most prestigious military academies, including the Royal Military Academy in Marche-les-Dames, Namur, in Belgium, where he was awarded a para-commando certificate. Bagosora was the first Rwandan to attend the French École Supérieure de Guerre Interarmées between 1980 and 1981 and the Institut des Hautes Études de Défense Nationale, from where he graduated in 1982 with a commendation. When the ICTR investigators looked further into his military career, they noted links with members of the French secret service, the Direction Générale de la Sécurité Extérieure (DGSE), but the line of inquiry was not further pursued. His highest rank was his promotion to a full colonel in October 1989.

Bagosora retired from the army and took a civilian post in September 1993, when he became the chef de cabinet to the Minister of Defence. At the time the Forces Armées Rwandaises (FAR) and the Gendarmerie Nationale (GN) did not have a unified command and came directly under the ministry. In this role, every decision went across his desk, and his wide-ranging responsibilities included formulating policy and filling in for the minister whenever he was absent. His job also entailed liaison with the military advisers provided by Belgium, technical advisers from Germany and senior French officers embedded in Rwandan army units. Seven months before the genocide began, all the Rwandan armed forces began to report directly to Bagosora.

The prosecution took five years to prepare the Bagosora trial. There was speculation that thirteen different investigative teams worked on the case, one replacing the other in succession. The undoubted highlight of the trial was the seventeen-day testimony Bagosora gave in his own defence that began on 24 October 2005, and in which he gave his own version of events.

The Bagosora testimony was a study in denial. Repeating claims made familiar in the diplomatic correspondence in 1994, he warned judges that a 'pro-Tutsi lobby' was fooling the world. The story of genocide was a propaganda ploy in a campaign expertly orchestrated by the RPF and its allies. Bagosora explained that in Rwanda in 1994 there was no plan for the killing, and the 'official history' was completely wrong.

As for himself, and his role within the chaos, he denied being in charge. For three days after the assassination of the president in his plane on Wednesday, 6 April, military leaders had faced a series of cataclysmic events and 'unexpected political violence'. On the systematic murder of politicians on the Thursday morning, Bagosora said it was due to a 'settlement of scores' arising from neighbourhood or political disputes or other reasons that he could not define.[9] There had followed an unplanned explosion of violence for which the RPF was responsible and which they, the Hutu, were powerless to contain.

The case itself had been designated ICTR-98-41. Bagosora was on trial with three other senior military officers as the tribunal was obliged to group defendants to try to speed up the judicial process. The other defendants were Major General Gratien Kabiligi, former head of the Rwandan army operations bureau (G3), Major Aloys Ntabakuze, the commander of the elite para-commando battalion, and Colonel Anatole Nsengiyumva, the commander of the northern Gisenyi sector, a former head of army intelligence.

All four officers pleaded not guilty, denying every charge. These included conspiracy to commit genocide, genocide, complicity in genocide, as well as murder, rape, persecution, extermination and 'inhumane acts' constituting crimes against humanity. The presiding judge was Erik Møse, from Norway, who sat with Jai Ram Reddy, a former attorney general of Fiji, and Sergei Alekseevich Egorov, a law professor from the Russian Federation.

Each defendant had individual defence teams. Each team was determined, energetic, and fought a comprehensive case. Every count on every charge sheet was challenged, every single date, time and place – including the testimony of prosecution witnesses, no matter how fearful their court ordeal. There was court time taken up with experts, for by now outside witnesses had started to come to Arusha, with their own revisionist theories for the court.

Some of them came from Europe, and experts in their field provided testimony and reports.

Getting a true picture of the first three days was decisive, as the prosecution lawyers explained to the court. At the time, Bagosora, as the acting minister of defence, assumed power of the highest military authority and exercised effective control over the Rwandan armed forces. Bagosora was in a position to intercede and, as a high-ranking official, had the means to avert the atrocities. Instead, he presided over the murder of ten UN peacekeepers, the elimination of the political opposition, mass murder, mutilation and rape of countless civilians, and these terrible atrocities during the first formative hours. This, then, ushered in the widespread killing everywhere else.[10]

In response, the defence strategy sought their own expert analysis of the opening days of the conflict. Bernard Lugan, associate professor of African history at the Jean Moulin University in Lyon, who published extensively on African politics, came to testify that there was no evidence to support the theory of planning for the killing. Instead, after the assassination of the president, the Hutu nationalists made the most of the resulting anarchy. Lugan explained how what happened was the result of years of violence by the RPF upon the Rwandan people. Thus, the years of terrorism and violence culminated in the death of President Habyarimana, the father of the nation. In a book published in 2004, Lugan described the conflict as a result of 'mutual hatreds'.[11]

Another defence witness was German political scientist Helmut Strizek, who told the court that the idea of planning made no sense. Strizek had lived in Rwanda between 1980 and 1983 working with the European Community (now EU) delegation as economic adviser. After he returned to Germany, he worked in the Ministry of Cooperation, in charge of the relationship between Germany, Rwanda and Burundi, and visited on several occasions.

It was obvious, he argued, that the RPF had brought down the president's plane and so the idea of planning was obsolete, and no more than a propaganda exercise. Only those people who claimed Hutu extremists brought down the plane believed in genocide planning. Why would Hutu extremists plan something when they did not know where such a thing might lead? Strizek described the genocide of the Tutsi as a 'unique type of genocide' in which there was no command and no planning but a spontaneous act by unruly, uncontrollable people who went on a killing spree.[12]

A Belgian priest, Father Serge Desouter, testified to the terrible impact of the civil war triggered by the Rwandan Patriotic Front (RPF) invasion in October 1990. A member of the White Fathers, Desouter lived many years in Rwanda, spoke Kinyarwanda, and claimed to have extensively studied the events of 1994.[13] He suggested that, rather than a plan for genocide, the 'mainly civilian-on-civilian violence' had been caused by people in fear. This fear was the result of the assassination of President Habyarimana and the consequent destabilisation of a new government.

The cross-examination of Bagosora was conducted by the Canadian lawyer Drew White. He suggested to Bagosora that if he removed the word 'Tutsi' in his evidence and replaced it with the word 'Jew', it would be considered racial discrimination. Bagosora refused to concede the point. There was a big difference between the Jews of Europe and the Tutsi, Bagosora responded. 'The difference with Rwanda was that, first of all, it was not the Jews who started the Second World War and secondly, it was not the Jews who took over power after the fall of Nazism. The Jews were victims.'

Bagosora, asked about the definition of Hutu extremism, replied: 'When people say Hutu extremist, it is in relation to whom? There are two extremes. Given that we were in a situation of conflict, you had the RPF on the one side, which, to a large extent, represented the Tutsi; and then on the other hand, you had the Hutu, who were opposed to the domination of the Tutsi through the RPF.'

While the Bagosora defence conceded that in the first few days certain elements of the military had been responsible for killing political figures, they disputed the level of organisation involved, and noted that none of these killings conformed to an 'organised military operation'. Bagosora was keen to reinforce the idea that he was in fact a serious and professional army officer, and when he was accused of visiting a number of roadblocks in Kigali, he sneered at the testimony of the witness, a night watchman. Bagosora told the judges he never went anywhere near road-blocks. He blurted out, 'Neither Hitler, Himmler nor [Göring] ever went running around in Berlin to flush out Jews to be killed. They would call their subordinates and juniors, give them instructions, and those instructions would be acted upon.'[14]

Bagosora said the disfranchised poor established the road-blocks on the initiative of local authorities. They had nothing to do with the Rwandan army. At that moment, all communication with the population had broken down. The armed forces lacked any control over the thousands of people who participated in the killing. The army was unable to engage civilians directly because it was too busy fighting the RPF.[15]

It was Judge Møse who raised the issue of large-scale massacres of Tutsi, and who wanted to know Bagosora's views on the subject of Kibuye, the *préfecture* where, pre-1994, the largest Tutsi population lived. During the period of the genocide Kibuye was also where the most widespread killing of Tutsi took place. At the end of April 1994, it was estimated that 200,000 people were murdered in Kibuye, and by the end of June, an estimate of only 8,000 Tutsi remained alive from the total population of a quarter of a million.

In those first weeks in Kibuye, local government officials and gendarmes had offered the Gatwaro sports stadium as a refuge to the frightened Tutsi who were fleeing massacres. On 18 April, however, soldiers arrived and threw grenades into the crowds, while machine-gun fire from the surrounding hills strafed the scattering families. When the ammunition ran out, the militia came in with machetes and nail-studded clubs to kill survivors. The next day, on 19 April, the militia returned, looking to finish off the wounded and loot the bodies. Some estimates put the number of dead people at the end of these two days at 20,000. It is believed that 12,000 people were killed in one day; one estimate calculated that 2,500 families were entirely wiped out at the stadium.

Later, the judge asked Bagosora how the 'Kibuye events conformed to the overall picture'. Bagosora said, 'If I said there were targeted killings in Kigali, there were also some in other *préfectures.*' The judge pointed out the targeted killings in Kibuye were Tutsi killings. 'Isn't that true?' Bagosora appeared confused. 'On the Kibuye dossier I am not an expert.' He hesitated. 'Because I was in Kigali and it is there I can give concrete examples of targeted killings. I saw the targeted assassination in Kigali and I had some information ... for example, in Gisenyi as well ... the massacres ... I think they started on the tenth and not the seventh. It was not systematic.' Leaning forward, Bagosora let out a long sigh before he slumped back in his chair. Later on, he offered: 'Me, I don't believe that genocide took place ... Most reasonable people think there were excessive massacres.'

Bagosora concluded that the massacres took place in an atmosphere of total disorder, with an absence of any political authority. The population of Rwanda turned on one another in chaotic circumstances.

'You claim to align yourself with Hutu people, but at the same time you blame them entirely for what happened in Rwanda in 1994,' the prosecuting lawyer Drew White pointed out. 'You say the ordinary citizen who took up arms and killed Tutsi in a spontaneous event had nothing to do with leadership and nothing to do with organisation. I am suggesting to you that perhaps it's time for you to free the Hutu citizens of Rwanda from the burden of all the blame that you put on them.' Bagosora made no response.

White told the court that from the outset Bagosora had been in a position of command as military units went house to house looking for pro-democracy politicians, journalists or lawyers – anyone who had advocated power-sharing with the RPF. Without the approval of the military, the prosecutor suggested, none of the events could have happened. In the early hours of Thursday, 7 April, when elite units in the army, including the Presidential Guard, eliminated Rwanda's pro-democracy politicians, Bagosora had already assumed official and de facto control of political and military affairs.

Next, Bagosora denied any role in the death of the prime minister, Agathe Uwilingiyimana, killed around 10 a.m. on Thursday, 7 April. Uwilingiyimana was thirty-eight years old, a former chemistry teacher, and when minister of education she had tried to end the quota system for Tutsi in schools. Throughout her political career she had been beaten up, threatened and frequently denigrated on the radio station RTLM. She was the subject of pornographic cartoons in the Hutu Power magazine *Kangura*. Bagosora claimed in court that Uwilingiyimana had been plotting a coup d'état and at a meeting on Tuesday, 4 April, she had planned with military officers from the south to rid the country of President Habyarimana and install a regime comprising only southerners. Unruly soldiers killed her, Bagosora said. Her UN Assistance Mission for Rwanda (UNAMIR) protection squad abandoned her.

These were more lies. Presidential Guards had disarmed her UN escort, which included ten peacekeepers from UNAMIR sent to protect her. They were all led to a minibus parked nearby and taken a short distance to the military base, Camp Kigali, where an adjutant who worked for G2 (Intelligence) told Rwandan soldiers outside the barracks that these Belgian troops had taken part in the assassination of the president the previous night. They were set upon, and one managed to disarm a Rwandan soldier. After an assault that lasted six hours, all ten peacekeepers were dead.

This was a 'spontaneous mutiny', according to Bagosora, and not planned or ordered. Instead, Bagosora blamed their deaths on Lieutenant General Roméo Dallaire, the commander of UNAMIR, who should have tried to rescue them. Nevertheless, as they fought for their lives, the Camp Kigali commander informed Bagosora, who was chairing a meeting in an adjacent building, of their plight. The prosecution viewed the deaths of the peacekeepers as part of an effort by certain members of the extremist political circles to provoke the withdrawal of the Belgian contingent. In this the extremists were ultimately successful.

The prosecution described how Bagosora engineered the creation of the Interim Government that was put together in the French embassy. There Bagosora presented a slate of candidates for ministerial posts in a new government agreed upon by Hutu Power extremists.[16] In his cross-examination, White reminded Bagosora that it should have been Judge Joseph Kavaruganda, the head of Rwanda's constitutional court, to swear in any new government, but the Presidential Guard had done away with Kavaruganda early on Thursday morning. In response, Bagosora claimed to the court that Judge Kavaruganda was killed 'in the crowd' by mutinous soldiers from the Presidential Guard.

Drew White asked Bagosora what was necessary to mount a successful coup d'état. 'As a matter of principle, a coup d'état is not legal,' Bagosora replied. 'It is double or quits. If you succeed, fine. If you fail, you are done in.' White asked the question again. Bagosora replied, 'You need to have enough military strength, as well as sufficient political credibility. You need a combination of both. You ... must be convinced that if you have to address the population, they will believe you.'

White continued: 'Colonel, I'm going to suggest to you that there was a coup on the night of April 6, 1994. It was a coup by the Rwandan armed forces over the political authorities of the Rwandan government. Moreover, you were the head of that coup. That you took over the power of the country of Rwanda on the night of April 6, 1994.'

White reminded the court that President Juvénal Habyarimana had come to power in a coup d'état in a similar fashion in July 1973, with Bagosora one of the senior military officers by his side. The plotters had created a Committee for National Peace and Unity to hide their transfer of power from one Hutu government to another. During the night of 2 July, a group of army officers had put a ring of steel around Kiyovu, the leafy residential enclave in the capital where government ministers lived, and arrested all of them, including deputies, their allied army officers and state functionaries. These people disappeared; the fifty-five dignitaries were put in the notorious Ruhengeri prison, beaten and slowly starved to death. The deposed president, Grégoire Kayibanda, placed under house arrest, also starved to death.

Twenty-one years later, in April 1994, in the hours following the assassination of Habyarimana, Bagosora also created a Crisis Committee with senior officers to 'coordinate the country's security and defence' until the creation of a provisional government, the Interim Government of Hutu Power hard-liners, and fraudulently claimed to adhere to the Arusha Accords, although not a single Tutsi was included.

White argued that although the prosecutor had not charged Bagosora with the assassination of Habyarimana, it had become necessary to challenge the insistence of Bagosora, and the other defendants in the trial, that the RPF was responsible for the crime. Bagosora blamed others, White claimed, to deflect attention away from himself. 'The prosecution feels at least a presumptive burden to put the propositions to this witness that he's incorrect in those assertions and that, in fact, the truth runs contrary to the evidence,' the lawyer proposed.

Bagosora counterargued, suggesting that the event of the assassination was a 'fateful day', and remarked how unlikely it was that so many people responsible for state security were killed in the presidential jet or were out of the country. In effect, the army was decapitated that day. The minister of defence, Augustin Bizimana, and the head of G2 (Military Intelligence), Colonel Aloys Ntiwiragabo, were in Cameroon. The head of army operations (G3), Colonel Gratien Kabiligi, was in Egypt. When first told of the crash of the aircraft, Bagosora said he feared a trap, or that they might be in the middle of a coup d'état.

While the Office of the Prosecutor at the ICTR ruled the assassination of Habyarimana outside the tribunal's jurisdiction, it nonetheless played a major role in proceedings. For the defence, it was the foundation stone of their case. Bagosora told the court that it was a known fact, accepted by all Rwandan experts, including expert prosecution witnesses, that the attack that triggered the tragedy in Rwanda was the responsibility of General Paul Kagame, the current president in Rwanda. This 'established criminal' should be on trial. The tribunal was a 'victor's court', putting only those 'Hutu who were vanquished' on trial. Bagosora also claimed that UNAMIR was an accomplice of the RPF in the missile attack.

In contrast, the reason why the Office of the Prosecutor excluded the president's assassination from the parameters of the case was the unreasonable chance of conviction. There was no point in bringing a case if it could not be won. 'There is so much information, disinformation and a lack of information that quite frankly the prosecutor does not believe that anyone could be convicted beyond a reasonable doubt of that crime. There is no point in bringing a charge. There would be no point in bringing charges if there was no likelihood of a conviction,' White said. Nevertheless, White reminded the court that Bagosora was a former commander of the anti-aircraft battalion in Camp Kanombe, adjacent to the Kigali International Airport (KIA). He was therefore more than aware that the flight path for the only runway went directly over the camp.

In the closing submissions on 28 May 2007, the prosecution accused the four military defendants of having prepared, planned, ordered, directed, incited, encouraged and approved the killing of innocent civilian Tutsi men, women and children, and others considered their accomplices. The prosecution reminded the judges of a decision made by the ICTR Appeals Chamber in the case of a politician, Édouard Karemera, and read it aloud to the court.

> There is no reasonable basis for anyone to dispute that, during 1994, there was a campaign of mass conscious participation in a nationwide government-organized system killing intended to destroy, in whole or at least in very large part, Rwanda's Tutsi population, which was a protected group. That campaign was, to a terrible degree, successful.[17]

No one had contributed more than the four accused to the success of that terrible campaign. The lawyers reminded the judges of the testimony of a direct witness to events, Lieutenant General Roméo Dallaire, who had told a military hearing that he believed the accused 'were implementing a plan that we had heard so much of from a variety of sources'. All information he received as force commander of UNAMIR led him to believe that a third force existed in Rwanda determined to subvert the peace process and scupper his UN mission.

When the genocide of the Tutsi got under way on Thursday, 7 April, Dallaire deduced from his experience that a plan was being implemented, and it was being 'implemented smoothly, because there was very little coordination, there was no excitement, no screaming down the telephone, nothing'. In response, the defence lawyers argued the question of intent, for in the 1948 Genocide Convention 'intent' was integral to the crime. In the Genocide Convention the wording read, 'the *intent* to destroy, in whole or in part, a national, ethnical, racial or religious group'. The defence argued there was no intent in 1994, no conspiracy, and no plan. Minus intent, the crime of genocide had not existed.[18]

They told the judges that not one scintilla of evidence was produced in court to prove the military defendants had taken part in the planning of massacres; not a trace of a conspiracy had been produced to prove their clients' involvement. The preparations and training was for civilian self-defence. The country had been at war with a Tutsi army, an army not serious about a peace agreement. The capital had been massively infiltrated by belligerent and well-armed Tutsi opposition. Therefore the killing between April and July, they argued, was indistinguishable from other human rights abuses in the region in recent years. They were part of the culture – a long and bloody ethnic conflict. The fear was the Tutsi RPA was coming home to conquer the country and once again enslave the Hutu.

The verdict, eventually announced on 18 December 2008, came after 409 trial days, 242 witnesses for the prosecution and the defence, and 1,600 exhibits, with innumerable pages of pleadings and 300 written decisions.[19] It took three judges eighteen months to evaluate the evidence. The courtroom was packed with press while a live feed was in place for international news organisations, with the camera focused on Judge Møse sitting in front of the UN symbol. As Møse read a summary judgement, Bagosora did not move, and only once or twice seemed to have difficulty swallowing, even when sentenced to a life term.

Judge Møse slowly read the crimes for which Bagosora was found guilty, including the murders of the prime minister, Agathe Uwilingiyimana, the head of Rwanda's Constitutional Court, Joseph Kavaruganda, the opposition politicians Frédéric Nzamurambaho, Landoald Ndasingwa and Faustin Rucogoza, and a bank director, Augustin Maharangari. Bagosora was guilty of the murders of ten UN peacekeepers. He was guilty of extensive military involvement in the killing of civilians in Kigali, of the organised murders at roadblocks, of the massacres at the Centre Christus, at Gikondo, Nyundo and Kabeza and other places of sanctuary where people had gathered.

Ntabakuze was found guilty of the crimes committed by the para-commando battalion, including the massacre at the École Technique Officielle (ETO). Nsengiyumva was found guilty of targeted killings in Gisenyi on 7 April, and at Mudende University, and of sending militia to Bisesero, in Kibuye.

It was probably at paragraph sixteen of the judges' sentence that the prosecution team must have started to feel queasy, for it was here that the statement expressly admonished them. 'Several elements underpinning the prosecution case about conspiracy were not supported by sufficiently reliable evidence.' A crucial accusation against the four military officers was unproven – that they had conspired together to commit genocide. The judges had determined that the evidence submitted for the charge of conspiracy to commit genocide was circumstantial and not sufficiently reliable.

Møse told the court that the defendants had 'not been found guilty of a considerable number of allegations with which they were charged'. It was possible that some military or civilian authorities did intend the preparations as part of a plan to commit genocide, but the prosecution had not shown that the only reasonable inference based on the credible evidence in this trial was that this intention was shared by the accused.

Møse continued:

The Chamber has found that some of the accused played a role in the creation, arming and training of civilian militia as well as the maintenance of lists of suspected accomplices of the RPF or others opposed to the ruling regime. However, it was not proven beyond a reasonable doubt that these efforts were directed at killing Tutsi civilians with the intention to commit genocide.

The Chamber accepted that some indications showed evidence of a plan to commit genocide, in particular when viewed in light of the subsequent targeted and speedy killings immediately after the shooting down of the president's plane. However, the evidence was also consistent with preparations for a political or military power struggle and measures adopted in the context of an ongoing war with the RPF that were used for other purposes from 6 April 1994.

The full judgement, released some days later, stretched to more than 600 pages, and explained that newly discovered information, subsequent trials or history may yet demonstrate a conspiracy involving the accused prior to 6 April to commit genocide. The Chamber's task was difficult because of the exacting standards of proof and the specific evidence on the record before it. The primary focus was on the actions of the four accused. The Chamber had considered the totality of the evidence. A firm foundation was not possible with fractured bricks.[20]

The criticism of the trial was harsh and the result considered an example of the appalling quality of the investigations. A reasonable court could no longer support the 'official, simplistic narrative of the genocide', wrote a journalist.[21] The judgement was described as 'a painful inventory of the mediocrity of the assembled evidence and its devastating effects. It was a measure of the extraordinary flimsiness of the work carried out by the prosecution to support such extraordinarily heavy charges.'[22]

To some, the judgement was alarming. It raised fears that the failure to confirm the conspiracy charge was valuable ammunition for deniers, those who sought to minimise or distort the facts.

By the end of the trial a handful of ICTR lawyers, academics and journalists in France, Belgium and Canada had become prolific in their support of the defence case as, increasingly, the génocidaires attracted an assortment of supporters loyal to their cause. There were books and academic articles written and conferences held to promote the idea that this was a question of 'collective madness'; that there was no coup d'état on 6 April; that the Rwandan military had been obliged to take charge to avoid a state of anarchy. The massacres that followed were but one episode in a long and bloody civil war.

On these terms, the only conspiracy concerned Anglo-Saxons plotting against the Hutu by using the RPF to undermine French interests in Africa. The conspiracies and theories spread far beyond the courtrooms amid claims that the entire history of the genocide of the Tutsi needed to be rewritten.

7

Monster Plot

A few weeks before the tenth anniversary of the 1994 geno-cide of the Tutsi, in March 2004, a news story on the front page of *Le Monde* caused a sensation. It claimed to have untied a Gordian knot, and offered new information about who assassinated President Habyarimana on Wednesday, 6 April 1994. The paper announced that after six years of investigation, a French judge determined that the responsibility belonged to the Rwanda Patriotic Front (RPF) and that the current president of Rwanda, Paul Kagame, gave the order.[1]

The story was timed to perfection, dominating the coverage of the anniversary and continuing into the following weeks. The information had come from the office of a French investigating magistrate, Judge Jean-Louis Bruguière, who, in March 1998, began an inquiry on behalf of the families of the three French aircrew whose salaries were paid by the French state and who had died in the missile attack on the Falcon jet. *Le Monde* claimed the judge had 'hundreds of witnesses' including dissidents, who had spoken of a 'network commando', a hit squad that was under the orders of Kagame and responsible for the attack.

The newspaper quoted a key witness, Abdul Ruzibiza, who explained, 'Paul Kagame did not care about the Tutsi living in Rwanda, and they had to be eliminated.' Ruzibiza revealed how he had helped to stake out the location for the assassins at a farm in Masaka some four kilometres from the airport. He saw them arrive in a Toyota, the missiles hidden in the back under rubbish and empty cardboard boxes. Ruzibiza eventually wrote a book which, published in 2005 at over 400 pages, provided a litany of alleged RPF human rights violations.[2]

When *Le Monde* published its scoop, the trial of Bagosora had been under way for two years at the International Criminal Tribunal for Rwanda (ICTR). This new element was quickly introduced into the courtrooms and used to support the idea that Hutu Power was the victim of a monster plot and that a French judge had proved it. The story in *Le Monde* supported the claims already suggested in the trial that the killing was an angry reaction to the death of the president.[3]

After the publication of his report two years later, on 17 November 2006, Bruguière wrote to Kofi Annan, UN secretary-general, to ask the then prosecutor of the ICTR, Carla Del Ponte, to take action. He lobbied Del Ponte to put Kagame and the RPF in the dock. The reaction at the ICTR came from spokesperson Everard O'Donnell, who told excited reporters the court was of the opinion that the assassination did not cause the genocide.[4] In response to the publication of the full report the Rwandan government severed diplomatic relations with France.

Later in November, Judge Bruguière issued international arrest warrants for nine members of the RPF he deemed responsible for the assassination. As a classified cable from the US embassy in Paris informed the state department in Washington, the judge could simply have gone to Rwanda and asked to interview the nine rather than make them the objects of international arrest warrants.[5] All nine were currently serving in senior government positions in the government. Kagame himself was immune from prosecution under French law as a head of state.

In early 2007, Judge Bruguière met the US ambassador, Craig Roberts Stapleton, in Paris. The judge admitted to Stapleton that he consulted President Jacques Chirac before issuing the warrants to ensure the French government was prepared for a backlash from Rwanda. Bruguière explained that the 'international community had a moral responsibility' to pursue justice. Stapleton reported how Bruguière did not hide his personal desire to see the government of Paul Kagame isolated and had warned him that closer US ties with Rwanda would be a mistake. Bruguière casually mentioned that he was standing for a parliamentary seat later in the year, and that a cabinet post as minister of justice would be his first choice.[6]

In the years to come, the story of the guilt of Kagame and the RPF filled books, newspaper articles and academic research. Not everyone was fooled.[7] Colette Braeckman, a member of the editorial board and African editor of the Belgian newspaper *Le Soir*, said she had heard the story before in an 'investigation' produced by an investigator at the ICTR, Michael Hourigan, an Australian prosecutor researching evidence against Bagosora. Witnesses had come forward just as Colonel Théoneste Bagosora made his first appearance in court, in February 1997. They approached investigators in a Kigali bar to say they knew all about the assassination and were part of a secret 'network' that was created by Paul Kagame. They were implicated in the assassination, they said. Strangely, however, none was subject to arrest, and Hourigan told superiors he could not 'provide any advice as to the reliability' of these informers.[8] Hourigan explained how his team members began to meet former members of the defeated Rwandan army in Kenya and Europe who urged them to investigate another 'possibility' and the secretive Paul Kagame. He seemed to believe without question what he was told.

For Braeckman, the only new element in the *Le Monde* article in March 2004 was testimony provided by Ruzibiza, the star witness. Braeckman met him a year earlier in May 2003 in Kampala, Uganda, at a time when he was peddling information about the assassination. Braeckman had spent the evening with him when he suggested they write a book together and look for finance. Braeckman asked about the topography of the places he mentioned; where had the team of assassins waited? How did they get there? How long had they waited? Who told them the plane's arrival was imminent? Ruzibiza was confused, said Braeckman, and unsure of details. She never saw him again and was told later he had gone to Paris. Braeckman thought the French intelligence service Direction Générale de la Sécurité Extérieure (DGSE) picked him up and, until the story broke in

Le Monde, she had no news of him.[9] Braeckman may not have known that a year earlier, Ruzibiza had been in touch with investigators from the ICTR, and had given a statement in Kampala in May 2002.[10]

One claim in the Bruguière report cast doubt on all the others, calling into question the thoroughness of his ongoing investigation. In his report, Judge Bruguière accused the RPF of the earlier assassination in February 1994, only weeks before the genocide of the Tutsi began, of the popular, moderate and conciliatory politician Félicien Gatabazi. Gatabazi was shot three times in the back as he ran from his vehicle to escape his killers. Bruguière claimed he had information from witnesses, and took this information at face value. As a result, he failed to acknowledge an investigation carried out by three members of an international unit of sixty civilian police officers from the UN Civilian Police (CIVPOL), a component of the UN Assistance Mission in Rwanda (UNAMIR). Their inquiries had shown Hutu Power operatives killed Gatabazi and the assassination was the subject of a high-level cover-up in an attempt to blame the RPF. Two vital witnesses, a female taxi driver and a driver for the International Committee of the Red Cross (ICRC) who saw the killers make a getaway, died soon afterwards, one in a grenade attack the following day and the other in a supposed suicide.

The CIVPOL officers had cooperated with the public prosecutor, François-Xavier Nsanzuwera, who conducted his own inquiries into the murder of Gatabazi immediately after the event. On 28 March, two CIVPOL officers witnessed his arrest of Faustin Rwagatera, the manager of the Las Vegas bar in Kigali who operated his own gang of Interahamwe, was a brothel-keeper, and allegedly accompanied the assassins. He was spotted with four suspects, three of them Presidential Guards.

When Rwagatera refused to provide information about the murder, Nsanzuwera charged him with obstruction of justice and sent him in handcuffs to the 1930 prison. Immediately afterwards, Nsanzuwera received a death threat and wrote the next day to General Augustin Ndindiliyimana, the head of the gendarmerie, for immediate protection.[11] At the same time, the minister of defence, Major-General Augustin Bizimana, warned the CIVPOL officers to find a 'new orientation' in their work.

Despite these attempts at the highest level to prevent their investigation, the CIVPOL police inspectors continued to make headway. They obtained access to the white Mitsubishi that Gatabazi had abandoned that night, fleeing a hail of bullets. The police officers retrieved four cartridges from the vehicle from R-4 rifles used by both Rwandan gendarmes and the army.

The CIVPOL investigation was further hampered by the Centre de Recherche Criminelle et de Documentation (CRCD), a corrupt criminal investigation branch of the national gendarmerie, a largely incompetent force. An officer of the CRCD refused to hand over an AK-47, complete with a shoulder strap, found hidden near the crime scene. The CIVPOL officers made sure their superior officers were aware of their difficulties and sent regular reports on the Gatabazi inquiry to the head of CIVPOL, Colonel Manfred Bliem, an Austrian police commissioner.[12] They copied their information to the UN special representative, the Cameroonian diplomat Jacques-Roger Booh-Booh. Their superiors were informed that in the course of their inquiries they needed to interview senior politicians, army officers and Presidential Guards and that there was interference with their investigation at the highest possible levels. No one seemed interested.[13]

Eventually, the CIVPOL police acquired the names of the alleged organisers of the assassination, as well as the identities of four suspects who fired the shots. Nsanzuwera believed that if events in April had not intervened, the case could have gone to trial. Instead, as the genocide of the Tutsi began, the gates of Kigali's prisons were opened, and Rwagatera was among the hundreds of prisoners released. He went looking for Nsanzuwera, breaking into his house in Rugenge, a residential district in the capital, on Tuesday, 12 April, along with a gang of Interahamwe, and found and killed a student, Médard Twahirwa, Nsanzuwera's brother-in-law. Nsanzuwera also discovered that gendarmes and Interahamwe had broken into his office and taken away his safe.[14] Inside were the files on the murder of Félicien Gatabazi that were now lost for ever.[15]

If Judge Bruguière had wanted to interview Nsanzuwera on what he knew of the assassination of Gatabazi, again he would have been able to do so. After the genocide, Nsanzuwera went to work in Arusha for the International Criminal Tribunal for Rwanda (ICTR). Here he wrote a landmark report on the Interahamwe for the prosecutors. It provided a valuable list of the terrorist crimes of this militia between 1992 and 1994.[16] From its early beginnings as the youth wing of the presidential party, Mouvement Révolutionnaire National pour le Développement (MRND), it had been transformed into a killing machine. Unlike the youth groups of the other political parties, this was a criminal organisation, he wrote, with an effective command structure, comprising a national committee divided into six commissions. It had support at the highest level, from the ruling Hutu elite, the senior ranks of the gendarmerie and the Presidential Guard.

There was no doubt that the Bruguière report was flawed. Another failure of his argument was the lack of forensic work, ballistics or on-the-ground investigation of the crash site. A credibility gap existed in the report's material evidence that only included five photographs showing parts of missile launchers and some serial numbers. These photographs had already been dismissed in a 1998 French National Assembly report, and could have come from anywhere.[17]

The story of missile launchers and serial numbers originated with Colonel Théoneste Bagosora.[18] The numbers were on missile launchers apparently discovered by chance on 25 April 1994 on Masaka Hill by an anonymous peasant. The missile parts were then taken to an army camp where a Rwandan soldier, Lieutenant Augustin Munyaneza, had examined them and written a report. The information on the launchers was given by Colonel Bagosora to a Belgian academic, Filip Reyntjens, who was writing a book about the assassination. By this time, inconveniently, the launchers had apparently been taken abroad and given to a Zairean general, where they had disappeared. According to the Bruguière report, the numbers on these missiles corresponded with missiles that could be traced, and had been 'sold by Russia to Uganda and then given to the RPF'.

The Bruguière investigators appeared not to have interviewed any of the direct witnesses to the event. Within minutes of the assassination, Colonel Luc Marchal, commander of the Kigali sector of UNAMIR, was aware of two eyewitnesses close enough to see where the missiles came from, both agreeing it was the military camp at Kanombe. Another witness, Dr Massimo Pasuch, a Belgian military doctor, was at his home in the heavily fortified Rwandan camp with all windows and doors open and so close that he distinctly heard the 'whoosh' as each missile left its casing. Pasuch described traces in the night sky as they went towards the plane. Lieutenant Colonel Walter Balis, the liaison officer between UNAMIR and the RPF, saw the missiles depart and believed it impossible for the RPF to infiltrate Kanombe camp. A Belgian corporal, Mathieu Gerlache, on the viewing platform of a disused air control tower, had a perfect view as the missiles left from the direction of Kanombe, the second scoring a direct hit, when the aircraft exploded.

As a result of these failings, Bruguière received wide criticism for his partial text. He seemed determined to accuse the president of Rwanda rather than seek the truth.[19] This did not prevent journalists from happily quoting him, while not apparently having read his report. For example, in 2007, the BBC's Stephen Sackur on *HARDtalk* accused President Kagame directly:

> You know that Judge Jean-Louis Bruguière has been working on that case for many, many years. You also know that he is one of the most respected judges in all France. He has a track record of tracking down terrorists, bringing them to justice. He has been working on your case and he has, I have it here, about seventy pages of documentary evidence ... Judge Bruguière comes up with this conclusion: 'the final order to attack the presidential plane was given by Paul Kagame himself during a meeting held in Mulindi on March 31 1994'.

That same year, in a major development, the investigating magistrate Marc Trévidic and his colleague Nathalie Poux assumed responsibility for the outstanding Judge Bruguière dossiers in

Paris. Bruguière had left the service, having been told that his political activity was incompatible with judicial duties.[20] Trévidic was to become one of the best-known investigating magistrates in France. In interviews, he made a point of saying that being a nuisance to governments was exactly what an investigating magistrate was meant to do. Old investigations never died, he said. It was often the case that with unsolved crimes, information could surface many years later. The dossier he inherited on the assassination of the presidents of Rwanda and Burundi proved his point.[21]

Trévidic suspended the arrest warrants for the nine Rwandan officials and, with a team of six French scientists and his colleague Nathalie Poux, he visited the crash site. The team included experts in missile technology and aviation, air accident investigators, a geometrician and an explosives expert. They carried out a series of tests on the Falcon 50 jet wreckage that remained where it had fallen sixteen years earlier. The investigation broadened in other ways. In the course of the visit, they interviewed previously ignored Rwandan witnesses who had seen the missile fire in the sky, and took them back to where they had been standing that night. They included the president's bodyguards and soldiers from Kanombe camp who had given evidence to Rwanda's own commission of experts established in 2008 to investigate the assassination. The commission, named after its chair, Justice Jean Mutsinzi, a former president of the Supreme Court, brought in experts from the United Kingdom's National Defence Academy for scientific advice and analysis.[22] In a detailed report in January 2010, it had concluded that the plane was brought down by Hutu extremists in an effort to destroy the Arusha Accords, and the missiles came from an area controlled by the Presidential Guard.[23]

The keen interest the French judges took in the Mutsinzi report was matched only by a concern to properly understand events in the immediate aftermath including the targeted killings of pro-democracy politicians, among them the prime minister and the president of the Constitutional Court. They asked for information on the circumstances of the murder of the ten Belgian peacekeepers. They asked for copies of Hutu extremist newspapers and magazines, and the transcripts of recordings of the hate radio station, RTLM, all of which predicted that the president would die for having agreed to share power with 'Tutsi rebels'.

An initial 400-page report published by the French investigating magistrates in January 2012 explained how the first missile missed the plane but the second ignited 3,000 litres of kerosene in the fuel tank.[24] The plane, travelling at 222 kilometres an hour and at an altitude of 1,646 metres, became a ball of fire in the night sky and, travelling onwards for some seven seconds, eventually hit the ground, disintegrating as it did so. The plane fell into the garden of the presidential villa, where the president's wife was preparing a barbecue for her husband. The mangled bodies of the twelve victims were in the wreckage.

The missile fire came, in all probability, from a 300-metre radius within the confines of the most secure army camp in the country at Kanombe, adjacent to the airport. This domain of some thirty hectares was under twenty-four-hour surveillance by platoons of soldiers operating a shift system and linked to the presidential villa by a private track. The missile fire could only have come from within the camp perimeter, mostly likely the scrubland to the south.

The new report effectively destroyed the Bruguière conclusions that the missiles had been fired from Masaka, a hill four kilometres east of the airport. The judge had relied solely on witness testimony and all of them, including several convicted génocidaires, convinced him that the missiles came from Masaka, where a peasant found the launchers. Bruguière apparently fell for an elaborately staged deception. It was fake news from the start, intended to cause a diversion, propped up with false statements, manufactured evidence, manipulated witnesses and forged testimony. Jean-François Dupaquier, author and expert on these matters, described it as having been the responsibility of malevolent people who had taken part in the corruption of the judicial process. Their aim was to 'lend support to their extremist Rwandan friends who launched genocide'.[25]

On the day of the release of the report, a series of filmed interviews became available, including one with survivor Esther Mujawayo, author, sociologist, psychotherapist and trauma specialist, who lived in Germany and worked for the Psychosocial Centre for Refugees (PSZ) in Düsseldorf.[26] Mujawayo wondered why so many people were taken in:

> At last. How could he [Bruguière] possibly have advanced such a thesis? How could anyone have believed this for an instant? The intellectuals, people in universities who were taken in like this? Even if the RPF had magic powers ... how could they have got into the camp? With this lie a million people died. They killed my husband. They killed my mother, my parents in law ... they killed everyone ... killed the Tutsi because of a fable invented for the purpose that said 'their' president was killed by us [the Tutsi] and they wanted revenge.

She had always known who was responsible: 'It was so obvious.'

But the suspicions persisted. A panel discussion on the English-language channel on France 24 included the journalist Stephen Smith, who broke the story in *Le Monde* in 2004. Now a visiting professor of African & American Studies at Duke University, Smith said that Trévidic provided a new thrust to the investigation, but one should not dismiss the serial number evidence that traced missiles to Uganda. The Trévidic report was, Smith argued, only part of an 'ongoing discussion' and was 'another element' to take into account. Smith also maintained his position that there was no master plan to commit genocide. 'The special court ... charged with trying genocidal planners and killers, has found no one guilty of conspiracy to commit genocide,' he claimed in the *London Review of Books* a year earlier.[27]

On 22 September 2010, the key witness for Bruguière, Abdul Ruzibiza, died in Norway, where he been granted asylum. He turned out to have been a nurse in the RPF and had pretended to have an inside track, claimed to have known all about the assassination but at the time was miles away in the north, in Ruhengeri. He eventually retracted his testimony, like some of the other witnesses involved with the Bruguière inquiry.[28]

In October 2006, another key witness, Emmanuel Ruzigana, had written to Bruguière to deny he ever belonged to a 'network commando' and to say he was ignorant about the plane. He did not speak or understand the French language and had been interviewed without an interpreter.[29] In an interview on 2 December, on Radio Rwanda, Ruzigana said he had wanted to go to Europe and a friend at the embassy of France in Dar es Salaam had helped him out. As soon as he arrived at the airport in Paris, there had been men who worked in the office of Judge Bruguière waiting for him.

Only later would it emerge that a Kinyarwanda interpreter used in interviews by Judge Bruguière, a man at the heart of his investigation, was Fabien Singaye. This man had operated a European spy ring for President Habyarimana and had occupied the post of first secretary at the Rwandan embassy in Bern, Switzerland. Some of his secret reports were discovered in the abandoned presidential villa.[30] His father-in-law was Félicien Kabuga, the businessman who provided large sums to finance the genocide and who remains a fugitive to this day. Singaye was thrown out of Switzerland in August 1994, and found a safe haven living comfortably in France.

Central to the Bruguière report, however, was testimony from Colonel Théoneste Bagosora. On 18 May 2000, Judge Bruguière spent a day with Bagosora in the UN Detention Facility outside Arusha, the first of two visits.[31] A transcript produced of the encounter showed the lack of precise questions that the French judge asked about the assassination. Furthermore, the transcript left a gaping hole in the story of the whereabouts of Bagosora on the evening of 6 April. Bagosora claimed that between 6:30 p.m. and 8:20 p.m. he had been at Amahoro Stadium with the Bangladeshi contingent at a reception. A Bangladeshi officer could not recall this event. Bagosora says he then returned home at 8:20, where he found his wife in tears on the doorstep, and she told him the news.

The sound of the destruction of the president's plane echoed all over Kigali, but Bagosora appeared to be the only person not to hear it.[32] Bagosora had even been unaware that the president was going to Dar es Salaam that day. However, in his testimony at his trial, he said he was already at home when his wife received a call from the general staff of the army informing her that the president's plane had been shot down.[33]

Bagosora told the judge the missile attack on the aircraft was an international plot abetted by UNAMIR. He suspected the ten UN peacekeepers, Lieutenant Thierry Lotin and his men, murdered on 7 April, had a role in this plot. On the day before the assassination they had escorted RPF personnel, taking the road that bypassed Masaka Hill, where the missiles were supposedly launched. Lotin and his men were seen at the airport at 8:30 p.m. only minutes after the missile fire. They should not have been there at all. They had stayed there until 3:00 p.m., when ordered to go into town to form an escort for the prime minister.

The RPF could not have accessed Masaka without a convincing escort, said Bagosora, and the most convincing escort was UNAMIR. The UN peacekeepers had freedom of movement. Therefore, UNAMIR escorted the RPF to the place from where the missiles were fired. 'There was a coup d'état by the RPF with UNAMIR as accomplice and with a part of the political opposition, which was pro-RPF, I tell you,' Bagosora said.

The most senior French officer in Camp Kanombe, Major Grégoire de Saint-Quentin, was an adviser to Major Aloys Ntabakuze, head of the para-commando battalion at Kanombe. The French officer was a tall and imposing figure who eventually commanded a brigade with the French army in Senegal and later in 2013 commander of French forces in Mali. He is today head of special operations. In April 1994, he was at his home in the Kanombe military camp when the missiles were fired at the presidential jet. His garden backed onto that of the camp commander, Félicien Muberuka, and he could see the comings and goings on the commander's driveway.[34] The three large windows in his living room overlooked the flight path, while the presidential villa was little more than 350 metres away. Saint-Quentin recalled that the launch of the two missiles seemed so close to him he thought the camp was under attack.

In a house nearby, a young girl thought the missile fire sounded like an American movie. She was sixteen and spent the rest of that night awake sheltering with her mother and brothers in the front room, just twelve metres from the road. She too thought the missile fire signified the camp was under attack but, strangely, there was no further activity. Normally there were tall and effective streetlights which were left on all night, and twenty-four-hour patrols, soldiers on foot and in vehicles, each group assigned individual zones to patrol. This evening, there was no activity, no trucks, no patrols and no sounds of soldiers. At dawn, they crept out and were told that all the families were leaving the camp, and transport was already arranged.

Saint-Quentin had wanted to retrieve the jet's black box and remembered two French officers in helmets who carried torches and searched the smouldering wreckage. The bodies of the casualties were laid out in a reception room in the presidential villa but were removed the next morning in an army truck to a cold store at Kanombe Hospital, where other bodies were piling up in the morgue.[35]

Saint-Quentin, in his interview with the judge, told Bruguière that the Rwandan forces did not have surface to air missiles.[36] Perhaps he was unaware of them. Human Rights Watch believed that when the Rwandan army retreated it took fifty SA-7 missiles and fifteen Mistral missiles into exile.[37] An army would not keep such an arsenal if it did not know how to use it. While France officially denied giving French-made Mistral missiles to Rwanda, this did not mean the Rwandan army did not have any.

A document found in UNAMIR archives and prepared by senior officers contained a list of the military hardware in the possession of the Rwandan government army, compiled in accordance with the peace agreement, a list dated 6 April 1994.[38] The list included fifteen French-made Mistral missiles and an 'unknown quantity' of SA-7 missiles. The force commander of UNAMIR, Lieutenant General Roméo Dallaire, confirmed the list as genuine and compiled with the greatest difficulty from sources within the military, this information gathered in accordance with his mandate. The missiles, fired at the plane from the Kanombe military camp, had effectively destroyed any hope of his resupply by air during the genocide. 'They had shot down one plane, and could shoot down another,' Dallaire said. The peacekeepers were unable to guarantee the safety of Kigali Airport, and no company was found willing to insure an aircraft that the UN had on standby.

In a declassified CIA report called 'Rwanda: Security Conditions at Kigali Airport – Capabilities and Intentions', dated 13 July 1994, there is information that Kigali's international airport was less dangerous once the RPF had driven out the troops of the Interim Government. 'Hutu regime troops, most likely including elements of the Presidential Guard, were almost certainly responsible for downing the airplane of the late President Habyarimana as it was landing at Kigali.' When the fighting broke out, the Hutu regime had some thirty-five pieces of air defence artillery, reported a classified informant, as well as the fifteen Mistral missiles.

Whole sections of this fascinating eleven-page CIA cable remain classified, and the US was clearly well informed.[39] The carefully planned operation to escort all the US citizens from the country on 9 April ensured they went by road. From Paris, information continued to arrive from the ambassador, Pamela Harriman, who told Washington at the end of April 1994 that her informant said the accusations of RPF involvement in the assassination were not credible, since the site from which the attack took place was near the president's residence and was secured by forces loyal to Habyarimana. The death of the president was a signal for a preplanned ethnic massacre to begin. The RPF offensive towards Kigali began only after the massacres of Tutsi had started.

The signals intelligence acquired by the US in the crucial first days was said to have included intercepted telephone calls from extremist officers in Kigali to counterparts in Gisenyi in the north as well as communications captured between politicians and militia and captured information about the downing of the presidential jet. It is likely that the tracking and recording of the entirety of the local and regional radio traffic was conducted by the National Security Agency (NSA) where, in the Maryland headquarters, people fluent in Kinyarwanda were known to have worked. The information gathered contained invaluable evidence of the activities of the génocidaires as they seized power. The US satellite imagery was such that burning tyres and bodies were visible at the roadblocks.

Despite the wealth of material that undermined the Bruguière conclusion, some people remained unconvinced and paid no heed to the retraction of the testimony of the witnesses upon whom the judge had relied. Ignoring the scientific evidence, a school of thought persisted that pronounced the RPF guilty of the assassination of the president. As a result, there had been no coup d'état.

In a book published in 2010 that bolstered the earlier Bruguière conclusion of RPF guilt, a Parisian academic, André Guichaoua of the Pantheon-Sorbonne University, dismissed the murder of the political opposition on Thursday, 7 April, as evidence of a coup and called it a 'recalibrated political transition', simply part of 'political infighting'. In this theory, the RPF downed the jet and deliberately sacrificed the Tutsi population. No plan had existed to exterminate Tutsi. Not until 12 April and the new Interim Government had been installed was a genocide policy adopted and a genocide begun. His theory took no account of the targeted killing of Tutsi at the roadblocks that began on Thursday, 7 April, nor the first large-scale massacres of Tutsi in Kigali – one in the church grounds in Gikondo in the morning on Saturday, 9 April, to which UN military observers were eyewitnesses. Another massacre of Tutsi families who had sheltered at the École Technique Officielle (ETO) on Monday, 11 April, saw an estimated 2,000 people killed.

These were early examples of the massacre of large numbers of people that would now recur in a pattern; Rwandan soldiers and gendarmes sealed exits where Tutsi people sought shelter, and then ushered in the Interahamwe to carry out the killing, thereby economising on bullets. It was in Gikondo, on the afternoon of Saturday, 9 April, that the chief delegate of the ICRC, Philippe Gaillard, recognised that genocide of the Tutsi was by now under way.

In his book published four years after the Bruguière report, Guichaoua expressed his belief that the genocide had been a desperate reaction by the most extremist faction in the face of a military advance by the RPF. Guichaoua categorised the killings as a crime against humanity committed by a government against a part of its population. Guichaoua wrote the preface for the book by Abdul Ruzibiza, the star witness used by Judge Bruguière, and indeed had first introduced the witness to the judge and had persuaded Ruzibiza to write a book.[40]

Another member of this school of thought is the acknowledged expert René Lemarchand, a French-American political scientist known for his work on Rwanda and Burundi and professor emeritus at the University of Florida. Lemarchand insisted the RPF downed the plane. He disparaged the Mutsinzi report and noted in 2018 that 'all facts pointing to Kagame's responsibility were conveniently ignored'. He failed to specify which particular facts he meant. 'The scantiness of the evidence notwithstanding, the notion of a criminal plot concocted by Hutu extremists is still the standard explanation advanced,' he wrote. Lemarchand believed it a subject fit for debate as people took up a number of 'contradictory positions'.[41]

Reyntjens, emeritus professor of law and politics at the University of Antwerp, remained an advocate for the Bruguière report and wrote about the existence of a 'whole heap of indications' that showed the RPF was responsible for the assassination. In an account of events published in 2017, Reyntjens omitted any mention of scientific reports about how missiles came from Kanombe military camp, which was inaccessible to the RPF. Reyntjens seemed unaware of the existence of witnesses in Kanombe camp that night. Reyntjens did not believe in genocide planning, and said the killing happened because of the aggression of the enemies of the regime that set off a chain reaction that led to it. The RPF had a historical and political responsibility in the extermination of the Tutsi.[42]

The story about Masaka Hill lingered on, the scientific and direct eyewitness testimony continually ignored. In 2017, in a book by Helen C. Epstein, *Another Fine Mess: America, Uganda, and the War on Terror*, the author accused President Paul Kagame of the assassination, repeating the claim in an extract from the book in the *Guardian*.[43] The missiles came from Masaka Hill, she wrote, and the weapons used were Russian-made SAM-16s because 'two SA-16 single-use launchers' were found near the launch site. She relied on the report by French investigating magistrate Jean-Louis Bruguière and pointed out that the serial numbers on the Masaka launchers came from a consignment shipped from Russia to Uganda. Her source was Filip Reyntjens who told Epstein the weapons were Russian-made SAM-16s and he said that 'two SA-16 single-use launchers' were found near Masaka Hill, a place more 'accessible' to the rebel fighters of Kagame's RPF than the Kanombe military camp. What Reyntjens may not have told her was that the information about launchers at Masaka Hill and their serial numbers originated with the prime suspect, Colonel Théoneste Bagosora, a convicted génocidaire.

With little fanfare, on 24 December 2018, French magistrates in Paris dropped the case brought against the nine senior RPF leaders suspected of the assassination of President Habyarimana and for whom there had been international arrest warrants issued. The twenty-year investigation had ensured the real culprits escaped scrutiny.

8

An Untold Story

Captain Pascal Simbikangwa disappeared in July 1994 into the refugee camps in Zaire (DRC), where his wife and mother had died. A former Presidential Guard and a member of the presidential family, Simbikangwa had been responsible for the Service Central de Renseignements (SCR), the security service attached to the office of the president. He earned the nickname '*le tortionnaire*', the torturer.[1] He was found selling forged passports in the French overseas department of Mayotte in the Indian Ocean, a fugitive from international justice and on the run for fourteen years.

The group of genocide fugitives who relied on France for a safe haven was noteworthy for the number and for the seniority of its members. After 1994, forty high-ranking alleged génocidaires were found to be working in France, living comfortable lives and integrated into society. Of the forty Rwandan suspects identified, thirty-three cases were in the hands of French investigating magistrates and some of these were left pending for more than twenty years.

The local police in Mayotte had first arrested Simbikangwa in 2006 for producing forged passports, and again on 28 October 2008, when he was found with hundreds of fake identity cards. There was a sizeable community of Rwandans in Mamoudzou, the coastal capital, and they accounted for half the requests for political asylum in the country. Simbikangwa lived under an assumed name, and even though he relied on a wheelchair to get around after a road traffic accident in 1986, no one seemed to recognise this Rwandan who was on an Interpol list, wanted for the 1994 genocide. In 2009, he was arrested once again, when he had 3,000 false passports in his possession.[2]

The news that Simbikangwa lived under an assumed name in Mayotte was relayed in a telephone call to a retired French schoolteacher, Alain Gauthier, and his Rwandan wife, Dafroza, a chemical engineer, who lived in Reims. Over the previous decade the couple had turned their apartment into an archive, cataloguing the numbers of genocide fugitives on French soil. The couple were indispensable in a growing citizens' movement seeking justice for genocide suspects in France. Alain was the right person to call. He was president of the Collectif des Parties Civiles pour le Rwanda (CPCR), a pressure group created in 2001 to 'provide moral and financial support for all those who bring legal cases against Rwandan genocide suspects, principally those on French soil'.

In the face of inaction from French judicial authorities, the couple had tracked fugitives and built cases, hoping that one day these suspects might end up in court. It was a mammoth task. The couple searched for survivors in Rwanda, investigated massacre sites, recorded testimony in prisons and listened to confessions of perpetrators. When the news reached them about Simbikangwa, they sent information from their files to the local police in Mayotte to show that the suspect was on an Interpol wanted list and was once high up in the génocidaire command structure. Simbikangwa was a Hutu Power ideologue, they confirmed, and a major shareholder in the radio station RTLM. He wrote fervently racist anti-Tutsi articles. As a result of this CPCR dossier, Simbikangwa was kept in custody and transferred in July to the prison of Saint-Denis on the island of Réunion, and arrived in France on 20 November 2009, at the prison in Fresnes, south of Paris. The trial, held at the Palais de Justice in Paris, began on 4 February 2014. It lasted five weeks and was heard before three judges and six jury members. It was twenty years since the genocide happened and the first time a Rwandan accused of the crime of genocide had appeared in a French court, the charges brought under universal jurisdiction. The French Ministry of Justice filmed the landmark trial in its entirety, only the sixth time in history for a trial to be officially recorded and available to view after the appeals process was exhausted, but only by application to the Tribunal de Grande Instance de Paris.

Without the pressure of citizen groups, the trial of Simbikangwa would never have taken place. There were hopes that the trial might help counteract an ever-growing movement of genocide denial. The senior public prosecutor, Bruno Sturlese, warned the jury of the effects of genocide denial, warned of its force and power. The prosecution had been obliged to prove genocide had happened in Rwanda, while the evidence of genocide was challenged by the defence.[3] It did not matter to the defence that the Appeals Chamber of the International Criminal Tribunal for Rwanda (ICTR) in 2006 held the facts of the genocide committed in Rwanda to be established beyond any dispute and thus constitute facts of common knowledge. Nor did it matter that this Appeals Chamber concluded it a universally known fact that, between 6 April 1994 and 17 July 1994, there was a genocide in Rwanda against the Tutsi ethnic group.

The prosecution lawyers in the Simbikangwa trial, and in the eventual appeal in 2016, called an unprecedented number of expert witnesses, historians and journalists in order to explain what exactly had occurred in 1994. An eminent French military historian, Stéphane Audoin-Rouzeau, told the jury this was not a familiar story: 'There is a huge lack of awareness; people who are supposed to be aware [with access to information, reading papers] have no idea either about the dates when the genocide occurred, or about who were the victims or the killers … How could our fellow citizens really know what is happening in this country?' Historians had been slow to understand the events. It was not until 2008, when Audoin-Rouzeau visited Rwanda for the first time, invited to attend a conference, that he realised what a massive event this was. He had barely noticed it at the time. He now believed it the most significant event of the late twentieth century to challenge the social sciences. In another fifty years, he told the jury, this debate would be of the greatest importance.

Only a state could support such a massive crime, he argued. It could not have been a 'spontaneous revolt'. While there was recognition of massacres in Bosnia, this was not true of Rwanda. There were 'unconscious' choices, he continued, a form of racism that we did not yet recognise within ourselves. In conclusion, Audoin-Rouzeau was critical of French government policy towards Rwanda. Nothing had done more to tarnish France's image as a beacon of human rights than the failure to respond to these events.[4]

The French government could not plead ignorance. Simbikangwa was a well-known figure, the subject of reports by at least two Western intelligence services, and his murderous behaviour was described in human rights reports. Belgian military intelligence in Kigali linked his name to a Hutu Power murder squad that targeted liberals and pro-democracy politicians. When the genocide began, the White House published his name as one of four military commanders, in a statement from the press secretary that called for an end to the massacres.[5]

His name was on a list of genocide perpetrators given to the US Congress in hearings of the Subcommittee on Africa of the House Committee on Foreign Affairs, when on 4 May 1994 Human Rights Watch activist Alison Des Forges revealed names of the Hutu Power military leadership.[6] Simbikangwa had been named a genocide perpetrator in one of the earliest reports into the crime published by a Rwandan commission of inquiry organised by a number of local human rights groups under the Comité de Liaison des Associations de Défense des Droits de l'Homme au Rwanda (CLADO). Published in December 1994, it listed fourteen people, members of the northern Hutu clique known as Akazu (little house), a group of extremists responsible for the most grave human rights abuses.

This publicly available material was of little concern to the prosecution. Instead, it relied on witnesses to show the individual role of Simbikangwa in mass murder. In the course of witness testimony, the mechanism of the killing outlined to the court showed how he enabled its progress and gave it legitimacy. The jury heard how Simbikangwa made decisions, resolved and gave orders to get rid of Tutsi people at the roadblocks established near his home in Kigali. He had helped prepare, order, direct, incite, encourage and approve the killing of innocent civilian Tutsi men, women and children, and others considered their 'accomplices'. He provided Interahamwe with weapons and was a liaison between the army and militia.

At the end of the prosecution's case, Bruno Sturlese told the jury that after this trial he would never be the same person again. The evidence in court had doubtless had the same effect on each of them. To bring justice, they had to recognise the complete lack of humanity of the executioners of such crimes. To that effect, he dismissed the claim from Simbikangwa that he saved fifty Tutsi, a tactic commonly used by Nazis and other Rwandan génocidaires to reclaim their humanity. Simbikangwa had cleverly manipulated reality and falsified history, but now he needed to face justice at last.

In Simbikangwa's defence, his lawyers claimed all was rumour and supposition, the prosecution witnesses had been coached and the trial was clearly political, orchestrated by the 'Tutsi government' in Kigali.

On the first day, they asked for a dismissal, arguing it was an unequal struggle. The prosecution had a total of nine lawyers: a public prosecutor, Bruno Sturlese; Aurélia Devos, head of a two-year-old international crime unit within the French judiciary; as well as prosecution lawyers representing the civil parties including the CPCR, the charity Survie that lobbied against French policy in Africa, and three human rights groups.[7] The judges refused the application.

The defence then attempted to play on the emotions of the jury and downplay Simbikangwa's command responsibility. He was a mere functionary, they argued, with no major influence over anything. In his own testimony, Simbikangwa himself refused to acknowledge there was a roadblock outside his house in Kiyovu in Kigali, where he spent April to July 1994. Despite the fact that he spent most of the period of the massacres at his home, he did not smell the burning bodies of victims abandoned on tyres outside his house. There may have been bodies, but he did not see any. In a statement, he pleaded with the jury not to be 'fooled by political manoeuvring'. He regretted that due to his disabilities he was not able to rescue more Tutsi. Going on the attack, he claimed the prosecution testimony was manipulated, the fault of the Rwandan survivors' group Ibuka, making up stories about him.

Next, the defence took advantage of the failure in the ICTR trial of Colonel Théoneste Bagosora to convict him for conspiracy to commit genocide. The lawyers for Simbikangwa asked the court how there could possibly be a conspiracy when the so-called brains of the plot had not been convicted of planning the crime. There was no conspiracy to murder: the killing was spontaneous.

The defence witnesses included a retired French gendarme, Lieutenant Colonel Michel Robardey, who blamed the leader of the Rwandan Patriotic Front (RPF), Paul Kagame, for having provoked inter-ethnic massacres. The killings had been carefully planned to justify the RPF's 'final assault' on Kigali. Robardey stated the assassination of Rwanda's president, Juvénal Habyarimana, was the decisive moment when he realised that this was a bid by Tutsi rebels to seize power.[8] He believed the RPF had perpetrated the assassination 'for strategic reasons'.

As a witness, the gendarme was not a neutral observer. Robardey had served in Rwanda from 1990 to 1993, where he was a technical adviser, assisting in the training of the judicial police. He also created the Centre de Recherche Criminelle et de Documentation (CRCD) within the national gendarmerie headquarters, a criminal records system reportedly under the guidance of Simbikangwa.[9] Robardey said that at the time he had investigated rumours about Simbikangwa and had been unable to corroborate any accusations of torture. The accusations against Simbikangwa came from unreliable informants.

His mission in Rwanda, he admitted to the court, was to track the terrorist enemy within – that is to say, RPF infiltrators – and investigate reports of genocide at the hands of the RPF.[10]

After the events of 1994, Robardey wrote copiously about them for a blog on the website Mediapart and promoted his ideas at public conferences. He regularly contributed to the work of the Association France Turquoise, created to 'defend and promote the memory and the honour of the French army and French military who served in Rwanda'. Its president was General Jean-Claude Lafourcade, the commander of the French military mission in

Rwanda in June 1994 known as Operation Turquoise which had allowed the génocidaires to flee. A website was created to post articles and videos that set out to defend the honour of the military and refute any idea that the French army was complicit in the events of 1994.

A French journalist, Pierre Péan, told a similar story and explained to the jury in the Simbikangwa trial that the 'thesis' of a conspiracy to commit genocide had been under attack for some time, and he reminded the jury that Colonel Bagosora had been cleared of that particular crime.[11] Péan had published a book in 2005, with information and guidance from Robardey, that suggested the human rights reports that focused on the events leading up to 1994 were 'fables'. There existed, in his words, 'an avalanche of false information, lies, tricks and disinformation', and he was ashamed of the French journalists who promoted this material.[12] He wholeheartedly endorsed the Bruguière thesis that conjectured that there had been massive manipulation by the RPF, whose leadership allowed the Hutu to 'cleanse the country'. His book bore all the hallmarks of the Hutu Power ideology, describing the 'Tutsi and their culture of deceit'. 'How can we still speak of the genocide of the Tutsis when, since 1990, the number of Hutus assassinated by the police or soldiers obeying the orders of [Paul] Kagame is far greater than the number of Tutsis killed by militia and government soldiers?' he wrote.[13]

The Paris court found Simbikangwa guilty of genocide on 14 March 2014, and he received a twenty-five-year sentence, confirmed on appeal two years later.

It was at the suggestion of the French journalist Pierre Péan that as part of the appeal brought by Pascal Simbikangwa's lawyers in 2016 the jury should watch a BBC 2 documentary, 'Rwanda's Untold Story', broadcast two years earlier in October 2014 as part of a series called *This World*. Péan told the court it would give the jury members a proper understanding of what really happened for it promoted the idea that the 'official history' of the 1994 genocide that everyone had accepted was no more than a construct of the current government, devised to win the world's sympathy.

BBC journalists argued in the documentary that an untold story existed, a story that everyone had missed. On 8 November 2016 the documentary was shown to the jury.

When first broadcast, 'Rwanda's Untold Story' prompted public demonstrations, including some by genocide survivors in front of the BBC offices in Portland Place, London, and in Kigali outside the UK High Commission offices. The BBC faced accusations of promoting genocide denial. The Rwanda Utilities Regulatory Authority (RURA) indefinitely suspended the BBC Kinyarwanda service that broadcast to an estimated 2 million people in the Great Lakes region, and had been established for twenty years.

In the documentary, the veteran BBC television journalist Jane Corbin states early on, 'We think we know the story. But do we?' Corbin interviewed two US academics, Allan Stam and Christian Davenport, who had conducted 'exhaustive fieldwork up and down Rwanda' and 'found a different side to the story'.[14] The academics said research showed more Hutu died at the hands of the RPF in 1994 than Tutsi. The academics said they discovered a 'totally new understanding of what had taken place'. According to their calculations 200,000 Tutsi had been killed, and vastly more Hutu. Stam concluded: 'Violence was committed in 1994 by almost every side and every participant in this war and break-down of social order. Random violence happened and hundreds of thousands of people died for no particular purpose.'

The statistics were nothing new. Twelve years earlier, attending an academic conference in Kigali in December 2003, Stam and Davenport had mentioned their statistics to fellow scholars. There was general 'astonishment and disbelief', wrote Alison Des Forges from Human Rights Watch. Later, Des Forges emailed prosecution lawyers at the ICTR in Arusha, Tanzania, and warned them to treat this new research with scepticism. 'Nice computer graphics, but based on data of highly variable quality,' she wrote.[15] In contrast, Stam and Davenport remember the conference in Kigali differently and claim that halfway into their presentation a military man in a green uniform stood up and interrupted, telling them that the Minister of Internal Affairs took great exception to their findings. The US academics further claimed their passport numbers were 'documented, that they were expected to leave the country the next day and that they would never be allowed back in'.[16]

Their figures were markedly at odds with a disputed death toll that varied between 500,000 and up to 1 million people murdered. The United Nations and the Western press generally accepted the figure of 800,000 people killed. The information contained in reports and inquiries confirmed that in the three-month genocide period, April to July 1994, the overwhelming majority of people killed were Tutsi. This finding was accepted as authoritative by the ICTR, and by reputable investigators, journalists and genocide scholars worldwide. Not one of these inquiries conclude, as Stam and Davenport did, that the number of Tutsi killed was 'no more' than 200,000. Nor that more than this number of Hutu people had been killed by the RPF.

In a 2009 article, the two academics described how they arrived at their estimates for the number of people who died 'during the 1994 massacre': these were 'an educated guess based on an estimate of the number of Tutsi in the country at the outset of the civil war and the numbers who survived the war'.[17] They further explained: 'Using a simple method – subtracting the survivors from the number of Tutsi residents at the outset of the violence – we arrived at an estimated total of somewhere between 300,000 and 500,000 Tutsi victims. If we believe the estimate of close to 1 million total civilian deaths in the war and genocide, then we are then left with between 500,000 and 700,000 Hutu deaths, and a best guess that the majority of victims were in fact Hutu, not Tutsi'.

The Stam and Davenport figures relied on a 1991 census that, they claim, calculates that there were approximately 600,000 Tutsi in the country when the killing started. The 1991 government population statistics, therefore, show a pre-genocide figure for Tutsi of 8.4 per cent of the population. A more widely agreed figure is 14 per cent, confirmed in the 1992 *Europa World Year Book* and in an article in the *Africa South of the Sahara 1994: Regional Surveys of the World*, by the Belgian academic Filip Reyntjens. Furthermore, the BBC makes no mention of the demonstrated unreliability of the 1991 government census figures, produced by a Hutu regime that had institutionalised a racist quota system against the minority Tutsi and was determined to reduce the numbers of Tutsi registered.[18]

When the BBC came to defend the programme against criticism, it claimed these 'controversial figures' were provided for viewers in the context of 'a debate with a wide range of views with many interpretations of data'. Another way of presenting this is to say that Stam and Davenport and the BBC simply ignored a weight of material evidence stacked against these calculations. Furthermore, the viewers were not given the full facts when they were told that the Stam and Davenport death toll estimate was at 'the extreme end of that spectrum'. Instead, the documentary suggested that 'a very wide range of figures have been muted', and 'problems with, and uncertainties over, its reliability have been expressed by those who looked at the total figure'.

The figure of 200,000 Tutsi killed was, in fact, at odds with a mass of evidence from other BBC journalists, as well as parliamentarians, human rights advocates, forensic scientists, academics, lawyers and judges, UN peacekeepers, and information in the archive of the UN Assistance Mission for Rwanda (UNAMIR), to say nothing of survivor and eyewitness accounts. It contradicted widely available research from Amnesty International, UNICEF, Oxfam, African Rights and Human Rights Watch. Corbin seems unaware of the massacre sites in Rwanda where hundreds of thousands of helpless victims sought shelter in cathedrals, churches, clinics and schools. She does not mention the overwhelming evidence showing how, during the 1994 genocide, the overwhelming number of victims were Tutsi.[19]

In sharp contrast, the Rwanda Ministry of Local Government in December 2001 published a preliminary report endorsed by the national government, and the figure of just over 1 million was cited. This figure was based on a census carried out six years after the genocide in July 2000, during which the names of 951,018 victims were established. The report recommended further investigation, saying that the census encountered 'constraints that mean it is not perfect'. It cited, for example, 'the lack of reliable information in some regions where entire families were wiped out; omissions due to memory lapse; refusal to talk for fear of being arrested; or, in certain urban areas, the indifference of the population'. This was why the eventual figure was thought to be more than a million.

The Rwanda research, generally ignored and rarely quoted, dates the start of the genocide to 1 October 1990 in the *préfectures* of Gisenyi, Byumba and Ruhengeri, as civil war broke out. The statistics show that 99.2 per cent of the victims were killed between April and December 1994. They show that 93.7 per cent of the victims were killed because they were identified as Tutsi; 1 per cent because they were related to, married to or friends with Tutsi; 0.8 per cent because they looked like Tutsi; and 0.8 per cent because they were opponents of the Hutu regime at the time or were hiding people from the killers. Of the victims, 53.7 per cent were between 0 and 24 years old, while 41.3 per cent were aged between 25 and 65 years. More men (56.4 per cent) were killed than women (43.3 per cent). The majority (48.2 per cent) of genocide victims were poor rural dwellers, followed by students in secondary and higher education (21.2 per cent). Pre-school children and elderly people over 65 represent 16.8 per cent of victims, according to the report. Most victims were killed by machetes (37.9 per cent), followed by clubs (16.8 per cent) and firearms (14.8 per cent). Some 0.5 per cent of the victims were women raped or cut open, others were forced to commit suicide, beaten to death, thrown into rivers or lakes or burned alive, infants and babies thrown against walls or crushed to death.[20]

Despite this overwhelming evidence, in the course of the programme, Corbin further questioned the motives of the Rwandan government in the memorialisation of the dead. She visited Murambi, one of six national massacre sites, where she asked why 'Paul Kagame keeps the flame of genocide burning at memorial sites' across the country. 'These places reinforce the official story that it was overwhelmingly Tutsi who died and Hutus that killed them,' she explained. 'These places reinforce the official story.' Corbin suggested that Kagame insisted on the genocide memorialisation for his own political ends, using the 'genocide card' in order to attract foreign aid. 'Nothing can prepare you for rows of mummified bodies preserved in the agony of death ... Why is it important to keep these bodies? People would find this macabre and strange.'

The bodies on display in the school at Murambi were tangible proof, the evidence of genocide rather than casualties of a civil war.[21] Layers of lime had served to mummify the corpses that showed evidence of sharp instrument trauma where multiple machete blows split open heads or sliced off limbs, and hammers crushed skulls. The bodies of an estimated 50,000 people murdered here were thrown into drainage trenches or bulldozed into pits. Later exhumation saw the lifting of 700 partly decomposed bodies from one of the trenches and laid out on display in dormitories.

The BBC faced unprecedented criticism. A group of historians, scientists, diplomats, genocide experts and journalists wrote a letter to Lord Tony Hall, the director-general.[22] 'In broadcasting this documentary the BBC has been recklessly irresponsible.' The programme had 'emboldened the génocidaires, their supporters and those who collaborate with them', they wrote and a detailed complaint followed. The documentary 'Rwanda's Untold Story' had breached a number of BBC editorial guidelines, including truth and accuracy, impartiality, serving the public interest, and distinguishing opinion from fact, and in addition it failed to understand the international importance of the crime of genocide.

The BBC staunchly defended the programme and in a secretive and labyrinthine procedure took more than a year to consider the complaint. The acting head of programmes, news and current affairs, Jim Gray, believed no offence had been caused to anyone and was the first to reject the idea that the programme promoted genocide denial. In defence of the programme, the executive producer of BBC 2's *This World*, Sam Bagnall, wrote, 'Unlike the Holocaust, the nature and extent of the planning prior to the genocide is open to significant debate.' The courts where the génocidaires were put on trial, he believed, 'cast serious doubt on many of the prosecution witnesses'. Bagnall claimed that everyone charged with a prior conspiracy at the ICTR had been cleared of the crime. This was untrue. A common claim among deniers, it had no basis in fact. The BBC hired an anonymous 'independent editorial adviser' to help them to address the issue and a year after the broadcast the adviser attended a secret meeting of the BBC trustees on 21 October 2015.[23] A background report on the complaint was presented at this meeting. This report failed to address the central and crucial complaint about genocide denial, and it introduced errors of fact and distortion. It showed clear bias. The anonymous adviser reduced the issue of genocide denial to a spat among academics about a controversial subject that created 'discord and disagreements'. The adviser defended the programme's misrepresentation of the Interahamwe and its failure to mention the Hutu Power ideology that underpinned the extermination programme.

As part of the complaint one of the signatories, Dr Roland Moerland, a criminologist from Maastricht University, wrote a report for the BBC to explain the dangers of genocide denial.[24] Denial was more complex than people imagined. Genocide denial was not just literally denying that something had happened but using a range of tactics to effectively engineer confusion and controversy and cast doubt about the genocidal enterprise. Deniers reinterpreted events and provided an alternative reality and tried to turn perpetrators into victims. Denial allowed the genocidal process to continue, making it a crime with no end.

One of the pre-eminent scholars of the crime of genocide, US Professor Gregory Stanton, who signed the complaint against the BBC, described the crime in ten stages, and said he believed the final stage was always denial. The crime of genocide proceeded with the classification of the population, symbolisation of those classifications, discrimination against a targeted group, dehumanisation of the pariah group, organisation of the killers, polarisation of the population, preparation by the killers, persecution of the victims, extermination of the victims and afterwards denial that the killing was genocide. Denial incited new killing. It denied the dignity of the deceased and mocked those who survived.

The BBC decision on the case came in a seventeen-page rejection published on the BBC website. An Editorial Standards Committee declared the programme had performed 'a valuable public service'. It explored 'credible alternative narratives' to the

'accepted version of events' surrounding 'one of the most disturbing and controversial conflicts in modern history, a conflict which
had unquestionably involved genocide on a monumental scale'.
The film did not 'diminish the full horror of the genocide' but
had 'appropriately signposted the controversial conclusions of an
academic study into the genocide death toll'.

The film gave a 'full account of the horror' and the script made
repeated references to genocide. How could the programme
promote denial? There were graphic images, and viewers would
have been in no doubt as to the 'enormous scale' of the atrocity.
The programme provided a 'different and challenging view'. The
film looked at a 'controversial conclusion on the relative numbers
of Hutu and Tutsi killed'. The trustees determined that the phrase
'genocide denial' was open to interpretation and there were no
BBC editorial guidelines that dealt exclusively with 'alleged genocide denial'; the trustees decided to consider the issue on the
grounds of impartiality, accuracy, harm and offence. They noted
the conclusion of the Editorial Complaints Unit (ECU) that conducted an investigation into the complaint, and the fact that
the programme was now posted on denial websites was not the
responsibility of the BBC and beyond its control. In any event,
'the film did not lend itself to misuse of the kind suggested by the
complainants'.

Like their anonymous adviser, the BBC saw the complaint as the
airing of different opinions: between the 'many stark differences
between the complainants' views' and 'those of the programme
makers (not to mention other experts)'. In their defence, the programme team cited 'several other academics who suggested a larger
number of Hutu died than is generally thought' but failed to name
them. The investigators at the ECU, who conducted the inquiry
into the programme, remained anonymous, the complaints procedure unaccountable. The BBC denied it discredited the established
historical record or sought to overturn material evidence that was
recognised internationally and capable of immediate verification
by resorting to sources of reasonably indisputable accuracy.

The BBC's final decision was made by the Editorial Standards
Committee; this marked the end of the procedure, and it was

published on 27 November 2015. It upheld one ground of the complainants' appeal and rejected all the others. Of the one complaint upheld the committee wrote: 'The programme failed to achieve due accuracy in its discussion of the assassination of President Habyarimana in April 1994 by omitting reference to a forensics and ballistics study that cast doubt on an earlier report discussed in the programme.'

The BBC programme had done more than provide a 'discussion about the assassination'. The journalists had assured their viewers that the current president of Rwanda, Paul Kagame, was guilty of the crime, and that over the years more and more 'evidence had come to light' that pointed to the RPF's responsibility for firing missiles at the jet. Yet the programme contained no material evidence at all. The scientific report of Judges Marc Trévidic and Nathalie Poux was simply ignored, as were the the direct witnesses to the missile fire, who had been close enough to hear them leave their casings. To support their accusation, the BBC relied on a witness, Kayumba Nyamwasa, who, Corbin said, 'knows all about the plane'.

Nyamwasa, upon whom the journalist relied, was a former military commander in the RPF and a known political opponent of Kagame who lived in exile in Cape Town, South Africa. Nyamwasa told Corbin that Kagame 'enjoyed killing his people' and that he had downed the plane. The BBC did not reveal the political links of Nyamwasa, or his stated ambition to overthrow the Rwandan government. There was no mention of his threats to Rwandan security, or of his links with an exiled opposition political coalition, the Rwanda National Congress (RNC), or of the corruption charges levelled against him. The BBC had relied on suspect testimony. In all the years Nyamwasa claimed to know about the plane, he produced no detail, and in October 2018 the investigating magistrates in Paris dismissed his claims as worthless.[25]

The BBC may not have realised quite how useful 'Rwanda's Untold Story' was among the deniers in their ongoing campaign. The BBC editors may have missed the full-hearted support given to the programme by Edward S. Herman and David Peterson, authors of a book published in 2010, *The Politics of Genocide*, widely condemned for its brazen genocide denial.[26] Six weeks after the broadcast, Herman and Peterson published an article fulsome in its praise, describing the documentary as 'the first of its kind in a reinterpretation of what really happened'.[27] The BBC had revealed the 'big lie' told by President Paul Kagame, who had so far managed to conceal his primary role in 'setting off the genocide in which most victims were Hutu'.

Edward S. Herman, professor emeritus of finance at the Wharton School of the University of Pennsylvania, and David Peterson, an independent journalist and researcher, argued events in Rwanda were misunderstood. The reason was a propaganda campaign waged by the Rwandan Patriotic Front (RPF) and its Western allies. Herman and Peterson argued the killing was 'triggered' by the RPF and the violence was justified as self-defence. The chief responsibility for Rwandan 'political violence' belonged to the RPF and not to the ousted coalition government, the Rwandan government army or 'any Hutu-related group'.

In a further publication, *Enduring Lies: The Rwandan Genocide in the Propaganda System, 20 Years Later*, in 2014, Herman and Peterson explained how a 'standard model' of the 'Rwandan genocide' was nothing more than a complex of interwoven lies and, when examined, simply unravelled. The truths embodied in this model were untrue, they said, and the preplanned genocide resulting in 800,000 deaths had no basis in fact.[28]

These authors praised the BBC for having given a voice to well-informed but marginalised figures whose views had been systematically suppressed and even ridiculed by the establishment media, historians and 'assorted political hacks from within the Kagame power lobby'. Most important, the BBC had given a substantial segment of the documentary to the work of two US professors, a break from 'twenty years of false and propagandistic storytelling in the Anglo-American world' that had buried the real history of the period.

The BBC documentary emboldened the deniers. 'Rwanda's Untold Story' remains widely quoted and available to view on various websites, reinforcing the arguments that the RPF started the genocide, then did nothing to stop it, and once having ignored it, had insisted on victory. These arguments, given the legitimacy of the BBC, minimise the crime and create confusion about what really happened.

BBC editors and journalists appear unconcerned at the use made of the documentary and several clips remain proudly displayed on the BBC website, under the BBC 2 *This World* series. It is described as a programme that 'challenges the accepted story' and, to this day, the broadcaster seems blissfully unaware of how the programme was used in the defence of a convicted génocidaire in a Paris courtroom.

9

Decoding

The minister of justice in the Interim Government, Agnès Ntamabyaliro Rutagwera, was one of the most important prisoners awaiting trial in Rwanda. Ntamabyaliro, a well-known Hutu Power figure, had been central to the events of 1994.[1] At the start of the year she had been the secretary-general of the Parti Libéral and had managed, with the help of President Juvénal Habyarimana, to split her party and create a Hutu Power wing.[2] Ntamabyaliro stood with Colonel Théoneste Bagosora when he helped to assemble the Hutu Power politicians in the French embassy and created the government that oversaw the policy of extermination.[3]

In the aftermath, Ntamabyaliro was a part of the government in exile in the camps in Zaire (DCR) and helped to devise policies to ensure the refugee population, an estimated 1 million people, once incited to flee the country, remained hostages of the génocidaires.[4] Ntamabyaliro helped to ensure that Hutu Power controlled camp administration at the local level, the Interahamwe entrenched among the people.

As the minister of justice, she was at the forefront of a revised propaganda campaign, devised in the camps, and she personally sent a tract to the United Nations Commission on Human Rights (UNCHR) in Geneva from the camp at Bukavu, Zaire. This twenty-page publication called *Le Peuple Rwandais accuse ...* ('The Rwandan people accuse ...') blamed the Rwandan Patriotic Front (RPF) for the entire catastrophe. The tract was to enable the world to reach a better understanding of what had happened, she explained.[5] It was a template of the denial campaign to come.[6] Ntamabyaliro waited ten years for her trial and was eventually sentenced in 2009 to a life term for genocide and crimes against humanity, confirmed on appeal. She was the only minister of the Interim Government to stand trial in a Rwandan courtroom.

While awaiting her trial, Ntamabyaliro received a visit from a young British academic who came to the 1930 prison to interview her. Dr Hazel Cameron is today a lecturer in the School of International Relations at St Andrew's University, Scotland. In the preface of an eventual book, the academic described the 'air of geniality' in the prison and the atmosphere of 'cordiality' between the perpetrators. In the same text, she raised doubts that apparently existed over the credibility of the prosecution witnesses who testified at the eventual Ntamabyaliro trial. Cameron said she took the advice of this former judge who gave her a warning. 'Look at the British,' Ntamabyaliro told her. 'They are guiltier than the French.' Cameron took Ntamabyaliro at her word. In 2013 she published *Britain's Hidden Role in the Rwandan Genocide: The Cat's Paw*. It argued that the US and UK used the RPF as a proxy, the 'cat's paw' of the title.

The author described how the RPF shrewdly created and sustained an overly simplified, politically correct view of history; a group of 'anglophone' Kagame-friendly journalists had promoted a story about a conspiracy to murder that involved planning, yet according to prisoners convicted of genocide no conspiracy had ever existed. These journalists were Fergal Keane, Philip Gourevitch and me, portrayed as suffering from 'political correctness RPF-style'. Cameron noted in her book: 'Such support from outsiders undoubtedly lends an air of authenticity to the RPF government of Rwanda's skewed version of history'. Cameron told her readers that prisoners had 'established their universal belief that the genocide committed by the Hutu of Rwanda was a spontaneous expression of popular anger'.[7] Cameron speculated whether the UK and the US had used the RPF to overthrow President Habyarimana as a means to install a government sympathetic to UK and US policies in Central Africa.

The idea of an Anglo-Saxon plot was not new. In 2010 in the US, Edward S. Herman and David Peterson argued in *The Politics of Genocide* that the idea of a genocide of the Tutsi was a political construct largely manipulated by Washington and its allies. These claims were no more than an excuse for 'so-called humanitarian intervention'.[8] Their book received an excruciating review by a Canadian academic, Gerry Caplan. Caplan was an expert, the author of *The Preventable Genocide,* published in May 2000, a report produced by the Organisation of African Unity following a two-year inquiry by a group of eminent personalities.[9] The Caplan review of Herman and Peterson's book claimed their work rested on a foundation of other deniers, statements by génocidaires, fabrications, distortions, innuendo and gross ignorance. Caplan wrote, 'Everyone who contradicts their fantasies is an American/ RPF pawn ... The main authorities on whom the authors rest their fabrications are a tiny number of long-time American and Canadian genocide deniers who gleefully drink each other's putrid bathwater.' It was the power of the internet that made them seem ubiquitous and forceful. Any online search gave them a dispro-portionately high pride of place.[10]

There were others who supported the Anglo-Saxon plot theory. President François Mitterrand of France thought it obvious that the RPF invasion of Rwanda in 1990 was an external aggression by an army supported, equipped and trained by Uganda. This justified French involvement.[11] The Anglo-Saxons clearly had eyes on French interests in Africa. Uganda was 'Tutsi-land' to some in the French military and their intelligence gathering in Rwanda centred on the 'Ugandan Tutsis'.[12] In this view of events, the RPF came from a social and ethnic minority, hungry for power, revenge and ethnic killing. The RPF was part of an elaborate US conspir-acy to gain a military presence in Central Africa.

The eventual RPF victory in July 1994 provoked strong reac-tions and some military officers and government officials in Paris felt that Rwanda was 'lost', the first in a series of regional dominos that would bring Burundi and Zaire under Anglo-Saxon domina-tion. How would France explain to other Francophone African heads of state that French protection was worth nothing? This was the view of the traditional officials in the Mitterrand inner circle, how they interpreted events.[13] The theory of Anglo-Saxon expansionism emphasised France's independence and perfectly asserted its international status and rank.

An Anglo-Saxon conspiracy was a favourite with Colonel Théoneste Bagosora. 'I think the US government is responsible for the genocide because they provided weapons to the minority and they knew that they would retaliate,' he said in an interview in Goma on 15 February 1995. He blamed the defeat on the US government and the European Community because of their imposition at the UN of a diplomatic and political embargo. Bagosora complained that the US had called for the arrest of former leaders before any investigations had taken place. This was old history, a revival of the Great Game, all about an English-speaking empire seeking advantage over the French hegemony.[14]

The Anglo-Saxon plot never existed, according to Herman Cohen, the assistant secretary of state for African Affairs (1989–1993). In testimony to a French inquiry established by the National Assembly, Cohen said that US aid to the RPF was non-existent. Appearing on 7 July 1998, Cohen said the only link was a dozen officers on courses in military colleges in the US, as part of cooperation with Uganda. 'We never gave arms to either Uganda or the RPF,' Cohen said. He found the idea of a plot decidedly regrettable as it prevented any real dialogue during the crisis.[15] The French inquiry later concluded that no US plot ever existed. The priority for the US was to restrict the role of the UN, for political and budgetary reasons.[16]

In the UK, the plot theory was fomented in the left-wing magazine *Living Marxism*, which reported Western complicity in an article in December 1995, rejecting the very idea of genocide. A press officer for CAFOD, the Catholic relief agency, Fiona Fox, visited Rwanda and wrote an article under the pseudonym Fiona Foster headlined 'Massacring the truth in Rwanda' that argued that the use of the word 'genocide' indicated an emotional over-reaction and obsession.

The Revolutionary Communist Party (RCP), which ran *Living Marxism*, claimed in a later piece in May 1997, 'Rwanda:

Myth and Reality', that the government of President Juvénal Habyarimana had been arm-twisted into relinquishing power, and took up machetes and 'whatever else came to hand'. His backers, Belgium, France, the US, the UK and Germany, progressively undermined his government. Furthermore, the peace agreement, the Arusha Accords, had been a means to consolidate an RPF takeover of power. The UN had mandated a tribunal that targeted all Hutu and 'Hutu extremism [is] a western inspired caricature'.[17]

Living Marxism described how inside and outside Rwanda the word 'genocide' was used 'to criminalize the majority of ordinary Rwandan people, to justify outside interference in the country's affairs, and to lend legitimacy to a minority military government imposed on Rwanda'. In a later issue, the idea that 'the Hutu-led government could plan and execute the deliberate annihilation of an entire people at a time when it could not even organize to sell the coffee beans seems a little short of incredible'.[18]

A subsequent article published in March 1996 with the headline 'Rwanda: The Great Genocide Debate', by Barry Crawford, claimed there was no genocide. Following that, a Marxist organisation that called itself Africa Direct distributed materials on the Great Genocide Debate at a number of African Studies conferences, including the conference at the Leeds African Studies Unit in London in July 1997.[19]

In his presentation, Crawford argued this was a civil war, a chaotic final attempt to stop the RPF and a case of 'every man for himself'. A struggle over state power took on an ethnic form. 'With Rwandans, apparently, you can conduct a genocide over the radio. This would be laughable if it were not such a deadly serious matter.'[20] The author continued in the same vein. In 2014, under the name Barrie Collins, he published *Rwanda 1994: The Myth of the Akazu Genocide Conspiracy and Its Consequences*.[21]

The Anglo-Saxon plot story circulated early in the post-genocide period. The idea promoted in the US magazine *Executive Intelligence Review*, best known for its publication of conspiracy theories, included the claim that the British secret services had been responsible. The president of Uganda, Yoweri Museveni, had been recruited by the UK and had geopolitical ambition. The plot devised by Baroness Lynda Chalker, the minister for overseas development, had obliged the French to rescue Rwanda.[22]

On 11 April 2013, in an effort to explain a growing campaign of genocide denial and its various manifestations, a Rwandan academic in the US gave an address at the Sheraton Hotel in Silver Spring, Maryland, at a public meeting held for the nineteenth commemoration of the 1994 genocide of the Tutsi. He called his address 'Deliberate and Unintended Ambiguity: The Relative Complexity of Decoding the Tutsi Genocide Denial'. He told his audience there were four distinct trends in the current campaign of genocide denial. The first was the erroneous description of the genocide as a civil war. The second was to deny it happened because of a lack of proof of intent and to claim that the killing had been spontaneous. The third was to claim that there had been a double genocide, that the Tutsi also killed Hutu in an inter-ethnic conflict and so each annulled the other. The fourth was to deny genocide by deliberate ambiguity and a lack of precision to spread confusion about what really happened. The intention of all denial was to erase memory.

Dr Gatsinzi Basaninyenzi was an associate professor of English at Alabama A&M University, where he taught African-American literature and literary criticism. The genocide claimed a number of his relatives in 1994, and afterwards he watched the growing campaign of denial with dread and fascination. In particular, he was interested in the role of Paul Rusesabagina, of *Hotel Rwanda* fame, who had been portrayed in the Hollywood film as a hero who, despite the odds, saved more than 1,000 people at the height of the killing. As a result, Rusesabagina had become an international sensation, gaining a world reputation for courage.

Basaninyenzi believed Rusesabagina was adept at the fourth category of denial: a deliberate ambiguity of language to spread confusion. In 2008, he watched Rusesabagina lecture to a packed auditorium at Birmingham-Southern College in Alabama, and later described listening for one long hour to a series of lies and half-truths.

For instance, Rusesabagina told the audience the roots of the killing were that Hutu had been enslaved by Tutsi for centuries, and when the Tutsi RPF invaded in 1990, they had killed thousands of Hutu. And so, he opined, the Tutsi were the first to pick up the machete. At the end of the lecture, Rusesabagina received a standing ovation. 'How come the American audience could not decode him and get a gist of his denial?' Basaninyenzi asked in his lecture in Maryland. Because of the ambiguity of his language, the audience had failed to see the true persona.

Rusesabagina became an entirely different person when interviewed by Keith Harmon Snow, a US journalist and a virulent and prolific denier to whom Rusesabagina gave a lengthy interview in 2007.[23] Harmon Snow had written often about the 'so-called Rwanda genocide', which he claimed was 'one of the most widely misunderstood events in contemporary history'. In the course of the interview, Rusesabagina told Harmon Snow how, when the RPF invaded from Uganda, they killed Hutu, and this was never qualified as a genocide. 'But it is one; until it is qualified as a genocide, me, I won't call it a genocide, but it is supposed to be one.'

Furthermore, the RPF infiltrated the militia, he said. 'Most of the guys on the roadblocks were Kagame people.' He blamed Paul Kagame for killing President Juvénal Habyarimana and therefore held Kagame responsible for the deaths of a million people. Rusesabagina explained that Lieutenant General Roméo Dallaire worked secretly for the RPF, and UNAMIR helped to smuggle soldiers into Kigali. The RPF carried out a coup and had been rewarded and protected for its trouble.[24]

The Hollywood film *Hotel Rwanda* released in 2005 briefly brought the genocide of the Tutsi into the public consciousness. It was billed as a film 'based on a true story'. Rusesabagina was portrayed as the Rwandan Oskar Schindler, a symbol of extraordinary courage in the most extreme circumstance. Played by Don Cheadle, he had been an ordinary man who found himself quite by chance in extraordinary circumstances and had faced down the killers. He could not watch the slaughter, and before long the four-star hotel with 112 rooms and five floors became a well-appointed refugee camp. In the years since, Rusesabagina had received the highest civilian award in the US from George W. Bush, the Presidential Medal of Freedom. He received the Lantos Human Rights Prize, an honour previously awarded to the Dalai Lama and Holocaust survivor Elie Wiesel.

The trouble was that the history of the Hôtel des Mille Collines told in the film did not accord with everyone's reality. It was a myth that the hotel manager had stood between the people in the hotel and the killers, and through cajoling, bartering and negotiation had kept the militia at bay and saved 1,268 people.

Rusesabagina was a friend to the architects of genocide, according to some witnesses. He had been parachuted into the job as manager at the start of the genocide. The hotel was not a place of refuge but, in fact, an impromptu military headquarters. He had come directly from the Hotel des Diplomates where on Saturday, 9 April, he helped organise celebrations to usher in Hutu Power's Interim Government.

One Rwandan who sought sanctuary in the hotel later wrote a memoir casting doubt on the nature of the protection afforded by Rusesabagina, a book that included the recollections of a number of other direct witnesses who survived in the hotel.[25] One Rwandan researcher, Alfred Ndahiro, looked into the story and sent a questionnaire to people who had sheltered at the hotel. Seventy-three replied, and only three believed Rusesabagina had saved their lives, and only because he had allowed them to drink water from the swimming pool.[26]

The people at the hotel had sent faxes complaining to the International Committee of the Red Cross (ICRC) in Kigali and to SOS International that they had to pay to shelter at the hotel.[27] The cheques, accepted by Rusesabagina for payment for the rooms, were cashed in Gitarama, where the Interim Government had established its premises when it left Kigali, and were taken to the formerly Kigali-based national bank by armed escort.[28] On 18 May, a fax from the Belgian office of Sabena, the owners of the hotel, signed by Michel Houtart, head of corporate development, addressed to Paul Rusesabagina, told him in no uncertain terms he was not to make anyone pay for the shelter, nor was he to charge for food.[29]

In contrast to the *Hotel Rwanda* story, the force commander the UN Mission for Rwanda (UNAMIR), Lieutenant General Roméo Dallaire, placed a group of Tunisian peacekeepers and an armoured personnel carrier at the entrance to the hotel, and he believed it was these troops who were ultimately responsible for deterring the killers. These UN peacekeepers were to report immediately any attempts by the militia or troops to enter.[30]

Some in UNAMIR believed it was expedient for Hutu Power to keep these people safe. The hotel was the focus of Western press attention and exempting the residents from violence became an integral part of a strategy to obscure the reality of the extermination elsewhere. With these people alive, it was harder to claim that a targeted and determined genocidal campaign was taking place.[31]

A Polish UN military observer, Major Stefan Steć, served in the UNAMIR headquarters and with six staff officers had created what they called the Humanitarian Assistance Cell (HAC), whose sole purpose was to try to save lives. Steć said that at the Hôtel des Mille Collines were prominent opposition politicians, both Hutu and Tutsi – doctors, lawyers and a senator, and he feared they would be killed secretly, picked off one at a time.[32] At one point, reports came from the hotel that Rusesabagina had provided the Rwandan army commander Lieutenant General Augustin Bizimungu with a list of the most important hotel guests and their room numbers. The UN observers managed to change the room numbers of those people most threatened. For the duration of the genocide, a Hutu Power military communications post was operational on the top floor of the hotel.[33]

The importance the Interim Government attached to the hotel became clear only later when, in his ICTR confession, Jean Kambanda, the prime minister in the Interim Government, admitted that the military and civilian authorities discussed the situation in cabinet meetings. The hotel, with its 550 refugees, was 'unfortunate'. These people were 'in full view' of the world's media, UN peacekeepers, medical teams from Médecins Sans Frontières (MSF) and the ICRC.

There was pressure placed upon the Interim Government to safeguard the sanctity of the hotel from a senior French government official and career diplomat, Bruno Delaye, head of the Africa Unit based in the Élysée Palace in Paris. Several times Delaye requested that army commanders and the Interim Government ensure the safety of the 550 people in the hotel. There was also evidence of French intervention in a failed attempt to get some of the people to the airport. A French journalist quoted an anonymous, despondent and guilt-ridden foreign office official who had admitted that this intervention was proof of the influence of the French authorities over events in Rwanda.[34]

The journalist, Alain Frilet, wrote how he had personally witnessed Delaye call Kigali from his office in Paris after a grenade attack on the hotel. Delaye told Frilet afterwards that the operation to evacuate some of the guests halted.[35] In his book *An Ordinary Man*, Rusesabagina confirmed that the 'Hutu Power government had direct links with France'.[36] It seems strange that when Bruno Delaye gave evidence in 1998 to the French National Assembly inquiry he claimed that after the assassination of President Juvénal Habyarimana any appeal for reason or any pressure at all on the Hutu camp would have been useless.[37]

On 3 April 2008, Paul Rusesabagina came to London to testify at Westminster Magistrates' Court. He was a witness in an extradition case concerning four alleged génocidaires living in the UK. Rusesabagina had been invited by defence lawyers as an expert about whether or not a fair trial in Rwanda was possible and the current position of human rights in the country. The case included Dr Vincent Bajinya, a medical doctor and alleged category-one génocidaire who lived with his family in London. He faced charges of genocide, crimes against humanity, leadership and participation in a criminal gang, and participation in acts of devastation, massacres and looting.[38]

The extradition cases listed before a specialist extradition judge, District Judge Anthony Evans, required the government of Rwanda to submit a prima facie case in respect of each of the four suspects. There were forty-two days of witness testimony in the Westminster court, thousands of pages of evidence served by both prosecution and defence, and several days set aside for final oral submissions.

The testimony of Paul Rusesabagina to the Westminster court before Judge Evans went largely unnoticed. He defended Bajinya, and explained that the 'Tutsi government' had brought the charges against the doctor as part of a policy to exploit genocide: it was a way for the current government to get rid of all Hutu opponents in senior positions, and the doctor was a political opponent. Asked about human rights in Rwanda, Rusesabagina said, 'I mean, there were killings before 1994 and after 1994. The difference is the ruling ethnic group. Before it was Hutu Power and people were dying. Now a Tutsi power and people killed. Either way the game is killing.'

He went on to explain that when the genocide broke out, the youth of all the political parties mixed and created a kind of anarchy in the whole country. He did not deny a story that roadblocks had included Tutsi killers and that there was no systematic, government-led genocide. He complained that the Rwandan government called him a 'negationist', a revisionist.

No need existed for Judge Evans to decode this genocide denial. In his eventual ruling, Evans wrote that to deny genocide as Rusesabagina had done was so contrary to all evidence and facts placed before the court as to be worthless. Not to accept genocide would be 'flying in the face of all international and humanitarian agency reports on the situation which pertained in Rwanda in 1994'.[39]

The judge duly noted Rusesabagina was a very strong opponent of the current government, even going so far as to claim that President Kayame was responsible for the genocide. The witness made other wild and exaggerated claims with no supporting proof for his allegations. He had a background strongly allied to the extremist Hutu faction and could not be considered either independent or reasonable, and therefore no weight should be attached to his testimony. His performance in court added questions regarding his direct links with Hutu Power – in 1994 and today. Although he claimed not to be acquainted with Bajinya, the magistrate noted that Rusesabagina had greeted him warmly when he entered the court.

In his testimony to the Westminster court on behalf of Bajinya about the human rights conditions in Rwanda, Rusesabagina claimed that any 'successful Hutu would be killed, imprisoned or forced into exile', although he gave only one example. Rwanda had a policy of sending its prisoners as 'slave labour' to the Congo, he said, and there were secret jails, unknown to journalists, humanitarians and human rights activists. He dismissed Rwanda's recent judicial reforms as a 'smokescreen'. The judge noted Rusesabagina had not lived in Rwanda since 1996, and estimated he knew nothing about the Rwandan judiciary or its detention facilities. Rusesabagina was a fantasist, he concluded, who made allegations in court about human rights in Rwanda with no supporting proof. In sum, he was an implacable enemy of the regime in Kigali.

Judge Evans further noted how well acquainted the witness was with leading members of the political party Mouvement Révolutionnaire National pour le Développement (MRND), as well as his links with the leading figures of Hutu Power such as Édouard Karemera, Mathieu Ngirumpatse and Georges Rutaganda. Rutaganda, the second vice president of the National Committee of the Interahamwe, was a good friend, while Major General Augustin Bizimungu, the army chief of staff, was described as a 'good man'. Bizimungu, one of the principal architects of the genocide, was a regular at the cocktail bar in the Hôtel des Mille Collines. The swimming pool outside where his soldiers washed their clothes was the only water available for those sheltering there during the genocide.

On 6 June 2008, Judge Evans advised that the extraditions should go ahead.[40] The lawyers for the Rwandans appealed the ruling to the Divisional Court. The attempt was successful, and extradition was blocked. In a ruling on 8 April 2009, while agreeing that the evidence put forward by prosecutors showed the four had a case to answer, the extradition foundered on the grounds that they would suffer a flagrant denial of justice if they were tried in Kigali. As a consequence, the four defendants walked free from court. The court had relied on a 2008 report prepared by Human Rights Watch, purportedly based on research conducted between 2005 and mid-2008 and critical of the justice system in Rwanda. Judge Evans had not trusted the work of this advocacy group because it lacked factual scientific basis and relied on anecdotal evidence without any hard facts.

It took another five years, until 13 May 2014, for the second arrest of the four Rwandan men by officers from Scotland Yard's specialist extradition unit. There was a fresh application from Rwandan authorities, accompanied by a statement in which prosecutors maintained the country's judicial system had made significant progress in the fairness of its trials. Rwanda pointed to recent extradition decisions by the European Court of Human Rights as proof that international bodies were sending alleged fugitives back to Rwanda for trial.

Bajinya, fifty-two, still lived in King's Cross, London, and was a former employee of a charity for refugees, Praxis, based in Bethnal Green. Célestin Ugirashebuja, sixty, was a care worker in Walton-on-the-Naze, Essex. He had been the *bourgmestre* of Kigoma *commune* in Gitarama. Charles Munyaneza, fifty-five, from Bedford, worked as a cleaner.[41] The ICTR had a file on him and in trials at the tribunal the prosecution had produced witnesses who had described his central role in bringing the killing to the *communes* of Kinyamakara, where he was *bourgmestre,* and to the *commune* of Karama in Gikongoro. Munyaneza allegedly took an active part in the killing.[42] Emmanuel Nteziryayo, sixty, from Manchester, had been *bourgmestre* in the *commune* of Mudasomwa, in the *préfecture* of Gikongoro, and was accused of provoking and leading the massacres in Murambi, starting on 21 April 1994, resulting in an estimated death toll of 50,000 people.[43]

A fifth man not previously arrested in the UK, Célestin Mutabaruka, fifty-seven, was detained on 5 June, joining the other four in the hearings. He allegedly had led a gang of killers in May 1994 that murdered many people on Muyira Hill in Bisesero. Mutabaruka now lived as a pastor and, with his wife, Rose, ran a church they had founded, located on a business park in Kent. The pastor and his wife were listed as directors of a charity called the Bells of Revival Worldwide Ministries, incorporated in June 2008. All five strenuously denied any wrongdoing. Human rights groups welcomed the arrests and criticised the amount of time allowed to elapse.

The Westminster Magistrates' Court again heard the case, this time before Deputy Senior District Judge Emma Arbuthnot. It included sixty-three days of evidence, during which more witnesses gave further expert advice, including expert testimony from John Philpot.[44] In her eventual ruling, Judge Arbuthnot described him as a lawyer who 'had worked extensively for the ICTR' and was the secretary-general of the American Association of Jurists.[45] There was no mention of his long-standing and early contributions to genocide denial.[46] In September 1995, Philpot had described the 'mutual bloodletting', and how when the RPF invaded, 'the majority Hutu population developed an acute phobia of the Tutsi population'. After the president's assassination on 6 April 1994, 'the Hutu population felt encircled and threatened with elimination', and the killing took place because of extreme fear, prompting self-defence by the Hutu.

Philpot had acted as the defence lawyer for Jean-Paul Akayesu in his trial at the International Criminal Tribunal for Rwanda (ICTR). The first person ever convicted of genocide in an international court,[47] Akayesu, from Taba *commune*, Gitarama, received a life sentence confirmed on appeal in September 1998, for nine counts of genocide, direct and public incitement to commit genocide and crimes against humanity – extermination, murder, torture, rape and other inhumane acts.[48] After the verdict at the ICTR, Philpot continued to defend his client on the internet, claiming it was wrong to vilify him.[49]

Philpot told the Westminster Magistrates' Court that he himself faced danger in Rwanda and was unable to travel there for fear of his own safety, because of 'the work he has done in the past' and the fact he was critical of the Rwandan government. There was no apparent awareness of breaches of the laws in Rwanda against genocide denial and the public promotion of its ideology. In Rwanda, a 2003 constitution criminalised revisionism, negationism and the trivialisation of genocide. A law punishing genocide denial stated that any person who negated genocide, minimised it or attempted to justify it by his or her words, writings, images or by any other means would be prosecuted and imprisoned from ten to twenty years.[50]

Another former defence lawyer from the ICTR who gave evidence to the Westminster Magistrates' Court was the Canadian lawyer Christopher Black, who believed the 'standard interpretation of genocide was incorrect'. Black, known for his denial of genocide in Bosnia, claimed that defence lawyers at the ICTR had 'accumulated massive evidence that paints an entirely different picture'.[51] He believed the word 'genocide' was used by the RPF 'as a term of art for their version of the war'. The RPF story was a pack of lies from start to finish. Black claimed the RPF began the war, committed most of the massacres and overthrew the democratic process.[52]

In order to explain just how dangerous Rwanda was for defence lawyers, the Westminster Magistrates' Court heard from Philpot of another lawyer from the ICTR no longer able to travel there. Peter Erlinder, a lead defence counsel in the ICTR Military One trial, had taught at the William Mitchell College of Law, and had been arrested in Kigali in May 2010.[53] Erlinder was apparently in Rwanda as a member of the defence team of Victoire Ingabire, who was arrested when she came back to Rwanda to participate in the presidential elections as the candidate of the Unified Democratic Forces (UDF-Inkingi). Ingabire was linked to the Republican Rally for Democracy in Rwanda (RDR), which was established as the political wing of the armed forces responsible for the 1994 genocide – Forces Démocratiques pour la Libération du Rwanda (FDLR), the remnants of the genocidal army determined to continue killing Tutsi and conquer Rwanda in the name of Hutu Power.

Erlinder was perhaps the best known of all the deniers, and in an explanation of his arrest, the Rwandan Minister of Justice, Tharcisse Karugarama, said that in Rwanda, genocide ideology was a deadly serious matter. The actions of Erlinder as a high-profile genocide denier and radical ideologue, the minister continued, were the reason why they devised these Rwandan laws. Left unchecked, the promulgation of the denialist worldview – that the genocide was a figment of Rwanda's imagination and that the victims were responsible for their fate – would cause unrest and disunity. In response to Erlinder's arrest, Christopher Black announced the 'alleged law under which the Rwandans arrested Erlinder was designed to suppress the truth about the war in Rwanda in order for a brutal regime to maintain its totalitarian control of a tragic country'.[54] Imprisoned for three weeks, Erlinder was released for medical reasons and did not face prosecution.

The Westminster Magistrates' Court on 2 December 2015 ruled not to extradite the five men. The court determined that each of the five had cases to answer, but there were concerns over whether they would receive a fair trial in Rwanda. The testimony of the deniers was probably of little note in the overall decision, but their participation in the hearings provided them with much sought-after legitimacy. Their arguments had been heard and they were accepted by experts in a British courtroom.

We may never know what swayed the judges, but most persuasive may have been a list of human rights abuses allegedly committed by the Rwandan government, called a 'Table of Violations', compiled for the defence by one of the British lawyers, Diana Ellis QC. Ellis was familiar with genocide cases, as she had been the defence lawyer at the ICTR for Hutu Power's propagandist-in-chief, Ferdinand Nahimana, who was convicted of genocide in 2003. Ellis was successful in November 2007 when the Appeals Chamber quashed some of Nahimana's convictions and helped to secure his release after twenty years in prison.

The decision made by Judge Arbuthnot not to extradite the men was appealed to the High Court in December 2016. The Rwandan government argued that changes made in the Rwandan courts system did allow for fair trials. A number of decisions by the ICTR Referral and Appeals Chambers and other non-Rwandan courts had permitted transfer or extradition of genocide fugitives to Rwanda. No court had refused to extradite, transfer or deport to Rwanda since 2009, in relation to those accused of genocide charges, although an exception arose in November 2015 when a Dutch court in The Hague refused to extradite a Rwandan citizen.

When the case reached the High Court in 2016, the judges complained about their workload on this appeal decision that was a 'truly formidable undertaking'.[55] There existed an enormous quantity of evidence, and its complexity and the disparate jurisdictions under consideration, the multiple levels of courts through which many of the cases passed, the fact that some of the evidence was incomplete and a great deal in writing only, were all factors adding to the difficulties.

The judges ruled on Friday, 28 July 2017. They accepted a report from a Dutch judge telling them of grave concern that if Bajinya was sent back to Rwanda he would not receive an adequate defence, with no adequate lawyers, and difficulties for defence witnesses. Two of the men, Mutabaruka and Nteziryayo, the judges concluded should not be returned as they had been the subject of earlier criminal proceedings in their absence in Rwanda, conducted by the local Gacaca courts, which the judges decreed did not amount to a competent judicial system. Regarding the other two, Munyaneza and Ugirashebuja, the judges concluded that 'the government of Rwanda should have a final opportunity to give firm and reliable undertakings to put in place conditions which would reduce the risk of unfair trial, so that they may lawfully be returned'.

The High Court wanted foreign lawyers and judges present in Rwandan courts to ensure compliance with human rights. It was a decision hard to fathom. By now, other countries had extradited Rwandan suspects. The ICTR had sent Rwandan suspects home for trial. In the end, the Rwandan government gave up trying to extradite the men and requested trial in the UK. The option of putting the men on trial in the UK had been legally available since 2010. In 2017 the Rwandan government requested the UK put these men on trial. It still awaits an adequate response. What continued to worry the Crown Prosecution Service lawyers was the number of genocide fugitives believed to be living in the UK, and the extent of the genocide fugitive problem.[56] There was a failure to understand the danger these fugitives posed, the gravity of their crime and how its true nature was deliberately distorted and confused.

10

Infiltration

The 11 January 1994 cable was difficult to ignore. As a piece of material evidence in court, it caused serious problems for defence lawyers. It was, perhaps, the most famous fax in UN history.[1] Sent from Kigali to the UN Secretariat in New York by Lieutenant General Roméo Dallaire, it gave details of preparations then under way to register all Tutsi families in Kigali with a view to their extermination.

The information it contained came from an informer, a coordinator with the Interahamwe militia who claimed an intimate knowledge of the activities of the Hutu Power movement. He said lists of Tutsi were being compiled in each *secteur*, going from house to house, noting every family member. Following this intelligence gathering, every *secteur* was provided with a militia of forty operatives trained to kill at speed.[2] Each group had been secretly trained in weapons, explosives, close combat and tactics. Within twenty minutes of receiving the order to kill, the militia in each *secteur* had the capacity to immediately murder 1,000 people. There were hidden stockpiles of weapons all over the city.

The informer warned that President Juvénal Habyarimana had lost control over his old party, the Mouvement Révolutionnaire National pour le Développement (MRND). Furthermore, the informer told of plans to goad the Rwandan Patriotic Front (RPF) in order to scupper the peace agreement and restart the civil war. In violent, coordinated and preplanned demonstrations, the Interahamwe would provoke Belgian peacekeepers and kill some of them in order to guarantee the withdrawal of the contingent, the backbone of the UN Assistance Mission for Rwanda (UNAMIR).

For two years, the cable with its warnings from the informer they called Jean-Pierre lay buried in the archive of the force commander which had been brought back from Kigali, with copies of the cable kept in the Department of Peacekeeping Operations (DPKO) at the UN in New York. The UNAMIR archive had been shipped back from Kigali to a storage facility in New Jersey.

However, the story of the informer's dire warnings broke not in New York but in Belgium. It emerged in an investigation by two journalists who wrote a series of articles in *De Morgen* in November 1995. They intended to reveal the extent of government information that was hidden from scrutiny and lost in archives. This was a way to deceive the public, they argued. One of the two journalists, Walter De Bock, gave an interview to the BBC World Service about his work.[3] He gave as an example how in January 1994 a man had warned UN officers of 'an April war, and genocide'. The UN had prevented Dallaire from dismantling the killing structure, he revealed in the interview.

'You are saying the UN had evidence that there was potentially going to be genocide in Rwanda, and they did nothing?' the interviewer asked. That is perfectly correct, the journalist replied. Bock revealed the Belgian military possessed the same information as UNAMIR. The faxes and cables sent from Kigali to the UN had found their way to the Belgian general staff in Brussels, where a special unit followed closely the activities of Belgian troops. The full text of the famous two-page 11 January fax to UN headquarters emerged in its entirety a few weeks later and received international press coverage to prove the extent of the failure over Rwanda. In later years the fax was part of the prosecution in the trials of the génocidaires at the International Criminal Tribunal for Rwanda (ICTR), disproving the many claims from defence lawyers that the slaughter had been spontaneous.

For this reason, the defence lawyers tried to turn the court's attention away from the information contained in the fax to the informer himself and launched a sustained attack on his reputation and motives.

One of the defence lawyers at the ICTR was the Canadian Christopher Black. In 2002, he had defended the former commander of the national gendarmerie, Major-General Augustin Ndindiliyimana, who in April 1994 was in charge of maintaining public order and who was accused of genocide in the trial known as Military Two.[4] In the courtroom, Black was determined to nullify the fax and told the trial chamber that Jean-Pierre was a double agent who worked for the RPF and had set out to smear President Juvénal Habyarimana.

Black did not limit his attack on Jean-Pierre to the courtroom. A little over a year after the Ndindiliyimana trial began in December 2005, Black published an article to claim a 'stunning lack of documentary evidence of a government plan to commit genocide'. He went on: 'There are no orders, minutes of meetings, notes, cables, faxes, radio intercepts or any other type of documentation that such a plan ever existed. In fact, the documentary evidence establishes just the opposite.' Black wrote that the lack of documentary evidence was the Achilles' heel of the 'RPF-western claims of genocide and something was found to fill this void'. The 'so-called genocide fax' filled that void, he ironically noted.

Black was keen to spread the idea that the famous fax was the single document upon which the prosecution claims of a planned genocide relied and an attempt by the prosecution to prove the discredited idea of premeditation. However, all the evidence presented at the tribunal and elsewhere established that, in fact, the fax was a fabrication, Black pronounced. It was a fraud committed on the people of Rwanda, the world and the judges of the Rwanda 'war crimes tribunal', as Black called the criminal tribunal.[5]

One defence witness who came forward to testify anonymously in the trial confirmed for the court that the informer Jean-Pierre was a manipulator. The anonymous witness was a former member of the National Committee of the Interahamwe and thought the figure provided by the informer of 1,700 militia in the city an overestimate, instead offering half that figure as a more probable number. The rate of killing at 1,000 per twenty minutes seemed 'too good to be true' and perhaps was created after the April events and not in January 1994.[6]

Black had not reckoned on Captain Frank Claeys, a prosecution witness, who had got to know Jean-Pierre better than anyone in UNAMIR. Claeys was a military information officer (MIO), a Belgian soldier and member of Dallaire's headquarters staff. Claeys met Jean-Pierre on the night he came forward and kept in contact with him until he disappeared from view on 15 March. In court, Black tried unsuccessfully to persuade Claeys to agree that the informer had set him up. Claeys told the court another MIO who worked for Lieutenant General Dallaire, Captain Amadou Deme, had his own informer and he had confirmed some of the information provided by Jean-Pierre. Deme wrote a longhand report about this and filed it in the archives of the Military Information Office, and it was produced in court.[7] The informer who was in contact with Deme said Jean-Pierre had stockpiled one hundred weapons at his house in Kanombe. Their stories tallied.[8]

'Captain, I put it to you that General Dallaire was – I put it to you this fax was fabricated, and I'm going to put it to you that all of General Dallaire's actions speak to the fact that he was very close to the RPF.' Black claimed that Dallaire was actually helping the RPF prepare for their invasion and the overthrow of the government. Claeys refuted the allegation.

'You and General Dallaire were very well informed on what the RPF was doing and kept this from the government,' Black said. 'UNAMIR was supposed to be a neutral party and, yet, were obviously helping the RPF infiltrate, and doing nothing about it, and meanwhile they made complaints to the world about some weapons cache the government would have had. It's quite one-sided.' Black said the Interahamwe leadership found UNAMIR biased and the national committee had approached UNAMIR and written to Dallaire on 19 January 1994, telling him they would be open to constructive dialogue. All to no avail. Again, Claeys denied the accusations.

Black claimed the original fax made no direct mention of killing Tutsi, and a second version of the fax had been secreted into the UN archives by a British army officer. Unlike the original, this fax referred to killing Tutsi. It was a fake.[9] Claeys denied this was the

case. He had met Jean-Pierre and had helped to write the fax to
UN headquarters.

For Black, writing in his 2005 article, the 'fabrication of the
"genocide" fax' was one more nail in the coffin of the Rwanda
'war crimes tribunal': 'It was ready to be buried under the weight
of accusations of selective prosecution, political bias, unfair procedures, trial by hearsay, perjured testimony and the cover-up of
the murder of two African heads of state, and all in the name of a
new colonialism masquerading as "international justice".'

After his service at the ICTR, Black continued to promote his
ideas and further embellished his story some years later in 2014
when he claimed how in the courtroom at the ICTR the translators were reading from scripts prepared by the prosecution instead
of translating actual testimony of the witnesses.[10] Furthermore,
he said, 'I received death threats throughout the trial from RPF
government officials, from Tanzanian secret police, and from the
CIA, who warned me I had stepped over the line. These have not
stopped even now, as the Canadian intelligence service visited me
in July to tell me I was on a Rwandan government hit list.'

Captain Frank Claeys appeared in several trials to defend the
reputation of Jean-Pierre and to testify to the veracity of the fax.
He testified in the trial of Colonel Théoneste Bagosora, whose
lawyer, Raphaël Constant, told him the arrival of the informer
seemed all too convenient. Constant reminded the court of the
reaction of Dallaire to the information. Dallaire thought the
informer had 'opened the doors to a secret world, an extremist
third force that until then had been in the shadows'.[11]

Constant pointed out that Claeys never actually saw the lists of
Tutsi to kill, and such lists may have been a part of the defence of
Kigali against the RPF. The arms caches, too, were for the defence
of Kigali. With the military occupied at the front, it was up to
civilians to defend the capital. Despite these accusations, Claeys
was adamant. The lists were compiled of Tutsi to be killed when
the time came. The informer spoke fluent French and used the
word *enregistrer*. The informer explained to Claeys how easy
the registration of Tutsi families was because of information on
every individual held by local authorities in the *cellules* and the

secteurs. The orders for registration came from the leadership of the MRND.

In his questioning of Claeys on behalf of Colonel Théoneste Bagosora, Raphaël Constant disputed the speed of any possible killing and asked how one could possibly kill 1,000 people in twenty minutes unless those people were together and one had a machine gun. 'Did he not explain this to you?' Claeys explained that Kigali was divided administratively and each area was allotted a certain number of militia. Once the order was given, 1,000 people could be killed in each area simultaneously.

Constant wanted to know from Claeys why he had not been suspicious that the informer was in contact with the RPF. His contact with the RPF would have proved the man a stooge. Claeys disagreed; the fact that Jean-Pierre had contact with the RPF did not surprise him at all. No one, not the UN nor any country, had offered to protect him. 'Where else could he go?' Claeys asked the lawyer.

'He was standing up against the extermination of the Tutsi, and nothing was going to prevent him from finding some help in his efforts to stop these plans,' Claeys said. In the event of discovery, Jean-Pierre may have arranged to seek shelter with the RPF battalion in Kigali. Constant disagreed. Dallaire and Claeys had too readily believed the informer. Claeys responded: 'It is easy to find weaknesses in the system afterwards. What is true is this plan existed. As events showed in the first hours and days after April 6.'

Claeys came to court again in the trial of Mathieu Ngirumpatse at the ICTR, the trial known as Government One, with three politicians including a lawyer, Édouard Karemera, who was the minister of the interior, and Joseph Nzirorera, national secretary of the MRND. In this instance, the lawyers suggested that Claeys had acted in haste in sharing the information in the fax sent to senior officials at the UN. He responded, 'Keeping this information for us and not informing others was not the way to do it.'[12] It was a set-up, the lawyers continued, this time against the MRND. Claeys was to blame for implicating the president and secretary-general of the party, Ngirumpatse and Nzirorera. Claeys denied it and said Jean-Pierre was not the only informer; others told of the locations of weapons and of plans to kill Tutsi.[13]

Twenty years later, at a conference in 2014, Lieutenant General Dallaire explained how the informer Jean-Pierre confirmed everything he had been hearing since he arrived in late November 1993. There was a risk in taking the informer at his word, which he gladly acknowledged. 'But if you read the fax, I wasn't asking for permission, if you remember. I was saying that's what I'm doing, and by the way I'm just changing my modus operandi from being defensive to offensive.' New York was correct in saying it was not in his mandate. 'But I never wrote it because I wanted them to tell me that I could do it. The biggest surprise, it was shot down. I must say, it was one of the fastest faxes I ever got back.'

The information provided by the informer about the stockpiled weapons was of the utmost concern. The commander of UNAMIR's Kigali battalion of Belgian troops, Colonel Luc Marchal, was responsible for ensuring a Kigali Weapons-Secure Area (KWSA) in which all armaments were subject to monitoring by UN personnel. Until the meeting with Jean-Pierre, Marchal had reported that the only weapons the Interahamwe possessed were traditional spears, clubs and machetes.[14] Dallaire did not know at the time that Marchal kept his own intelligence network which he outlined in a statement to ICTR investigators in 1997. Marchal admitted that his Kigali battalion had paid informers, and he handed over a list of their names. He said that he got the list from Lieutenant Mark Nees, who ran this secret network for him.

Some of the information obtained by Nees leaked to the press, and Belgian journalists discovered how well informed he was. For example, in 1993, Nees had become aware of a meeting on 5 November at the Hotel Rebero. In the course of the meeting, chaired by President Juvénal Habyarimana, a decision was taken 'to distribute grenades, machetes and other weapons to the Interahamwe and to CDR young people'. Nees heard 'the objective was to kill Tutsi and other Rwandans who are in the cities and who do not support them [i.e., the Interahamwe and CDR]. The distribution of the weapons has already begun.'[15]

Colonel Luc Marchal had listened with increasing concern to the information supplied by Jean-Pierre. Marchal had met him with Captain Frank Claeys on the night of 10 January 1994. The informant wanted safe passage out of Rwanda for him and his family. In exchange, he could provide lists of names of the Interahamwe who had already received military training, their workplace, photographs of each and their addresses. He could provide the prepared lists of Tutsi families.

In a television interview ten years later, Marchal spoke about the meeting: 'Jean-Pierre gave me a very good and clear description about the Interahamwe organisation. He described the cells, the armaments, the training, and he told me that everybody was suspected ... and then the reaction will follow immediately, and the reaction was to kill a maximum of Tutsis. And each family, each house, was located in Kigali, so everything was being prepared ... And [based] on what Jean-Pierre told me of the Interahamwe organisation, I felt it was a real killing machine because the objective was very clear for everybody – kill, kill and kill.'

'Did he mean civilians?' the interviewer asked.

'Yes, of course, civilians, Tutsis, of course. Jean-Pierre used the word Tutsi ... There was no specification about the person, just Tutsis must be killed.'

Marchal said that for Jean-Pierre it was a matter of conscience.[16]

To test the informer's claims, Marchal sent a member of UNAMIR headquarters staff, Captain Amadou Deme, to the MRND headquarters, where he found 50 AK-47 assault rifles and sealed boxes of ammunition waiting for distribution. Jean-Pierre later took Deme to see smaller caches of arms hidden in bushes and undergrowth at strategic crossroads in Kigali. Marchal sent military observers to a demonstration held outside the Nyamirambo stadium and they watched as the informer, with his Motorola radio, acted in a leadership role and directed the activities of groups of Interahamwe militia.

The 11 January fax was sent to the secretary-general's military adviser, a Canadian, Major General J. Maurice Baril, in New York. In the fax, Dallaire expressed his intention in the next thirty-six hours to take action over the caches of weapons hidden all over the city. The response by return from senior officials at the UN headquarters instructed him to refrain from any pre-emptive action. Officials at the UN wondered why UNAMIR, with some 1,500 troops, was taking the responsibility for seizing weapons when the Rwandan government army had 28,000 troops and 6,000 gendarmes.[17]

Marchal was stunned at the refusal. The whole point of the mission was to secure a weapons-free area in Kigali. 'It was the worst thing for us,' Marchal said, 'just to stay, and to watch, without reaction.'

The officials in New York insisted Dallaire tell President Juvénal Habyarimana about this information as quickly as possible. Dallaire did so and met the president of the MRND, Mathieu Ngirumpatse, and its secretary-general, Joseph Nzirorera, and both men denied the party militia was involved in violence and were bewildered by how specific the information was.[18] The president of the MRND seemed unnerved and, according to the informer, reportedly responded with an accelerated distribution of weapons.

Dallaire met the ambassadors from the US, France and Belgium, the papal nuncio, Monsignor Giuseppe Bertello, and the dean of the diplomatic corps to tell them what Jean-Pierre had said. The three ambassadors expressed serious concern about the information and promised to consult their capitals. At a further meeting with the ambassadors on 13 January, Dallaire presented a letter from Jean-Pierre with more information. The next day the three ambassadors met with President Habyarimana to express their own concern.

In the days to follow, Marchal and Dallaire tried to find a country that might offer Jean-Pierre refuge, or even an embassy in Kigali where he could seek asylum. Not one country extended an invitation, and Marchal decided to let the informer go. Dallaire decided otherwise; he had created his own small intelligence unit in headquarters and ordered Frank Claeys to continue to see the man informally.

Captain Claeys never doubted the importance of the information Jean-Pierre provided. However, he thought the intention of the famous 11 January fax to UN headquarters had been to ensure his protection. After all, its subject heading was 'Request for

Protection for Informant'. It was nonetheless imperative to obtain the information Jean-Pierre promised, including his documentary evidence – the lists of Tutsi families and the names of those in the Interahamwe who received military training. Despite this, officials in New York refused to help Jean-Pierre. They told Dallaire the organisation did not want to get involved in 'covert activities' and such action was against his peacekeeping mandate.[19]

For two months, until 15 March, Claeys continued to meet the informer, continued to gather the information that Jean-Pierre was still willing to provide. He told Claeys of the secret communications between certain members of the Rwandan army, the gendarmerie and Interahamwe, how they communicated using Motorola radios. A direct link existed between the army chief of staff, Colonel Déogratias Nsabimana, and the president of the MRND, Mathieu Ngirumpatse. Ngirumpatse was a former ambassador to Germany and minister of justice, the informer's immediate superior who gave him orders.

The informer told Claeys that UNAMIR was infiltrated by the extremists, and Ngirumpatse was aware of every high-level decision UNAMIR made: a Hutu Power mole existed on the staff of Jacques-Roger Booh-Booh, the UN secretary-general's special representative in Rwanda. Jean-Pierre claimed to have listened to tape recordings of the mole, a non-Rwandese African who spoke French, as he gave his latest report.[20] In this particular recording, the mole speculated whether UNAMIR would react to indiscriminate killing, and whether UNAMIR had the stomach for a fight. In addition, Jean-Pierre told Claeys the local civilian staff working in the UNAMIR headquarters provided a stream of information directly to Ngirumpatse.

In later years, the Jean-Pierre fax was scrutinised by the Belgian Senate, a parliamentary commission created to look into 'the events of Rwanda'. The proceedings lasted more than a year, through 1996 and 1997, with some of the testimony broadcast on Belgian TV. There had been anger in the Belgian Senate at ignored warnings and the obvious risks to the Belgian soldiers who served in UNAMIR. The commission called Major-General M. Verschoore, the deputy chief of service of the Service Général du Renseignement et de la Sécurité (SGRS) to testify. He told the commission he was unaware of the existence of the informer Jean-Pierre and thought too much attention had been paid to his information. Major Hock, a member of his staff, an analyst in charge of Central Africa, had evaluated Jean-Pierre and reported that he had a poor reputation and was a deserter. Hock told the Belgian commission that people regularly offered their services for financial advantage or hoped to obtain the status of applying for political asylum. In the commission report, the Belgian senators criticised Hock and the SGRS for not paying enough attention to Jean-Pierre and declining his requests for asylum.

Some years later, Colonel Luc Marchal changed his mind. In April 2006, Marchal testified for the defence in the trial of General Gratien Kabiligi at the ICTR in Arusha. He visited the former head of the national gendarmerie, Major General Ndindiliyimana, who was on trial there, and Marchal became convinced this man was innocent. Marchal now believed the RPF allowed the genocide to happen because 'it was convenient'. At the end of the year, Marchal gave a wide-ranging interview to the Flemish weekly news magazine *Knack,* in which he expressed his belief that Jean-Pierre was a double agent sent from the RPF to discredit President Juvénal Habyarimana. 'We were manipulated,' he said.[21]

The story of Jean-Pierre did not end there, and continual doubts have been cast on his motives. In January 2014, a senior fellow of the US Holocaust Memorial Museum, Michael Dobbs, launched an in-depth article for the museum website called 'The Failure to Prevent: International Decision-Making in the Age of Genocide', with a simultaneous op-ed article in the *New York Times* head-lined 'The Shroud over Rwanda's Nightmare'. The main theme of the work was to question the motives of Jean-Pierre, together with suggesting he played a double game as an RPF agent. If this turned out to be the case, Dobbs had suggested, then the information he supplied to UNAMIR in January 1994 was worthless.

There was consternation when the article was published. Bizarrely, it seemed, the museum had based the evidence of whether the genocide had been planned on one informant's bona fides. The author seemed unaware of the details of the planning in reports and inquiries produced by governments, the UN, the Organisation of African Unity (OAU) and Human Rights Watch.

Dobbs' work was produced to coincide with the twentieth anniversary of the genocide. The museum's special research project, alongside the National Security Archive, produced an online collection of declassified material, hoping to draw proper lessons from the events of 1994. 'We first have to assemble all the available facts and declassify any remaining secrets,' the brief promised.

In a six-part feature posted on the museum website in January 2014, Michael Dobbs wrote how Jean-Pierre was altogether 'a more complicated figure' than at first supposed: 'Half-Hutu and half-Tutsi, he operated on both sides of Rwanda's political and ethnic divide.' Dobbs rested some of his claims on a supposed interview from 2003 with the wife of Jean-Pierre 'that had never before been officially released', although it was submitted by defence counsel at the ICTR. The statement claimed that in late March, two weeks before the president's assassination, the informer moved to a rebel-held enclave in northern Rwanda, where he was 'in very good books with senior members of the RPF'. In an article posted on a denial website, his wife told investigators, 'I do not know how he died and where'. His wife apparently claimed 'Kagame's team' killed Jean-Pierre.[22] The author thought it certain that Jean-Pierre joined the 'Tutsi-led rebel group'.

Dobbs found it curious that Jean-Pierre was married to a Tutsi and the product of a mixed Tutsi–Hutu marriage, but that this did not seem to have affected his advancement in the Interahamwe, at least until the end of 1993. Dobbs seemed unaware that the leader of the Interahamwe, Robert Kajuga, was Tutsi. Dobbs claimed Jean-Pierre had fallen out with party leaders who suspected him of selling arms to rebels in Burundi, and some witnesses accused Jean-Pierre of having been an agent of the RPF assigned to penetrate the Interahamwe. Dobbs claimed these connections caused French and Belgian analysts to suspect that Jean-Pierre might be spreading 'disinformation'.

Dobbs claimed the final meeting between Jean-Pierre and UNAMIR was on 10 February, when he told the general's aides he planned to go to Zaire, for 'commando training'. Instead, he went to Tanzania, where he joined the RPF. This did not accord with the testimony of Claeys, who last saw Jean-Pierre on 15 March. Dobbs wrote that the fact that several of his predictions came true in April 1994 is not by itself proof of the reliability of his information in January 1994. The museum, perhaps unwittingly, had given an endorsement to a central plank of the defence case.

It was with anger in his voice, at an address at the UN in New York for the twentieth anniversary, that Lieutenant General Dallaire, aware of the doubts raised in the material posted by the museum, made a point of saying: 'It was a deliberate, well-planned, well-executed plan to exterminate an ethnic group and we saw it coming.' The predictions of Jean-Pierre came horribly true.

It was too easy to forget that the Jean-Pierre affair was only one of literally hundreds of pieces of available evidence demonstrating that a conspiracy to eliminate the Tutsi was in place. Indeed, it was precisely because of Lieutenant General Dallaire's keen awareness of these countless ominous signs that he was prepared to take Jean-Pierre's information seriously.

There was an instant rebuke for the museum report and Dobbs' work. A group of academics, ambassadors, journalists and scholars wrote a joint letter to the museum, highlighting the lack of understanding of the crime of genocide, how its inexorable process showed it to be entirely predictable.[23] In the letter to the museum director, Sara J. Bloomfield, the group pointed out that overwhelming evidence existed of a conspiracy to murder Tutsi. In posting the material, the museum provided people who sought to minimise and diminish what had happened with an unparalleled platform and invaluable legitimacy. Nevertheless, the material remains posted to this day.

It seems extraordinary that after convictions at the ICTR for conspiracy to commit genocide, trials in which the arguments of a lack of planning failed to persuade the judges, some academics have continued to argue the opposite. Professor André Guichaoua remains convinced the RPF assassinated the president, and he also denied the existence of genocide planning. Guichaoua, a French sociologist and specialist in the Great Lakes region, and a professor at the Panthéon-Sorbonne University, wrote two great tomes on Rwanda. His second book, *Rwanda: De la guerre au génocide*, published in 2010, is some 600 pages. In the French edition, Guichaoua wrote how the testimony of Jean-Pierre was incoherent, and he noted the absence of any verification of his assertions by UNAMIR intelligence officers and Lieutenant General Dallaire. His own source was an Interahamwe, a protected witness, who in May 2004 told Guichaoua that the informer Jean-Pierre was 'a traitor'.[24]

René Lemarchand, professor emeritus at the University of Florida, who is widely published on Rwanda after a lifetime of study, praised the work of Guichaoua. It showed a 'somewhat improvised, belated attempt at planning made by a handful of actors to organize a final solution, against the consensus of the pro-pacification moderates'. Lemarchand wrote how the outcome was not 'foreordained by the existence of a long-standing conspiracy to kill all the Tutsi'. What came into focus from a 'welter of personalities, institutions, factions, bloody encounters and settlings of accounts described by the author' was the crucial role played by individual personalities. This version had no room for the predictions of Jean-Pierre.

In response, in an acclaimed critique of the work of Guichaoua, the French scholar Hélène Dumas wrote that he paid no heed at all to the killers – those who carried out the genocide.[25] Guichaoua did not address the nature of the killing, nor did he consider the importance of the racist Hutu Power ideology. The impression from the work of Guichaoua was that the military and political leaders were personally ambitious, as though the massacres were part of political infighting and political opportunism determined events. This version depended on the chaos and intrigues that the assassination of President Habyarimana caused at the heart of government.

One further piece of material evidence is hard to ignore. Similar to the 11 January cable, this too was submitted in the trials at the ICTR as proof of planning, and was intended to show this had not depended upon political infighting, or chaos or intrigue. As evidence for the criminal conspiracy to commit the genocide of the Tutsi unravelled, the investigators from the ICTR had found a list of shareholders of the commercial radio, RTLM, created in 1993.[26]

The radio station, known afterwards as Radio Machete, had conducted a vile campaign against the minority Tutsi in the months before the genocide, and the radio was the voice of the genocide of the Tutsi as it progressed. The shareholder list, with fifty original shareholders, showed President Juvénal Habyarimana at the top, with a majority share. The greatest sums of money came from people either related to him, his wife, Agathe Kanziga, her family and other Hutu Power fanatics. These included bank managers, journalists, army officers and politicians.

The radio had mobilised the population, circumventing key clauses in the Arusha Accords in which incitement to violence and hatred were barred from the political process. The incitement to ethnic hatred that poured from this radio station was a fundamental part of the genocide conspiracy, the result of a careful strategy adapted and elaborated by political, civil and military authorities. There was a plan, organised at the highest level, and its object was the extermination of the Tutsi population of Rwanda.

11

Identity

The broadcast of atrocity speech was central to the commission of the 1994 genocide of the Tutsi. As a consequence, the
radio station Radio-Télévision Libre des Mille Collines (RTLM)
can be considered a modern psychological operations weapon, part
of a propaganda campaign intended to spread a racist message of
hatred. The message was clearly and effectively disseminated before
the genocide began on 6 April 1994, and it was part of a genocidal
process. RTLM's programmes were designed to appeal to a largely
illiterate and impoverished society. Such coordination must be seen
as proof of planning on the part of the Hutu Power movement.

From the first broadcast on 8 July 1993, the popularity of the
new radio station was evident.[1] As the Swiss journalist Jean-
Philippe Ceppi saw for himself: everyone – whether soldier,
peasant, rebel or intellectual – was tuned in. 'In cars, in the fields,
the Rwandans spend their time with their ears glued to transis-
tor radios, in families or in gangs, at each roadblock militia are
listening …'[2] Ceppi noted the sudden and large-scale distribution
of cheap portable radios, sometimes given away free of charge in
remote and rural communities.[3] At first, programmes aired only
a few hours a day, restricted to certain regions. Nevertheless, by
February 1994, transmission covered most parts of the country.

The radio caused a broadcasting revolution. The first licensed
commercial station, RTLM's programmes were a world away
from the dull state broadcaster, Radio Rwanda. There had never
been Western-style entertainment and now shock jocks, phone-ins

and the much-loved Zairean music 'Lingala' competed for attention. Having attracted their attention, the announcers appealed
directly to the youth of the Interahamwe militia.

The majority of broadcasts on RTLM were in Kinyarwanda, a
beautiful, elegant and flexible language. It was with poetic flourish
that the journalists on RTLM issued murderous threats and double
entendres over the airwaves.[4] The on-air denigration of Tutsi
included visceral scorn, ridiculing laughter, sneering and disdain.[5]

While the language of polarisation already existed, in the
months before the genocide began, some Kinyarwanda words
attained a new popularity that gained power through repetition
on radio RTLM: 'kumara' (to eat up), 'gutema' (to cut), 'irondo'
(nocturnal patrols), 'utsembatsemba' (to exterminate), 'gutsemba'
(to massacre).[6] On air, the word Tutsi was replaced with 'inyenzi',
cockroach: 'The Inyenzi have always been Tutsi. We will exterminate them. One can identify them because they are of one
race.'[7] The announcers criticised the idea of a single Rwandan
people. It was no more than a trick to divide and weaken the
Hutu by destroying their sense of identity. The anti-Tutsi rhetoric
paraded as entertainment and soon developed into stereotyping in
a manner that promoted contempt and hatred.

Over the airwaves, the future génocidaires used news bulletins
to spread false information. They denigrated the UN Assistance
Mission for Rwanda (UNAMIR) and its peacekeepers. The
journalists accused the prime minister, Agathe Uwilingiyimana,
appointed under the peace agreement as part of a transitional
authority prior to elections, of preparing a coup with southern
army officers. Three days before the assassination of President
Juvénal Habyarimana on 6 April 1994, the radio announced that a

little thing was going to trigger the final struggle. They have dates.
We know them, then you will hear the noise of bullets and thunder
of grenades ... Let the RPF [Rwandan Patriotic Front] know it
will be held accountable before the people and before history and
one day it shall explain before the people and mankind as a whole
how they hastened these children of the country to their deaths
... All is fair in war.[8]

The tone then changed. The message now addressed the Hutu, called upon them to rally and unite to head off the enslavement that awaited them if the Tutsi army won the civil war. The UN would be unable to help them, they were told.

Two years earlier the génocidaires had shown exactly how to influence the rural masses with fake news.[9] In March 1992, they had engineered the massacre of Tutsi in farming communities in Bugesera in the southwest using disinformation over the airwaves to instill fear and whip up hatred.[10] The killing that month cost an estimated 300 Tutsi lives, the bodies found in latrines, marshes and ditches. The official government line was that the killing resulted from Hutu peasants rising up 'spontaneously' and killing their Tutsi neighbours out of fear. However, the repeated broadcast by Radio Rwanda of a news item days beforehand played a crucial role. It had warned of a terrorist plot by 'the Inyenzi [cockroach] enemy' to kill local Hutu officials and politicians. The listeners were told the plot was uncovered by an organisation called the Inter-African Commission for Non-Violence based in Nairobi. In fact, the press release upon which the news was based was a forgery, the address for the 'commission' in Nairobi nothing more than a PO box number. It was a simple, crude and effective piece of propaganda.[11]

In Kigali, diplomats went to see President Juvénal Habyarimana to express concern. All but the French ambassador to Rwanda, Georges Martres, joined the demarche.[12] Four human rights groups issued a public statement to explain Radio Rwanda had been 'used with great efficiency by the country's fascists', who were 'co-responsible for loss of life in a series of killings in Bugesera, calling for hatred and ethnic division'.[13]

The state prosecutor for Kigali, François-Xavier Nsanzuwera, travelled south to see for himself.[14] He had family in Bugesera and therefore knew the peasants were unlikely to rise up 'spontaneously'.[15] He was certain that they were pawns in a Machiavellian plan. Perhaps this was state-sponsored killing; the local authorities passive at best, and, at worst, endorsing the violence.

Once there, he heard about a squad of French-trained Presidential

Guards, based in Kigali but on this occasion dressed in civilian clothes, who offered encouragement to the Hutu population to kill Tutsi in acts of 'self-defence'.[16] Back in Kigali, Nsanzuwera met with the then minister of justice, Mathieu Ngirumpatse, who told him that the Tutsi in Bugesera were 'arrogant and needed a lesson'. Some months later, when Ngirumpatse became secretary-general of the Mouvement Révolutionnaire National pour le Développement (MRND), he called Nsanzuwera complaining about the arrests of Interahamwe militia for murder and other violent offences and insisted on their release.[17]

The concerns of the diplomats in Kigali increased after news emerged of the murder of Antonia Locatelli, a Roman Catholic Italian missionary and educator who had lived for twenty-two years in Bugesera. On 9 March 1992, Locatelli had sheltered an estimated 7,000 Tutsi families in her girls' school. She gave an interview to Radio France Internationale telling journalists this was not 'spontaneous' killing, as the government claimed. The massacres were prepared, she said. The killers were organised. She had witnessed them arrive in vehicles with official number plates. The next day a gendarme shot her, firing a bullet in her mouth and another in her head.[18]

The Roman Catholic Church, an institution that had tolerated anti-Tutsi policies, stayed clear of any controversy and issued a statement that placed the blame firmly on the Rwandan people. 'Trust is missing in people's homes, to the point that certain communities have known massacres: Hutu and Tutsi are fighting each other and the regions are set one against the other.'[19]

In the criminal investigation into the Bugesera killings, there were prosecution witnesses who dared not testify, or simply stopped talking. More than 500 arrests took place, but after keeping them some months in custody, the authorities freed the alleged killers who were driven home from prison in buses from the Rwandan transport office. The authorities made no secret of their contempt for survivors.

The diplomatic community in Kigali was well aware a plot lurked behind the crime, and noted the involvement of Interahamwe militia and local administrators. They also noted the involvement of the director of Radio Rwanda, the country's most eminent history professor, Ferdinand Nahimana. A confidant of President Juvénal Habyarimana, Nahimana often wrote his speeches.[20] A skilled propagandist, he eventually gave academic legitimacy to the ideology of Hutu Power.[21] It was clear that Nahimana himself had ordered the broadcasts, and the ambassadors insisted he be relieved of the directorship of the Office Rwandais d'Information (ORINFOR).[22]

Softly spoken and appearing to be a mild-mannered academic, Nahimana seemed an unlikely génocidaire. He had a doctorate awarded at a French university, Paris Diderot, and had planned a scholarly life devoted to teaching a new generation of historians at the National University of Rwanda, where he became dean at the Faculty of Letters. A popular figure at the French embassy, he was appointed a member of a committee planning how Rwanda was going to commemorate the two hundredth anniversary of the French Revolution in 1989. The French wanted exhibitions in schools and universities, a new Rwandan postal stamp and for the French Revolution to be the theme of a forthcoming book festival. Nahimana was on the guest list at the French embassy for the official commemoration in Kigali on 14 July where, on immaculate lawns, and with a backdrop of tropical gardens, there were champagne toasts for 'liberté, égalité, fraternité' and 'the promotion of these very same values in "French Africa"'.[23]

Nahimana's career continued its meteoric rise.[24] When the new French ambassador Georges Martres (1990–1993) arrived, he invited the professor to diplomatic events, and admired his proficiency in the French language. Nahimana spoke of his love of France, and was full of praise for President François Mitterrand. His removal from office as the director of ORINFOR in 1992, a few months after the broadcast of the incendiary news bulletins that led to the Bugesera massacres, made no difference to his social standing. 'I kept regular contact with the ambassadors of the US, Belgium, Switzerland and France, and the Papal Nuncio. Some of them invited me to dinner,' he told his biographer.[25]

The decision to force him from office in 1992 was unpopular among leaders of the Interahamwe militia, and they came to his defence.[26] He found support from the regime's spy chief and interrogator, Captain Pascal Simbikangwa, who wrote a glowing endorsement of Nahimana as a man 'giving himself body and soul ... so that our fatherland may not lose its soul'. Captain Simbikangwa pleaded, 'Do not aggravate these brains that awaken the masses ...'[27] Nahimana toured European capitals to explain to journalists that the massacres were the sole responsibility of 'local officials' and savage 'inter-ethnic' confrontations. He was a useful envoy, sent abroad whenever the extremists needed to deliver a message to the outside world, and on this occasion Nahimana treated any suggestion of a coordinated criminal enterprise with derision.[28] Today, Simbikangwa is serving a twenty-five-year sentence in a French prison, found guilty on appeal of genocide in 2016.

In 1993, Nahimana published a book based on his university thesis, called 'Rwanda: the emergence of a state', dedicating it to the French Ministry of Cooperation and Development, who financed his two-year study in Paris and the book's publication.[29] The author claimed to present an untold story of northern Hutu kingdoms and clans, a fiercely independent people that constituted the last strongholds against white colonisers. These noble Hutu had first resisted the Germans, from 1897 as part of German East Africa, and in 1916 resisted the brutal Belgian military forces with command in Katanga, in the neighbouring Belgian Congo.[30] The colonisers only defeated the northern Hutu because of help from the army provided by the Tutsi monarchy. The northern resisters were 'resilient and remarkable people', and only when the north was conquered were modern political boundaries established.[31] Nahimana therefore presented the north as the 'real Rwanda'.[32] And, in contrast, he relegated the tales from the Tutsi, told by their dynastic poets, musicians and ritualists, conveying the struggles of Tutsi dynasties in forty-three reigns, to no more than stories.[33] Nahimana was not the first historian to characterise every problem in Rwanda in ethnic terms. He sought to revise national historical memory in accordance with his own bigotry and bias. In response, many scholars accused him of exaggeration and falsehood.[34]

At the same time, after he had returned from his tour in Europe, Nahimana created the new commercial radio station, RTLM. Later known as the 'Goebbels of Rwanda', just like the Nazi master propagandist, Nahimana defined radio as a main instrument of a propaganda policy.[35] Over the airwaves, RTLM reinforced his distorted notions of Rwandan history.[36] Here is an example from 2 December 1993:

> Tutsi are nomads and invaders who came to Rwanda in search of pasture, but because they are so cunning and malicious, the Tutsi managed to stay and rule. If you allow the Tutsi-Hamites to come back, they will not only rule you in Rwanda, but will also extend their power throughout the Great Lakes region.[37]

An exploration of the degree of influence of RTLM and its success as a modern psychological operation came in an expert report by Jean-Pierre Chrétien, the director of the National Centre for Scientific Research (CNRS) in France and specialist in the Great Lakes region of Africa.[38] He believed Nahimana became a political ideologue who used the radio as a propaganda tool. His hate propaganda cloaked in faux-scientific objectivity promoted horribly racist views.[39] Chrétien believed the reach and influence of the ideology of Hutu Power was far greater than even that of Julius Streicher and his Nazi anti-Semitism.[40]

Chrétien was a part of the successful prosecution of Nahimana at the International Criminal Tribunal for Rwanda (ICTR).[41] On 8 December 2003, the fifty-three-year-old professor stood motionless in the dock as he received a life term in prison, found guilty of genocide, direct and public incitement to commit genocide, conspiracy to commit genocide, crimes against humanity (persecution) and crimes against humanity (extermination).[42]

Among the three presiding judges, Navi Pillay was a renowned South African justice, later UN High Commissioner for Human Rights and among the first judges appointed to the International Criminal Court.[43] She read out the judgement and sentence in court. 'Without a firearm, machete or any physical weapon,' Pillay told Nahimana, 'you caused the deaths of thousands of innocent civilians.' Nahimana betrayed a special responsibility to society – as a renowned academic, a professor of history at the National University of Rwanda.[44] 'You were fully aware of the power of words, and you used the radio, the medium of communication with the widest public reach, to disseminate hatred and violence.'

Nahimana had pleaded not guilty and had told the judges he was a scapegoat. He complained that Western journalists compared what happened in Rwanda to Hitler's final solution, which was 'pure fantasy'.[45] He told his French biographer how, as the youngest of nine children born to subsistence farmers in Gatonde, it was God who made him who he was.[46]

There is a short documentary film showing an interview with Nahimana in his cell as his trial progressed.[47] In it, he claims the prosecution case against him was 'all propaganda', which 'conquered international opinion'. The stories in the Western press of an 'ideologue of genocide' and an 'African Hitler' were wrong. They left an impression that without Nahimana there would have been no 'genocide'. He was fighting such lies with a 'very competent team of lawyers and their assistants', and would prove his innocence. In his cell, there is a desk crowded with papers and a computer. There is wall-to-wall shelving filled with books, files, ring binders and documents.

In the courtroom, Nahimana sometimes assumed an air of bafflement, alternating with moments of arrogance. At other times he showed disdain for the international legal proceedings. He was a 'serious academician, gentleman, lucid intellectual and scholar'. Once the killing was under way, he had no power over the broadcasts on RTLM calling out against Tutsi. He found out only afterwards what terrible things RTLM journalists were saying. Nahimana was, after all, absent from the country. His own family was safe from the sounds and scenes of the genocide of the Tutsi when it began. They had initially sheltered in the French embassy, then flown out of Rwanda on a French aircraft to neighbouring Burundi. Nahimana said he returned only later as political adviser to the newly created Interim Government.

The judges concluded Nahimana had manipulated evidence, that he was evasive. Gaps existed in his testimony, and the judges did not accept his version of events.[48] In his position as chair of the RTLM 'technical and programming committee', he was clearly able to determine the content of RTLM news broadcasts. He was therefore undoubtedly a dangerous racist ideologue.

The chief prosecutor was US lawyer Stephen Rapp. He later served in the administration of President Barack Obama as United States ambassador-at-large for War Crimes Issues in the Office of Global Criminal Justice. He recalled that the trial was critical in the history of international law. 'This is our Nuremberg,' he said.

At Nuremberg, each of the four Allied countries that had formed the International Military Tribunal – the United States, France, Great Britain and the Soviet Union – provided one judge and one alternate. The criminal tribunal for Rwanda was more international. The judges were chosen in a transparent procedure by the UN General Assembly, three judges for each of the four trial chambers. The tribunal was larger than Nuremberg: there were 1,000 employees from eighty-five UN member states.

The media trial was the first time since the trials at Nuremberg in which defendants stood in an international courtroom charged with using words to kill. On the earlier occasion, it was the German Nazi Julius Streicher, notorious for his anti-Semitic weekly journal *Der Stürmer*, who was in the dock. Streicher, although he did not directly participate in the extermination in the Holocaust, was found as culpable for the crimes as those who had a direct hand. He poisoned the German mind with racist propaganda. As a result, he was hanged for crimes against humanity on 16 October 1946.

In addition to Nahimana, there were two other defendants in the trial, each charged on separate indictments, but all involved in print and broadcast media, twisting history into propaganda and promoting racist hatred. Together all three defendants faced criminal charges of genocide, conspiracy and incitement to commit genocide.

Jean-Bosco Barayagwiza, a northerner, a diplomat and an adept politician, was the chairman of the executive committee of RTLM. He was also director of political affairs in the Rwandan Ministry of Foreign Affairs. He was responsible for Rwanda's extreme political party, the rabidly anti-Tutsi Coalition pour la Défense de la

République (CDR).[49] The group excluded Tutsi from membership
and was a vehicle to promote the notion of a Hutu nation state.
Barayagwiza refused to attend the trial and forbade lawyers to
represent him before the court, denouncing the 'parody of justice'.
Instead, he spent the time working on a second book and cor-
responding with the outside world, bemoaning his fate in the
hands of victors' justice. He wrote a letter of complaint to the UN
secretary-general, Kofi Annan.

If Barayagwiza and Nahimana were ideologues, the third
defendant in the trial, Hassan Ngeze, was a demagogue. A prominent journalist and the founder and editor in chief of *Kangura*
('Wake it Up'), a bimonthly tabloid newspaper that featured com-
mentary, and articles depicting Tutsi as enemies of the state using
venomous cartoons and salacious scandal. A collector's item today,
its December 1990 issue included the Hutu Ten Commandments.
Printed in French, the article called for contempt and hatred of
the minority Tutsi. Any man who married a Tutsi woman was a
traitor. Tutsi used their women and their money as weapons to
fool Hutu.

On 17 December 1990, the French ambassador to Rwanda,
Georges Martres, reported to Paris on the *Kangura* article with
the words, 'The radicalisation of the ethnic conflict can only inten-
sify. The newspaper *Kangura*, mouthpiece of Hutu extremists, just
published an issue resurrecting the ancient hatred against Tutsi
feudalism: the "Hutu commandments".'[50] On the back cover was
a full-page photograph of President François Mitterrand with the
caption: 'A true friend of Rwanda'.

The Hutu Ten Commandments insisted on the need for religious zeal to maintain Hutu purity and avoid any contamination
from Tutsi. For, in the pages of *Kangura*, the Tutsi were seeking
to dominate and enslave Hutu, and bring back their monarchy.
In *Kangura*, the Tutsi population was described as inherently
evil, forcing the argument of their extermination as a 'preventive
measure'. *Kangura* also took to naming Tutsi 'who owned a dis-
proportionate amount of wealth' as a way to stir up animosity. An
issue in November 1990 exposed a so-called conspiracy in which
Tutsi had attempted to colonise the entire region.

Ngeze had charisma and egotism, winning him unexpected supporters. On 4 July 1990, as *Kangura* was preparing for its third edition, the police arrested him for disturbing the peace. In response, Reporters Sans Frontières waged a campaign to get him freed. Meanwhile, from prison, Ngeze produced a third edition of *Kangura* with a print run of 13,000.[51]

In his trial, Ngeze told the court he was an investigative journalist, and his role in life was to tell the population news that it did not know. He spoke of the importance of press freedom. His US defence lawyer, John Floyd, argued that the anti-Tutsi writings were protected speech, and he proposed US law, with its strong protection of free speech, be adopted as a standard by the tribunal. The judges disagreed, telling the court national laws on freedom varied, but international standards were well codified. The judges told Floyd that even US domestic law recognised incitement to violence, threats and other expressions of hate as beyond the boundaries of protected speech.[52]

As she read out the judgement, Judge Navi Pillay noted that in the case of Julius Streicher at Nuremberg, there was no requirement for a direct effect to prove incitement, and that incitement to violent crime was not protected speech even in the most liberal countries, such as the United States. At the same time, she noted that the three not guilty pleas in the trial were supported by publicly funded defence teams and were fought vigorously every step of the way.[53] In the judgement and sentence, the three defendants were pronounced guilty, and received lengthy prison sentences. Nahimana and Hassan Ngeze received life terms, and Jean-Bosco Barayagwiza, a thirty-year term. All three appealed their sentences on various grounds of errors of fact and law.

In a defiant statement, Floyd, Ngeze's defence lawyer, said that freedom of expression had stepped backward by fifty years. 'This would have never lasted in the US court. These men would have had their rights to democratic expression.'[54] The chief prosecutor, Stephen Rapp, believed the historic guilty judgements established an international standard to govern the responsibility of those who would control the media for hate-spewing broadcasts and articles.

~

In the years since, in Western academic scholarship, doubts have persisted on the degree of influence of RTLM upon the course of the 1994 genocide.[55] For example, Scott Straus, professor of political science and international studies at the University of Wisconsin–Madison, proposes the radio station had less influence than supposed, as noted in his 2006 book: 'I find that the mechanisms driving individuals to kill were not primarily about ethnic prejudice, pre-existing ethnic antipathy, manipulation from racist propaganda.'[56]

Straus interviewed 210 perpetrators in prison, the 'avoués', those who had confessed their crimes throughout Rwanda. He interviewed a further nineteen people who claimed leadership roles. None of this sample admitted to membership in the Interahamwe. Straus further cast doubt that the Hutu Ten Commandments had diffused to rural areas. Only 6.5 per cent of his respondents agreed that Hutu had hatred for Tutsi. Some told him that 'pawa' was a foreign word they did not understand. Only 4 per cent of his sample understood 'Hutu Pawa' to refer to an anti-Tutsi 'pro-Hutu coalition'.[57] Straus concluded racist propaganda did not instill racism.

Notable about this research was that 71.5 per cent of the Straus respondents said they did not kill anyone at all. Only sixty people in his survey admitted to murder. This would mean that certain killers were responsible for hundreds of deaths each and that most people had stood and watched. This was not at all how direct witnesses and survivors remember it. However, eleven years after the publication of his book, Straus raised doubts about whether perpetrators of genocide could be trusted. In the first issue of a new publication, the *Journal of Perpetrator Research*, Straus wrote: 'Do perpetrators ever tell the truth? Even if they are not lying directly, they may not be able to understand or live with the horror of their mentality at the time of the violence. These are all real concerns.'[58]

The research of Rwandan scholar Charles Mironko, cultural anthropologist at the Hutchins Center for African and African American Research, Harvard University, found different concerns. Mironko was able to interview prisoners in Kinyarwanda without the necessity of translators. He spoke to nearly one hundred people in six different prisons throughout the country who had confessed to taking part in the genocide. He discovered that the first response to questions was often to claim ignorance of RTLM, to know nothing of the message or incitement to violence and to say that the radio was something foreign to the rural peasantry.

Mironko believed this was denial. It was a means to claim they had been incapable of participating in the political project that the radio represented, because they were no more than bystanders or even victims. Mironko found these perpetrators offered ample evidence that they understood the messages on RTLM, and they were themselves a specifically targeted audience. 'I did not own a radio because I am a cultivator, but some people used to say that RTLM was urging us to kill.' As a consequence, Mironko believed RTLM created whole communities of listeners.

Subsequent research published in the US in 2010, the work of an economist and public policy professor, David Yanagizawa-Drott, indicated in a statistical study that the murder of Tutsi was 65–77 per cent higher in places that received the full RTLM signal versus those that did not. The radio broadcasts increased militia violence, directly influencing behaviour in isolated communities out on the hills, and increased local participation.[59]

As the genocide progressed in 1994, discussions about RTLM took place in the Security Council and, although aware of its insidious power, in May 1994 the US administration refused any action to jam the broadcasts. The Pentagon decided the cost of US$8,500 per flight for airborne equipment was too high, and the wisest action was to provide relief in the way of blankets and plastic sheeting for refugees in neighbouring countries.[60]

In the course of a discussion about RTLM in an informal meeting of the Security Council on 27 June 1994, when member states expressed exasperation at the lack of response to their earlier call for this media outlet to stop its dissemination of ethnic hatred and its anti-UNAMIR campaign, the Rwandan ambassador, Jean-Damascène Bizimana, said RTLM was a private enterprise and not controlled by the Interim Government. He said this was a question of press freedom.[61]

It was obvious that the broadcasts of RTLM were central to events. Dallaire thought the songs played as the genocide of the Tutsi got under way must have been pre-recorded and people knew what was coming.[62] The disinformation campaign over the airwaves against UNAMIR had been continuous. Dallaire described a 'very determined propaganda campaign' in which the local media were used 'to incite ethnic, partisan and anti-UNAMIR activities'. He soon came to realise that the content of the broadcasts in French and those in the Rwandan language Kinyarwanda were markedly different. He believed it was because of the disinformation from the extremists over the airwaves and in the propaganda sheets that UNAMIR lost the respect of the local population and put the lives of his troops at risk.

12

Moral Equivalence

The idea of comparable wrongs quickly took hold. On 13 April 1994, a week after the genocide of the Tutsi began, at a ministerial meeting in Paris, the head of the French armed forces, Admiral Jacques Lanxade, asked by President François Mitterrand about massacres in Rwanda, had replied, 'They are already considerable. But now it is the Tutsi who are massacring the Hutu in Kigali.'[1] According to the minutes of this meeting, another description given to the president was 'inter-ethnic massacres'. In late May that year, according to a biographer of Mitterrand, the French president, when speaking to German Chancellor Helmut Kohl, dismissed the 'one-sided' idea that it was only Tutsi killed.[2] In June, the French foreign minister, Alain Juppé, also promoted the notion of moral equivalence, writing in the newspaper *Libération*, on 16 June, that there needed to be justice for all 'these genocides'.[3] President Mitterrand, later on in the year, said, 'The genocide or genocides. I don't know what I should say.'[4]

The idea of Rwandan Patriotic Front (RPF) massacres of Hutu was nothing new. Since the start of the civil war in October 1990, numerous reports appeared about RPF killings, including in Hutu Power's house magazine, *Kangura*.[5] When the genocide of the Tutsi began in April, the idea of massacres committed by the Rwandan Patriotic Army (RPA) was a constant refrain from the Interim Government, and its ambassadors repeated the accusation regularly in the UN Security Council. It was an early attempt to conceal the crime of genocide by seeking comparable wrongs, to claim each 'side' was as murderous as the other. In May, the Interim Government officially informed the UN Security Council that the RPF had slaughtered 'hundreds of thousands of Hutu'.[6] Human Rights Watch (HRW) described these accusations as a smokescreen intended to distract foreign attention from the genocide against the Tutsi.

The idea of two genocides in Rwanda, the first nearly wiping out the Tutsi minority and the second secretly committed by the Tutsi-dominated RPF, would have been a sensational news story, if true. There were numerous rumours. Following the RPF military victory in July, a US journalist, Mark Fritz, spent nearly a month looking but he never found any evidence of the systematic killing of Hutu.[7] The UK journalist Mark Huband of the *Observer* noted only 'secondhand reports' from the UN High Commission for Refugees (UNHCR) from the camps about RPF killings.[8] A BBC journalist, Mark Doyle, who reported from Rwanda, wrote a dispatch to London explaining there was no convincing evidence of the RPF massacring civilians. Doyle warned the BBC news desk not to broadcast claims about RPF abuses until some convincing evidence emerged. 'I used to take regular calls from BBC editors in London asking me to make sure I put the other side,' Doyle wrote later. Doyle told them this was not a balanced picture, and there was no moral equivalence.[9] The issue, however, dominated the final months of 1994.

In July the sudden exodus of 1 million people incited to flee Rwanda pushed the country to the top of the international news agenda. In stark contrast to the reporting of the genocide of the Tutsi from April to July that was hardly ever on newspaper front pages, within three days of the exodus into Goma there was a media frenzy and graphic reports described epidemics of biblical proportions that swept the land. The flight of the Hutus made for extraordinary television pictures, and there was a blurring in the perception of events. The plight of the refugees became confused with the civil war and the genocide.

For Anne Mackintosh, the Oxfam regional representative for Rwanda, Burundi and Kivu (Zaire) from 1991 to 1994, the refugee crisis overshadowed the genocide. The refugees were not, as some journalists and aid agencies claimed, fleeing the genocide; instead many of those fleeing were the Interahamwe militia, and the thousands of people who perpetrated the genocide. A rigorous propaganda campaign waged by radio RTLM had urged the 'Hutu nation' to take refuge in Zaire. The production and widespread distribution of propaganda in the camps was under way within weeks and included the production of copies of *Kangura*, with its usual racist propaganda and fake news. In the camps, a disinformation campaign waged by Hutu Power warned if anyone returned to Rwanda they would be massacred by the RPA.[10]

The refugee camps were unprecedented in size. By the end of 1994 in Tanzania, an estimated 500,000 people settled at a camp called Benaco. Around 200,000 refugees fled to Burundi. An estimated 1 million people passed into Zaire at Goma, and 200,000 more into Bukavu.[11] In these vast refugee camps, the Hutu Power authorities kept control using violence and murder. Anyone expressing a wish to return home was killed. Those same administrative structures that existed in Rwanda were swiftly recreated – the *préfectures*, *communes*, *secteurs* and *cellules*.[12] Hutu Power kept control through the *bourgmestres*, the same men who had issued the orders to kill Tutsi during the genocide. Soon a web of Hutu Power committees, neighbourhood security units and associations embraced almost all segments of refugee society.[13]

It was quickly obvious that the exodus was another strategy devised by the Hutu Power leadership aimed at undermining the credibility of the new Rwandan government installed in Kigali following the July military victory of the RPF. The refugees gave Hutu Power an asset with which to claim legitimacy, and a way to attract international sympathy. One potential solution to this massive humanitarian catastrophe came in the parting advice of Lieutenant General Roméo Dallaire at the UN Secretariat in September 1994, given to those countries with troops serving in the UN Assistance Mission for Rwanda (UNAMIR II). Dallaire suggested the deployment of overwhelming military force to identify those in the camps who were intimidating the refugees. There needed to be broadcasts via a UN radio to persuade the population of a safe return home. Dallaire suggested a large fleet of vehicles to transport people back to Rwanda. At UN headquarters, senior officials called it 'Dallaire activism', and it got nowhere.

In late July and early August, there was a trickle of refugees back to Rwanda, but the movement soon slowed. Rumours about massacres carried out by the RPF began to circulate. This scare-mongering by Hutu Power leaders in the camps reinforced the idea of sinister Tutsi duplicity, and reminded people of a supposed age-old and secret Tutsi plan to eliminate Hutu. There were anon-ymous pamphlets distributed claiming that none of those who returned to Rwanda had survived.[14]

UN peacekeepers made one practical attempt to counteract the Hutu Power propaganda in the camps. Leaflets that visually por-trayed Rwanda as a lush and fertile place of safety were dropped from UN helicopters. The leaflets encouraged refugees to return home to security, fresh water and food. The plan badly backfired when at the last minute the UN plan to guarantee safe passage to returning refugees was put on hold; possession of the leaflets in the camp brought an automatic death sentence.

In September everything was thrown into disarray. In New York the UN secretary-general, Boutros Boutros-Ghali, had received a panicked call from the UN High Commissioner for Refugees, Sadako Ogata, based in Geneva. She had received reports from a US consultant hired by her agency alleging that RPF troops had slaughtered thousands of Hutu in a preordained campaign as they had made their advance leading up to August 1994.

To the RPF courts martial and punishment of some soldiers for revenge killings suggested there was no such campaign, as did the lack of information in UNAMIR reports. Regardless, this unveri-fied allegation spread like wildfire.[15] The consultant, a US national Robert Gersony, had been contracted by UNHCR for sixty days to organise a voluntary repatriation programme for refugees, and he claimed to have acquired information about RPF massacres while conducting a series of interviews over a period of five weeks in a third of Rwandan *communes*.[16] That there had been revenge killing by RPF soldiers was not in dispute; what was shocking was the claim that massacres of Hutu had been systematic, with a death toll of 30,000 people.

In Washington the Gersony figures were greeted with surprise. In the US State Department, the information ran counter to the intelligence received; the RPF killed Hutu in battle, and while it admitted targeting extremist Hutu who it believed to be responsible for the massacre of Tutsi, generally the RPF protected Hutu within the territory it controlled. A partly declassified memorandum from Toby T. Gati to George Moose, the assistant secretary of state for African affairs, on 16 May 1994, informed him of the killing of Tutsi behind government lines with systematic executions by government-supported militias. Unlike the government forces, the RPF did not appear to have committed what was called in the cable 'Geneva Convention-defined genocidal atrocities'.[17]

At the UN, the figures produced by the UNHCR consultant caused consternation. 'It was a major crisis on our doorstep,' recalled the recently appointed UN Special Representative for Rwanda, Ambassador Shaharyar M. Khan, a former foreign minister of Pakistan, who arrived in Kigali on 4 July 1994. Gersony challenged the credibility of the UN and cast doubt on the competence of the new force commander of UNAMIR II, Canadian General Guy Tousignant, who arrived on 16 August 1994.[18] Tousignant was keen to explain how the UN had tried to foster a climate of trust and confidence to prepare for safe refugee return.

The news was so disturbing that Kofi Annan, under-secretary-general for peacekeeping operations, was dispatched immediately to Kigali. There he met Gersony, who gave an oral briefing and described how the RPF used 'subtlety and finesse, covering their tracks with greater dexterity than the militia' when they carried out their killings. Gersony believed that between 25,000 and 45,000 people had been killed by the RPF, including 5,000 people in August. Listening to these accounts with some disbelief was UN Special Representative Ambassador Khan. He was aware that UN military observers and aid agencies were present in the areas Gersony mentioned. Khan wondered how it was possible to massacre 30,000 people without attracting attention. In any case, the RPF did not travel with hoes and machetes. When he briefed members of the new Rwandan government the following day, Gersony described 'a mass genocide by the RPA'.[19]

At a later meeting at UNAMIR headquarters in Kigali, the deputy force commander, Brigadier-General Henry Anyidoho, and Colonel Isoa Tikoca, head of the UN Military Observers (MILOBS), decided to verify the Gersony information and sent MILOBS to the places Gersony mentioned in his briefings. They discovered the reports were exaggerated. These UN officers were convinced that Gersony and his two colleagues were the subject of planted and dramatised evidence. Charles Petrie, deputy director of the UN Rwanda Emergency Office (UNREO), who had also heard rumours about RPF massacres, carried out a careful investigation with aid agencies in the region, and he rejected the idea of preordained massacres. UNAMIR information officers investigated three out of seven cases of alleged RPF abuses, and all three were inaccurate, if not outright fabrications.[20]

Annan and Khan personally visited some of the sites mentioned by Gersony and asked the peacekeepers, doctors and engineers working there at the grass-roots level in the communes about the treatment of returning Hutu to the region. They were told Hutu who left in panic were returning, but there were pockets of territory still under the control of Hutu Power. Khan recalled that the descriptions given to Gersony were generally accurate, but the identity of the perpetrators and victims had been transposed. Khan visited a team of US and Canadian doctors in a region Gersony identified as 'the massacre belt', and none of the medical staff confirmed the claims.

The US also wanted to put the Gersony claims to the test. In Kigali, the US military attaché Tom Odom believed that 10,000–15,000 secret killings a month inside a UN-monitored area as small as Rwanda was a startling figure.

At the direction of the force commander, a Canadian intelligence officer, Phillip Drew, was tasked to set up an investigation to verify the reports about RPF massacres Gersony claimed had taken place. An inquiry was launched, and a multinational team of intelligence officers was recruited together with criminal investigators, taken from several UN contingents and non-troop-contributing nations, some of them serving undercover. Under the protection of members of the Canadian contingent they left

Kigali in a three-vehicle convoy and headed first to the village of Zaza. The team included a forensic entomologist from the US Naval Criminal Investigative Service (NCIS), there to determine the approximate date of death from the human remains. The first massacre site was in the south-west, near Kibungo, where Gersony had reported many Hutu had been slaughtered in the school a few weeks earlier. Drew recalls that on their arrival at the school the team found partially decomposed bodies everywhere, including in cisterns, wells and latrines. Many of the bodies found in the classrooms and outdoor compounds had skeletonised, and identity cards found on some of the bodies identified the victims as having been Tutsi.

A forensic examination of the bodies by the entomologist established the killing took place from mid- to late April, during the period when Hutu Power was in control of the area as the genocide of the Tutsi progressed. In the days to follow the intelligence team visited every site Gersony mentioned and failed to corroborate any of his claims. Many places had seen large numbers of killings, but of Tutsi. The intelligence officers concluded that Gersony and his colleagues were duped by people in the refugee camps in Zaire. It was apparent to them that the génocidaires were trying to pin the blame on the RPF while hiding from justice in the camps, knowing exactly where in Rwanda dead bodies were located. Some doubted Gersony set foot in Rwanda, believing that he relied entirely on information gleaned in the camps. To this day, the reports written by members of this unique intelligence mission remain hidden in government archives.[21] Odom never did believe the RPF was systematically killing Hutu in Rwanda.[22] 'We found old massacre sites but nothing new,' he wrote later. Odom believed there were killings, but they were probably isolated acts of revenge. Meanwhile, Odom reported, Hutu Power was rearming in the camps.[23]

Declassified documents released by the US State Department show the French were also dismissive of the Gersony death toll. A French diplomat in Kigali, Jacques Courbin, told a US counterpart the UNHCR had bungled the Gersony report. The information pointed to serious lapses and the collection of inaccurate data. 'In some cases, they had charged the RPF with site-specific atrocities on dates when the sites were not yet in RPF hands,' Courbin reported. 'The non-report was flawed, and he doubted that the RPF had engaged in preplanned systematic killing as it advanced,' a US diplomat reported to Washington.[24]

As a result of the numerous investigations that had been conducted by various teams and officials, the senior UN officials on the ground, Major General Tousignant and UN Special Representative Shaharyar Khan, along with the US ambassador David Rawson and others, eventually dismissed the Gersony allegations. Gersony, invited to take part in a joint investigation team established with four Rwandan ministers and four UN representatives, had declined. No Gersony report emerged. His claims came only in uncorroborated verbal testimony and ran counter to a tide of overwhelmingly contrary evidence. Three days after Robert Gersony had met Kofi Annan in Kigali, when the latter assured him there would be an investigation into his claims, the Gersony figures suddenly appeared in the *New York Times*, describing 'an unmistakable pattern of killings and persecution' by soldiers of the RPF, 'aimed at Hutu populations'. Gersony had given a private briefing to US officials, and told them that there was no Hutu intimidation in the refugee camps, for this was not borne out by his interviews. Gersony also believed little evidence existed of Hutu Power forcing refugees to remain in the refugee camps, and he wanted the entire UN policy of assisting them to return home to be reconsidered.[25] Gersony achieved his wish and in a reversal of UN policy the peacekeepers of UNAMIR II stopped further efforts to encourage return.

Gersony continued to promote his claims, and on 11 October 1994 gave a briefing to the Commission of Experts established by the UN Security Council to investigate the 1994 genocide of the Tutsi. Here he spoke of systematic and sustained killing and persecution of the civilian Hutu populations by the RPF between April and July 1994. He claimed large-scale indiscriminate killings of men, women and children, including the sick and elderly, had been consistently reported to him. The only publicly available written account of the Gersony claims comes in a précis of what he said at this meeting.

In 1999, the Gersony figures were published in the work of Alison Des Forges after he had given her a personal briefing.[26] She described the figures as the 'first convincing evidence' of wide-spread, systematic killings by the RPF and claimed that the UN suppressed 'the Gersony report' by claiming it did not exist.[27] Des Forges described how Gersony had spoken to a wider number and variety of witnesses than any other foreigner working in Rwanda during this period. She somehow forgot the UN MILOBS and the peacekeepers of UNAMIR, present in Rwanda in some cases since October 1993, some of whom had thoroughly investigated Gersony's claims and had dismissed them as not credible. In the years that followed, there were dramatic increases in the death toll for these supposed RPF killings. In February 1996, *Libération* published an investigation by journalist Stephen Smith of Hutu people allegedly killed by the post-genocide regime and estimated that there were more than 100,000 victims during the RPF's first year in power. *Libération* published a supposed eyewitness account of a Rwandan nurse who described sites, one near Kigali, where prisoners were put to death (their skulls were crushed), and another in a game reserve, the Akagera National Park, where scores of Hutus were cremated.

It did not end there. In a sensationalist book published in 2018 called *In Praise of Blood*, a Canadian journalist, Judi Rever, claimed genocide of the Hutu took place and that the methods used resembled those of the Nazis. According to her account the RPF had established death camps and cremation pits and, Rever further alleged, hundreds of thousands of Hutu had been killed, burned or dissolved in acid, their ashes dispersed with bulldozers. Rever claimed that the Hutu genocide was carried out in total secrecy, the mass murder leaving barely a trace, and that the Western allies lent a hand in the cover-up.[28] She also made the noxious claim that during the genocide RPF commandos infiltrated Hutu militia and 'assisted directly in killing Tutsi at roadblocks'. In her acknowledgements, Rever thanked her sources – the defence lawyers and known genocide deniers Christopher Black and Peter Erlinder. Rever thanks Robin Philpot, whose own book argued that the 'accepted narrative' was false and that the

RPF and the United States were entirely to blame for the catastrophe in 1994.[29]

Rever thanked Professor Filip Reyntjens for his help. After the publication of the Rever book, he was jubilant and claimed her book was proof at last of a 'double genocide'. Reyntjens was arguably the most vocal proponent of moral equivalence in the circumstances of the 1994 genocide of the Tutsi. Reyntjens liked to explain that the story was not the politically correct one of good guys and bad guys. 'It was a story of bad guys, period,' he said. Reyntjens considered the trials of the génocidaires at the International Criminal Tribunal for Rwanda (ICTR) as pathetic instances of victor's justice. He condemned the failure to bring to court the RPF, whom he blamed for massacres in 1994 and for what he termed a 'strategy of tension' in the years beforehand.

In June 2014, at an international commemorative conference at The Hague on the occasion of the twentieth anniversary of the genocide, Reyntjens blamed the RPF for what had happened. 'I would not say that they were forcing the Hutu extremists towards genocide. That would be too strong, but certainly they were creating conditions that helped in that direction.' Reyntjens claimed the RPF 'strategy of tension' included the assassination in February 1994 of Félicien Gatabazi, executive of the Social Democrat Party.[30]

After his presentation, Reyntjens listened politely to me telling him it was not true that the RPF killed Gatabazi. There had been an investigation by officers from the UN CIVPOL, a part of UNAMIR. These experienced European police inspectors concluded that Gatabazi's killers were Presidential Guards; the CIVPOL reports on their investigation into the Gatabazi assassination were available in UN archives if he wanted to research further. Reyntjens smiled. He appeared mildly amused but unpersuaded. He remained unshakeable in the belief that the RPF had assassinated Gatabazi. He also stuck to the belief that the RPF assassinated President Juvénal Habyarimana, whose murder he called the 'coronation of this strategy of tension waged by the RPF'. The RPF 'had sacrificed hundreds of thousands of Tutsi lives on the altar of military victory and a grab for power'.[31]

A Belgian professor of African law and politics at the University of Antwerp, and professor emeritus at the University of Anvers, Reyntjens, a constitutional lawyer, was widely regarded as an expert in Rwandan history, politics and law. He had first visited Rwanda in July 1976 and became a popular source for journalists. He appeared in the BBC 2 documentary in October 2014, 'Rwanda's Untold Story', in which he told viewers that by the end of 1993 'the RPF had decided they would take power by the bullet'.

While he was in Rwanda, however, Reyntjens had been keen for a personal role in politics. In 1978, at the request of President Habyarimana, Reyntjens had helped draft a constitution for the Second Republic that had institutionalised the quota system in society, whereby a certain percentage of Tutsi had places in higher education and state employment. Reyntjens once told an interviewer he did not believe the quota system was rigorously enforced, that it was informal. He claimed the proportion of Tutsi in public, parastatal and private sector employment greatly exceeded the government quota.[32]

Reyntjens was seeking influence again in October 1990 when, as he notes in his memoir, he offered his services to President Habyarimana following mass arrests of Tutsi and political opponents in the wake of the RPA invasion from Uganda. 'I could help them manage a disastrous situation from the point of view of public relations,' he wrote. At this time, he started to cooperate with a former colleague, the Rwandan historian Ferdinand Nahimana.[33] In November 1990, the government sent a delegation to Europe led by Nahimana with the purpose of countering 'RPF propaganda'.

Reyntjens remained involved with Rwandan affairs and became one of the harshest critics of the ICTR. He never allowed an occasion to pass without complaining of its 'tarnished legacy' for failing to bring the RPF to justice for its 'massacre of Hutu'. At a symposium in Geneva in 2009 to consider the sixteen-year legacy of the ICTR, he had castigated the assembled judges, lawyers, translators and members of the registrar for their failure to bring RPF military leaders to court.[34] Justice was one-sided, he claimed. He told the symposium of his exchange in July 1996 with the first ICTR prosecutor, South African Judge Richard Goldstone: Reyntjens told him he possessed 'compelling prima facie evidence of RPA crimes'. When Goldstone became irritated, stating emphatically that no such evidence existed, the brief conversation ended.

Reyntjens continued: 'Clearly, the office of the prosecutor was not starting its operation with an open mind, and this mindset has handicapped it ever since.' Reyntjens claimed a cover-up, telling the symposium that the US had buried the special investigations at the ICTR into RPF killings. He blamed the stewardship of Pierre-Richard Prosper, the former member of the office of the prosecutor turned American ambassador-at-large for War Crimes Issues, publicly accusing him of making a deal with the RPF that none of its members would face trial at the ICTR. Ambassador Prosper had listened quietly to the accusations levelled. He then explained to the symposium the difficult attempts made to reach an agreement between the tribunal and the government of Rwanda, how the ICTR had offered help to Rwandan justice to prosecute individuals for acts of revenge by its troops. There was a minute to this effect available in archives, available to researchers, he told Reyntjens.

William Schabas, professor of international law at Middlesex University and an internationally recognised expert on genocide law, responded to Reyntjens' claim of 'victor's justice'. Schabas had visited Nuremberg a year earlier and told the symposium that he had not heard Germans saying the Nuremberg trials of the Nazis were defective, that they inhibited reconciliation because they only prosecuted one side. He wondered what balanced justice at the end of World War II might have looked like.[35]

Schabas was not arguing there was no RPF responsibility for crimes against humanity, but that they were not responsible for genocide, and added: 'Let's look up close a little more at this idea that if you only prosecute one side that you create terrible impediments of reconciliation. Because I think Germany, probably in all of Europe, has probably done the best job now of addressing the crimes of the past. How much symbolism is required to beat back the charge of victors' justice?'

The tribunal did not set out to please public opinion, recalled former deputy prosecutor and Cameroonian lawyer Bernard Muna. It did not set out to please Amnesty International or Human Rights Watch. The intention was to render justice. It would be a pity if the work of the criminal tribunal was constantly put through the process of some conceived impartiality between the two warring factors in Rwanda. 'This was not the job of the tribunal,' said Muna.

Nor was the ICTR intended as an inquiry commission, said Caribbean judge and former ICTR president from 2004 to 2011 Sir Charles Michael Dennis Byron. Judges were not historians. The purpose of a criminal trial was to establish individual guilt, not to establish the historical truth of conflict. The tribunal had established a factual record of the genocide and atrocities and had proved individual criminal responsibility. Judge Byron believed that in this way the work of the ICTR had denied space to the revisionists. The ICTR had put on trial a prime minister, ministers of government, the president of the national assembly, préfets, *bourgmestres,* other senior political public servants, businessmen, leaders of the Interahamwe, senior military officers, media representatives, a doctor and members of the clergy. In sum, the tribunal had held accountable those in positions of power and privilege. One final challenge to the idea of moral equivalence came from Hassan Jallow, the chief prosecutor of the ICTR, who reiterated that the primary mission of the tribunal was to address the crime of genocide. He believed the pressure to prosecute the RPF military leaders was driven by political considerations.

Reyntjens remained unconvinced. He produced further evidence to reinforce his argument for equal and comparable wrongs. He turned to the murder on 7 June 1994 of twelve Roman Catholic clergy by RPF soldiers near Kabgayi and told the attendees at the Geneva Symposium in 2009 that the RPF leadership was responsible for this massacre and had escaped justice. Only soldiers of low rank had stood trial for the crime in Rwandan courts that were unsuitable for obtaining justice for this crime against humanity.

The killings of the clergy at Kabgayi is today more widely known than the death camp bearing the same name located nearby. In June, BBC reporter Mark Doyle recounts, newsrooms around the Western world seized on the story of the RPF murders of the twelve clergy 'with undisguised glee'. It was proof at last that the 'other side' was just as evil. Doyle wrote, 'The problem was that this was not the proof of moral equivalence that could make the world feel okay about dismissing the whole Rwandan business as African chaos. This was not the balancing item that would make it okay to forget about the genocide.' The prominence it got was misleading.[36]

When RPF troops liberated the Kabgayi death camp, they found an estimated 30,000 emaciated people. There were unburied corpses everywhere.[37] The dying and chronically sick were in a huge storage barn, people suffering machete injuries or starvation, dehydration and disease.[38] The people were survivors and victims of genocide who had fled, seeking sanctuary at the Vatican of Rwanda, with its imposing cathedral on a site a few kilometres square.[39]

In fact, Kabgayi was a trap. Every day, soldiers and Interahamwe abducted and killed young men. They systematically selected and abducted Tutsi women and girls for rape.[40] At least twelve people died of starvation every day. One estimate suggests that some 70,000 people had died in total in Kabgayi. During this period, the ICRC delegates were forbidden to go inside the camp perimeter and instead rented a house with a view across the terrain. The powerless delegates listened to the screams of murder victims at night and tried to pick up the bodies in the morning.

For the US journalist Scott Peterson, the motivation of the RPF murders of the clergy was clear. The RPF soldiers believed the clergy had organised the killing at Kabgayi that looked like a death camp in Germany during World War II.[41] Furthermore, the archbishop who was killed was Vincent Nsengiyumva, closely attached to the Hutu Power structure, for fifteen years a member of the Mouvement Révolutionnaire National pour le Développement (MRND) central committee, who had presided over the social affairs committee. He had helped implement policies of discrimination and demonisation of Tutsi that laid the ground for genocide. Once the genocide of the Tutsi began, the archbishop did not once call the massacres a genocide, let alone condemn politicians and military officers. In May 1994, the Vatican in Rome was calling for 'both sides to come to the table'.

Dallaire explained in his book that the RPF soldiers who secured Kabgayi had travelled for weeks and encountered the 'Hutu scorched-human policy', and they were aware how intimate the Church was with the Habyarimana family and former government. 'Quite simply, they killed the princes of the church out of vengeance, their discipline frayed to breaking point by the atrocities they'd witnessed. At a ceasefire meeting on 9 June, the RPF acknowledged a total breakdown of military control at Kabgayi and a group of its soldiers had viciously slaughtered the clerics, all of whom were Hutu.'[42]

At the symposium in 2009 in Geneva, Hassan Jallow, today chief justice of Gambia, responded to Reyntjens' complaints about the injustices at Kabgayi. He told the gathering that the RPF soldiers who shot the priests had stood trial in Rwanda in 2001. Two captains pleaded guilty to murder, and a major and a brigadier general pleaded not guilty to complicity to murder. The two captains were sentenced to eight years in prison, a sentence reduced to five years on appeal, while the judges acquitted the senior officers. Jallow explained the indictments charged the defendants with offences under Rwandan law but also under the Geneva Conventions. Two were on trial for murder, and the senior officers were charged with complicity and command responsibility. These four soldiers had opened fire in the course of a meeting and in the presence of other senior military officers.

Jallow had ICTR monitors at the trial of these men, a senior trial attorney and a senior legal adviser who attended every day of the trial and had studied the evidence. As a result, Jallow gave an assessment of the trial to the United Nations Security Council on 4 June that year and it was found to be open, public, free and fair. Jallow said he had other priorities. Hundreds of génocidaires remained at large, and this was not a good situation. 'We have had our target lists pruned to less than a hundred people,' said Jallow.

~

Reytnjens was not alone in his views that the ICTR system was rigged and that it failed in its quest for justice. The executive director of Human Rights Watch since 1993, the New York–based US attorney Kenneth Roth, also called the ICTR reputation tarnished.[43] William Schabas encountered Roth at a conference in 2008 in Florence, at which Roth announced that the work of the ICTR would not end until it had dealt with the crimes of the RPF. Roth, Schabas recalled, cited a figure of 25,000 people as RPF victims, and argued that if the ICTR hoped to fulfil its mandate and do its job properly, it should prosecute those responsible.[44]

Roth had lobbied the tribunal and had written a letter to Hassan Jallow to tell him that the failure to prosecute the RPF undermined the legitimacy of the tribunal. 'Do the wounds left by massive crimes such as the genocide in Nazi-occupied Europe or Rwanda heal better if the victims or those who liberate them acknowledge a part in the wrongdoing?' he asked. Roth claimed massacres by the RPF 'were as evil and as deserving of prosecution as the crimes they were fighting to stop'. To assign blame to one side was meaningless. In a response to Roth's letter, Jallow said, he was told the decision to indict was based solely on the availability of credible evidence and the law, and not on feelings of maintaining 'balancing acts' by indicting 'all sides' to the armed conflict.[45]

Schabas concluded that HRW was not a neutral investigative body. It was now an advocacy organisation. It took positions at a political or policy level, then marshalled the evidence, such as it existed, in order to support its views.[46] The organisation seemed more concerned to prove RPF guilt than to chase recalcitrant governments who had genocide suspects on their soil, or to encourage government to fulfil their obligations under treaty law and abide by the 1948 Genocide Convention, which provides for the punishment of the crime.

While HRW had assisted at the trial of four genocide fugitives in Belgium in 2001, it had since neither helped nor encouraged smaller civilian groups to track the hundreds of genocide fugitives who lived at large with refugee status in the US, the UK, France, Belgium and the Netherlands. Some fugitives were known and their addresses were available in France, in Belgium and in the Netherlands.

Since 1995, HRW had exerted no pressure on French authorities to address issues of complicity, whether politically or judicially. As a book by a former US diplomat, Richard Johnson, pointed out, HRW seemed blissfully unaware that Hutu Power ideologues continued from exile to promote their racist ideology and spread denial and disinformation; it was a network wielding a continuing and pernicious influence. It appeared the organisation had abandoned the idea of seeking justice for genocide victims.[47]

There was serious criticism of HRW from Roelof Haveman, a policy adviser of law in the Netherlands Ministry of Foreign Affairs who had worked in Rwanda and later highlighted the factual errors in HRW reports and complained that rumour and stereotypes replaced reality. He alleged a failure by HRW to distinguish between opinion and fact; the organisation was investigator, accuser and judge, and unaccountable to anyone, most importantly the people of Rwanda.

Furthermore, HRW nurtured an anti-RPF bias. In 2006, the advocacy group welcomed with enthusiasm the report of Judge Jean-Louis Bruguière that the RPF downed the president's plane in April 1994, but eventually the group was forced to produce a half-hearted retraction, stating that some parts had obvious merit while other parts were not fully substantiated. There had been no serious effort to check the work of the French magistrate, and HRW had fallen into the trap that placed undue reliance on inadequate, unverified and scant witness testimony used as primary source material. The organisation devoted more resources to documenting revenge killings by the RPF than investigating the worst crime since the creation of the human rights movement and bringing the killers to justice.[48]

It was notable how active HRW was in 2008 at the extradition case heard in the London courts. In the first hearing, Judge Evans had dismissed HRW arguments, accusing the organisation of relying on anecdote and lacking hard evidence for claims, and calling its amicus curiae not reliable. However, the High Court in 2016 thought the HRW reports plausible and this contributed to the failure to extradite the genocide suspects. The judges had believed HRW's claim that the men would not get a fair trial in Rwanda. This went against the prevailing judgements made since 2011 where the ICTR, the European Court of Human Rights, and the national courts of Norway and Sweden had no objections to the extradition of suspects to Rwanda.

For the lawyers at the UK Crown Prosecution Service (CPS), who had brought the extradition case to court, the reliance on the HRW amicus brief was unfortunate. A lawyer who worked on the case for the CPS, Anne-Marie Kundert, wrote of the HRW report submitted to the High Court judges: 'On analysis many of these (HRW) sources rely on the same limited number of concrete examples, in relation to which bad faith has often been presumed but not proved. None of the footnotes were produced.' Kundert recognised there were sometimes failures in legal protection in Rwanda, and this was hardly surprising in a society that was emerging from autocratic rule, genocide and civil disorder. The government of Rwanda needed assistance in their judicial efforts in order to avoid the development of an impunity gap.[49]

Kundert was not alone in her criticism. There were other challenges to the HRW way of working, an organisation run by lawyers using institutional money to document, publish and exploit the media in order to pressure politicians and, in London, prevent extradition. One early critic of HRW and its relationship to Rwanda and the genocide, the author Alex de Waal, wrote in 1997 that while Rwanda was a watershed for human rights activism in Africa, in this case it had not worked. In the aftermath of genocide, there was more outrage at the prison conditions of the perpetrators in Rwanda than outrage at the genocide.[50] It was an imbalance justified by 'a principled refusal to calibrate or compare abuses' because one killing was as bad as another was. It was an approach, wrote de Waal, that minimised past abuses, as HRW defined the genocide, to focus on current abuses, largely problems attributable to the aftermath of the genocide. Some demanded that justice for the genocide be overlooked in the name of reconciliation.

In his book published in 2013, *The Travesty of Human Rights Watch on Rwanda*, Richard Johnson claimed that the organisation had failed in its primary task – to pressure recalcitrant governments to fulfil their legal obligations under the 1948 Genocide Convention, to punish the crime of genocide. Johnson warned that as a result, a network of fugitives wielded a continuing and pernicious influence, using in exile the skills that had proved so useful during the genocide – propaganda and disinformation.

13

The Mechanism

In September 2016, the chief propagandist of Hutu Power, Ferdinand Nahimana, walked free from prison, having served twenty years and six months in international custody.[1] It was thirteen years since his conviction to a life term imposed in a courtroom at the International Criminal Tribunal for Rwanda (ICTR), where he was found guilty of genocide, direct and public incitement to commit genocide, conspiracy to commit genocide, crimes against humanity (persecution) and crimes against humanity (extermination).[2]

For the survivors of the genocide of the Tutsi, his release was a devastating development. The decision betrayed a lack of understanding of the crime of genocide and failed to acknowledge its magnitude. Nahimana continued to claim his innocence, and, given the Hutu Power propaganda produced by Nahimana and his fellow génocidaires, these prisoners continued to promote the same poisonous and racist ideology that motivated their criminal acts in 1994. To have released Nahimana at a time when genocide denial was more entrenched than ever was irresponsible. The decision showed contempt for the survivors and their continued suffering.

The Rwandan minister of justice, Johnston Busingye, called for the removal of the US judge responsible, Theodor Meron. In coming to his decision, Meron had held no hearings, had taken no account of the views of the survivors, and had given no say to the government of Rwanda. His decision was secret and unaccountable. No appeal was possible. A brief official explanation came in the form of a short, redacted report that provided basic background information.[3] It included glowing testimonials from prison wardens who described Nahimana's impeccable conduct. In the course of his prison career, Nahimana had lived 'in perfect harmony' with fellow inmates and the prison administration. He was polite, disciplined and would quickly reintegrate into society as someone 'humble and courteous'.

Nahimana served his sentence in a community with his colleagues, a group of Rwandan génocidaires who lived together in a purpose-built compound within the high security Koulikoro prison, some thirty-five miles (fifty-seven kilometres) from Bamako, the capital of Mali.[4] The special compound, constructed at United Nations expense, was segregated from the misery found in the rest of the prison. Within yards of this 'international wing' there were unsanitary conditions, overcrowding, a lack of medical care and not all the prisoners had access to potable water. The génocidaires, on the other hand, had separate cells, showers, a gym, a well-stocked library, a dining room and a church.

The UN, an organisation intended by its founders to uphold human rights, required that the Rwandan génocidaires live in conditions that met the UN Standard Minimum Rules for the Treatment of Prisoners (SMRs). Initially adopted by the UN Congress on the Prevention of Crime and the Treatment of Offenders in 1955, they were given final approval by the UN Economic and Social Council in 1957.[5] Conditions had to comply with the Body of Principles for the Protection of all Persons under Any Form of Detention or Imprisonment, approved by UN General Assembly resolution 43/173 of 9 December 1988, as well as the Basic Principles for the Treatment of Prisoners, affirmed by UN General Assembly resolution 45/111 of 14 December 1990. These requirements are non-binding on UN member states. To ensure the proper application of these international standards, the special compound in the Koulikoro prison received visits from international humanitarian groups, including the International Committee of the Red Cross (ICRC).

In this special community, according to the wardens, Nahimana had a crucial role. 'It was quite an achievement among a group of intellectuals in which each member is intent on promoting his own ideas.' They praised his character and personality. A former warden noted the contribution of Nahimana to the smooth running of the unit: he helped to 'restrain and keep his compatriots in check'. Even the Ministry of Justice in Mali weighed in with a letter to support his early release, telling Judge Meron that between 2009 and 2013 Nahimana was the 'Rwandan group' representative, helping his fellow inmates to 'resolve many issues'.

A psychosocial report described his behaviour as exemplary. He was 'always willing to listen to his co-detainees'.[6] Furthermore, Nahimana submitted his own petition for release, written by three lawyers. They stressed his family ties, which he managed to maintain, and that he hoped to 'work for peace and reconciliation' in Rwanda, although it was not explained by the lawyers how this might be achieved.[7] Meron wrote in his report that the prisoner showed 'some signs of rehabilitation'. The judge seemed not to care that Nahimana continued to deny his own responsibility in 'these crimes'. While his lawyers maintained that their client did not question or minimise 'the genocide', or his 'profound regret' for the 'crimes committed in Rwanda', what he did not accept was a role in the criminal nature of the broadcasts of RTLM. Nahimana had not once offered to help the office of the ICTR prosecutor. This was something Meron regarded as a 'neutral factor'.

It remains unclear whether the judge critically assessed the information he received about Nahimana. His short report contained no detail at all about the ways in which the prisoner was 'rehabilitated'. Afterwards, there were doubts expressed about the capacity of the prison authorities in Mali to develop rehabilitation programmes for these Rwandan prisoners, particularly given the language and cultural differences.[8]

In their special compound, the génocidaires kept in touch with world events, received frequent visitors, and were interviewed by journalists and academics. They received $2 a day to buy newspapers, and payment was provided for telephone calls. They posed no problems for the prison authorities. They spent their time working on their campaign of denial, and the facilities provided for them helped them to write books and communicate with

publishers who were willing to produce their work. The prison
warders noted how educated these prisoners were and how they
kept to themselves and worked on their 'political activities'. A
member of the Koulikoro prison management gave a radio interview in which he explained that these prisoners demanded 'justice
for all victims without exception', whether Tutsi or Hutu.[9]

From the special compound in Mali and another prison in Benin,
the génocidaires continued to protest their innocence, influence
newcomers to the subject, find new and receptive audiences, and
seek out conspiracy theorists and gullible journalists and academics. Their written work repeated the familiar stories of genocide
denial – how more Hutu people died than Tutsi, how the killing
was self-defence, the deaths not intentional, there was no planning and no central direction, and the Hutu were the real victims.
From this special compound, the chief propagandist, Ferdinand
Nahimana, had two books on sale on Amazon (in France), and
the author described himself as a political prisoner.[10] In their community, the génocidaires spent time analysing numerous ICTR
and UN documents and wrote appeals to the authorities. Only the
truth could save the people of Rwanda, wrote Nahimana.[11]

The supporters of their campaign of denial praised the Mali
prison authorities for not succumbing to 'the demonisation of
Rwandan Hutus' that had turned them into monsters in Western
public opinion. These men deserved our pity. They had been up-
rooted from the lush green lands of home, to a hot, dry and dusty
Mali. Furthermore, Rwanda was Christian, and Mali Muslim.
The Montreal journalist and publisher Robin Philpot wrote: 'For
prisoners convinced of their innocence, the worse problem is the
distance from their families.' Philpot wrote about 'the colonial
nature of these new forms of UN-sanctioned penal colonies'. How
could they make their cases known and hope to reopen them?
This was nothing less than banishment, and these prisoners were
condemned to a long slow death. Philpot reported complaints
from the génocidaires that they 'had been made to disappear from
the news'.[12]

This was not strictly true. An invaluable glimpse inside the
special compound in Mali where the génocidaires lived came

in filmed footage broadcast on ITV news in the UK on 21 July 2015. It was billed a world scoop, and was an interview with Jean Kambanda, the world's first head of government to plead guilty to the crime of genocide. The Africa correspondent for ITV, John Ray, had gained access to a top security prison, he said, that housed the men behind Africa's 'final solution'.

The on-camera interview with Kambanda, economist and banker, the prime minister of the Interim Government that oversaw the extermination programme of the Tutsi, took place in the library. Kambanda was the world's highest-ranking political leader held to account for the crime of genocide, and he was serving a life term but he had later retracted his plea. In the television footage, Kambanda walked through gardens with a briefcase, and talked and laughed with the British journalist. He appeared portly, having gained weight since the last day of the trial in September 1998. He began the interview in faltering English, 'I cannot express any regrets for something I have not done. Someone else did it.' The truth was still in dispute, the journalist said at the end. Kambanda admitted to Ray that he had distributed weapons, but only so people could protect themselves. His conscience was clear. He had been a 'puppet' and felt no sense of guilt. 'We are fighting to be free,' Kambanda told Ray.

Just a few weeks after the announcement of the release of Ferdinand Nahimana from the special compound in Mali, I spoke with Justice Navi Pillay, the South African judge who presided in the media trial at the ICTR. The trial saw the conviction of three defendants, Ferdinand Nahimana, journalist Hassan Ngeze, and director of the hate radio Michel Barayagwiza, for their role in using the media in the incitement of genocide. Pillay, in December 2003, had read Nahimana his life sentence.

Pillay said no one had consulted her about the early release of Nahimana and, as the presiding judge in the trial, she thought this would have been appropriate. Pillay expressed concern at the lack of any post-release conditions imposed on Nahimana and wondered why no realistic possibility existed to monitor him, to supervise his activities, or to find out whether his racist propagandising continued. Meron had simply granted 'an irreversible and unconditional form of release, an unconditional reduction in sentence' that had resulted in complete freedom. The decision threatened the credibility of international justice, Pillay believed.

'The trials of the génocidaires were not to make us all feel good,' Pillay told me. 'They were for the people of Rwanda.'

That Meron had decided the fate of Nahimana after having earlier played a role in reducing his sentence on appeal was of concern. On 28 November 2007, the Appeals Chamber had reduced Nahimana's life sentence to thirty years. Meron had written a dissenting view in the appeal judgement, wanting to reduce even further the thirty-year sentence agreed upon by the two other appeal judges. He thought the sentence of thirty years too harsh. In his dissenting view, Meron was scathing of the media trial and pointed to the 'sheer number of errors' in the trial judgement. He called for a new trial because 'mere hate speech' was not the basis for a criminal conviction.[13] Meron believed that the liability connected to hate speech was illegitimate in light of freedom of expression, and this was explicitly grounded in the free speech guarantee of the US First Amendment.[14]

> I believe that the only conviction against him that can stand is for direct and public incitement to commit genocide under Article 6(3) and based on certain post-6 April broadcasts. Despite the severity of this crime, Nahimana did not personally kill anyone and did not personally make statements that constituted incitement. In light of these facts, I believe that the sentence imposed is too harsh, both in relation to Nahimana's own culpability and to the sentences meted out by the Appeals Chamber to Barayagwiza and Ngeze (co-accused), who committed graver crimes. Therefore, I dissent from Nahimana's sentence.

Fellow ICTR judges were not alone in their concerns at these developments. Professor Gregory S. Gordon, professor of law at the Chinese University of Hong Kong (CUHK) Faculty of Law, worked on the media trial from its beginnings and was an expert on atrocity speech in the circumstances of the 1994 genocide of the Tutsi. Gordon, who had helped gather prosecution evidence, believed that the media trial was so significant that from a historic perspective it had helped to define the distinction between hate speech and speech used to incite genocide.

Gordon published *Atrocity Speech Law: Foundation, Fragmentation, Fruition* in 2017. In an interview in London that year, he explained the crucial role of Ferdinand Nahimana and claimed that, without him, the hate radio RTLM would not have existed. The connection between hate speech and atrocity in Rwanda was so strong that the media trial 'served as a virtual laboratory for the development of atrocity speech law'.[15] Ideology and propaganda were integral to the crime of genocide, and the 1994 genocide of the Tutsi of Rwanda showed how mass media was a causal factor in mass atrocities.

A direct challenge to the views of Meron on free speech came in a foreword to Gordon's book, written by a Nuremberg prosecutor, Benjamin B. Ferencz. Ferencz believed a failure to criminalise hate speech served only to encourage fanatics, for example those responsible for the genocide of the Tutsi. He added: 'The first amendment to the US Constitution that guarantees freedom of speech was never intended to justify the violation of fundamental human rights designed to protect everyone.' Hatred generated by vicious propagandists such as Julius Streicher was one of the main reasons the Nazi crimes could be committed.

Curbing hate speech was a way to prevent genocide, for it was the case that arousing public fears could incite it. 'We have still not recognized that you cannot kill an ingrained ideology with a gun,' wrote Ferencz. From the start of the media trial, Gordon recalled, there was a dearth of jurisprudence to guide them. As the tribunal geared up in 1996, on one set of shelves in an almost empty library was a complete set of the transcripts of the trials at Nuremberg.[16]

Judge Theodor Meron had never sat through a genocide trial. He served only on the Appeals Chamber, and so did not experience the agonising testimony in the trials. He did not take part in the debates among the judges about the appropriate length of sentences imposed on the génocidaires for their unspeakable crimes. In her interview, Judge Navi Pillay carefully explained why the judges had decided to impose life sentences in the courtrooms of the ICTR, something the trial judges had discussed at length and taken seriously. The scale and magnitude of the crime were never in doubt from the very first trial, Pillay explained, nor its brutality.

Pillay was one of three judges in the world's first genocide trial held at the ICTR to hear the case of Jean-Paul Akayesu, a middle-ranking official in local government, a *bourgmestre,* a teacher and schools inspector. Found guilty of nine counts of genocide, direct and public incitement to commit genocide and crimes against humanity – these included extermination, murder, torture, rape and other inhumane acts – his life term was confirmed on appeal.

The trial of Akayesu made legal history in another way. The crime of rape was not initially in the indictment but in the course of the trial, and after questioning from Pillay, the testimony from prosecution witnesses had revealed the level of sexual crimes that took place in the genocide. Without Pillay, the courts might never have addressed this aspect of the genocide, and she went on to ensure groundbreaking jurisprudence on rape as a crime of genocide. It was a significant milestone and determined that sexual violence was an integral part of the process of destruction: the Akayesu judgement noted, 'Rapes resulted in physical and psychological destruction of Tutsi women, their families and their communities.'[17]

The collection of data to determine instances of rape and sexual violence had been fraught with problems. Today, an accurate number cannot be set. Most experts believe it to be in the region of 250,000 rapes and sexual assaults.[18] The sexual violence in Rwanda included sexual slavery, forced incest, deliberate HIV transmission, forced impregnation and genital mutilation.[19] The intention of the sexual attacks was to humiliate, demoralise and enslave. The evidence in the Akayesu trial had shown Tutsi women targeted for sexual violence, and this had contributed to the destruction of the Tutsi group as a whole. In the media trial in 2003 over which Navi Pillay presided, there was expert and witness testimony that confirmed Hutu Power propagandists had targeted Tutsi women, the targeting woven into the planning of the genocide in 1994.

In the light of all this evidence and the magnitude of the crimes, the imposition of life sentences was appropriate, said Pillay. This was widely accepted by ICTR judges who expected the génocidaires to serve their sentences in full. Only those who confessed and cooperated with the prosecutor were eligible for early release. The tribunal attached significant value to 'voluntary, substantial and long-term cooperation with the prosecutor'.

When appointed president of the International Residual Mechanism for Criminal Tribunals (MICT) in 2012, known as the Mechanism, Meron had assumed responsibility for the supervision of all international prisoners. Meron was now in charge of making new rules and judgements upon these cases. A Polish-born US citizen and an international lawyer with a stellar career, Meron was a recipient of the French Légion d'Honneur and a Shakespeare scholar. The first president of the Mechanism, Meron served from its creation in 2012 until January 2019.

The Security Council established the Mechanism to complete the work of two international criminal tribunals when they closed – the ICTR and its forerunner, the International Criminal Tribunal for the former Yugoslavia (ICTY).[20] A part of the mandate of the Mechanism was to supervise those convicted of grave violations of international humanitarian law in Rwanda and in the former Yugoslavia.

Meron had served on the Appeals Chamber used by both the ICTY and the ICTR. He was widely considered one of the world's most distinguished specialists in international human rights law and international penal law, his numerous books and articles contributing to the advance and development of the discipline, and he gave advice to the US government and State Department. In his job as president of the Mechanism, Meron maintained high-level contacts with the governments of UN member states in order to facilitate and improve cooperation with the Mechanism: he was required to make annual reports to the General Assembly and biannual reports to the Security Council.[21]

With Meron as president of the Mechanism, the prospects of the imprisoned Rwandan génocidaires improved considerably.

Meron took advantage of his powers as president to alter the internal procedures already in place. He used a device known as 'practice directions' to adopt new rules for the procedure for the determination of applications for pardon, commutation of sentence, and early release of persons convicted by the ICTR, the ICTY or the Mechanism (PDER). Meron, the only full-time judge on the Mechanism, ensured approval of his new rules by a plenary of judges via remote communication in June 2012.

His changes had significant results.[22] Meron was no longer required to make public his decisions on early release and could now take into account humanitarian and health issues. He was no longer required to consult survivors nor to ask the original trial judges for an opinion, although when the Security Council created the ICTR, the enabling resolution mandated that in early-release cases there must be consultation with trial judges.[23] This was also a requirement written into the statute of the ICTR.[24] Although the statute of the Mechanism did not refer to consultation with trial judges, its rules and practice specified that the president should consult with any judges of the sentencing chamber, but only those who continued to serve as judges on the Mechanism.[25] This provision disappeared and by 2016, when the time came to release Ferdinand Nahimana, Judge Meron was no longer required to consult any judges at all. One legal scholar noted drily, 'Perhaps release is considered to be an administrative or executive task at the MICT (Mechanism), but this should not preclude judicial review of decisions.'[26] Another factor that greatly improved the prospects of the génocidaires was the decision made by Judge Meron to apply the same rules to the Rwandan prisoners as those that governed the imprisonment of those responsible for war crimes in the former Yugoslavia. There was a need for 'equality among international prisoners, irrespective of the court that sentenced them'.[27] At the ICTY, convicted prisoners were eligible for release after they had served two-thirds of their sentence. The two-thirds eligibility rule henceforth applied to the entire prisoner population over which he, as president of the Mechanism, supervised. While conceding this could 'constitute a benefit for the Rwandan prisoners', he wrote, 'this alone could not justify discrimination between the groups of convicted persons under the jurisdiction of the Mechanism'.

When in October 1994 informal negotiations had taken place in the Security Council to discuss the establishment of a criminal tribunal, the Rwandan ambassador who was representing the new government established in Kigali wanted those convicted by the tribunal to serve their sentences in Rwanda. He sought a voice for the Rwandan government on any pardon or commutation of sentence and warned that the members of the former Hutu Power government might 'be sent to serve their time in France and would be able to wangle their way out of jail early'.[28]

It did not turn out this way. Only in June 2018, and facing criticism for the first time in his six years as president of the Mechanism, did Judge Theodor Meron consult the Rwandan government about the next three proposed early releases. Rwanda's justice minister, Johnston Busingye, wrote directly to Meron to object in the strongest terms to any further releases. The severity and gravity of the crimes should be sufficient to deny the prisoners' applications.[29] 'Nothing about these people has changed,' he said. 'They have shown no remorse, not even acknowledgement of their crimes.' There were objections elsewhere and Toby Cadman, the co-founder of a human rights organisation in London, Guernica 37 International Justice Chambers, thought that early release of anyone convicted of the crime of genocide served only to undermine the process of international law.[30]

One of the three prisoners under consideration was journalist Hassan Ngeze, the editor of *Kangura*, convicted in the media trial at the ICTR of genocide and public incitement to commit genocide. Just as for Ferdinand Nahimana in the same trial, the Appeals Chamber had reduced Ngeze's life sentence to thirty years. One of the media trial lawyers, the prosecutor Simone Monasebian, on hearing of the possibility of Ngeze's release, wrote to Meron. She explained that *Kangura* and radio RTLM had fuelled the genocide, and both had been more potent and dangerous than bullets or machetes. The génocidaires were unrepentant violent extremists, she told him.

The survivors' organisation Ibuka announced that Meron was the 'epitome of all things wrong following the aftermath of the 1994 genocide'. The organisation had repeatedly called for an investigation of every controversial decision taken by Meron, either reduction in sentence or early release. Any decision that served to benefit genocide perpetrators also benefited their campaign of denial. Every decision that diminished the status of the crime of genocide needed investigation.[31]

There were several cases worth consideration. Meron was the presiding judge of five justices on the appeal that reduced the life sentences of Colonel Théoneste Bagosora and Colonel Anatole Nsengiyumva, both originally sentenced to life in prison for genocide, crimes against humanity and war crimes. The sentence of Lieutenant Colonel Anatole Nsengiyumva, the northern commander, former head of army intelligence, reduced to fifteen years, saw him freed with time served taken into account. In November 2009, Meron was the presiding judge in the appeals chamber decision to acquit Protais Zigiranyirazo; he was the notorious brother of Agathe Kanziga, the wife of President Habyarimana, and convicted of genocide and extermination as a crime against humanity. Judge Meron said that the original trial erred in its handling of evidence. In 2013, Meron presided over the appeal that acquitted and released Justin Mugenzi and Prosper Mugiraneza, initially sentenced to thirty years for genocide, both ministers in the Interim Government.

Meron also granted the early release of the Roman Catholic priest, Father Emmanuel Rukundo, who served fifteen years of a twenty-three-year sentence, convicted in February for genocide, murder and extermination as crimes against humanity. Meron was already familiar with the Rukundo case when he granted him early release. When a member of the Appeals Chamber, he was one of five appeal judges who in October 2010 had reduced Rukundo's sentence from twenty-five to twenty-three years. The appeal reversed his genocide conviction and blamed the original trial for not having proved genocidal intent in the mental harm he had inflicted with his sexual assault on a twenty-one-year-old woman.

Some tried to find reasons for Meron's leniency towards the génocidaires. A few months after the release of Nahimana, in January 2018, Gregory Gordon gave a paper, 'On the Early Release of the "Rwandan Goebbels": American Free Speech Exceptionalism and the Ghost of the Nuremberg-Tokyo Commutations'. In the paper, Gordon questioned whether the decision-making of Meron was an example of exactly how American power influences the operations of international criminal justice. Gordon thought similarities existed with other occasions when US political interests affected the treatment of war criminals. In the early 1950s, US High Commissioner for Germany John J. McCloy pardoned or commuted the sentences of numerous high-level Nazi defendants convicted at Nuremberg, and that same year, General Douglas MacArthur began releasing high-level Japanese war criminals convicted by Nuremberg's sister Tokyo Tribunal. The shifting Cold War policies favoured rapprochement with the Germans and Japanese.

Others considered the possibility of US influence. They recalled the controversy that surrounded Meron's decisions in ICTY cases. In 2013, in a leaked confidential letter, a judge at the ICTY, Frederik Harhoff, had complained that Meron had exerted 'persistent and intense' pressure on his fellow judges to allow Serb and Croat commanders, prisoners convicted at the Yugoslavia war crimes court, to go free. Meron had wanted increased proof of 'specific direction' by an accused military or senior political leader, a higher burden of proof for those in command.

On that occasion, there had been complaints from international lawyers and human rights groups. Some judges said in private that the rulings had abruptly rewritten legal standards and would now serve to protect military commanders. The changes Meron made, however, were to quell fears from the US government in particular that it could face legal action against senior leaders for war crimes. Still others speculated that this was a question of economics, and that the US, retreating into isolationism, did not want to continue sending money to the UN to pay its share for the upkeep of international prisoners.[32]

The harshest criticism came in the UN Security Council in an address by the Rwandan ambassador, Valentine Rugwabiza. On 6

June 2018, she spoke of the failing credibility of the Mechanism, condemning its secret procedures and lack of accountability. The Council was due to discuss an application by Judge Meron for a renewal of his two-year contract as president.

Ambassador Rugwabiza told the Council that since its establishment in 2012 under the personal direction of Meron as president, the Mechanism had released more than ten masterminds of the genocide before the end of their sentences.[33] Their release was unconditional. There was no way to ensure they would not re-engage in criminal activities. This would be the legacy of the Mechanism and its current president. In a grave admonishment, the ambassador told the Council that in allowing a secret and unaccountable process to develop to provide these early releases, it had strengthened the génocidaires in their desire to minimise and diminish the crime. She warned that some of the released génocidaires had regrouped and once again were propagating their genocide ideology. These were dangerous and unrepentant individuals who dismissed entirely the factual basis of their criminal conspiracy. Allowing them their freedom, the Mechanism had enabled an ongoing campaign of denial.[34]

Rugwabiza was not against the principle of early release but believed the purpose of incarceration was to rehabilitate individuals. She said, 'There was no country on earth that had commuted more sentences, given early release to more convicts of genocide, than Rwanda.' In Rwanda, the trials of more than a million perpetrators over nearly a decade had taken place in Gacaca courts. In Rwanda, early releases came only after confession and contrition. In these local courts, the remorse shown required proof through action, and the accused sometimes revealed the location of buried bodies. These same rules must apply to high-profile international prisoners, she said. In order to be eligible for early release, a prisoner should provide a public acknowledgement of guilt, public support for peace projects, and public apology to victims, or victim restitution. A lack of consideration of the gravity of the crime, and a failure to consider the absence of remorse, was to blame for these early releases. While the Mechanism released génocidaires, it had failed in its other main task and had not apprehended or prosecuted a single genocide fugitive – also a part of its mandate from the Council.

That afternoon the Council held a secret and informal meeting to discuss the matter.[35] The Council membership was divided over the issue and a compromise decision allowed the eighty-seven-year-old judge six further months in office. In the course of those six months Meron approved the early release of one more unrepentant génocidaire, a former military officer, Aloys Simba, thereby ignoring the strongest objections from the government of Rwanda. Simba had been convicted at the ICTR for the crime of genocide and extermination, arrested while hiding out in Senegal in November 2001. Four years later he was sentenced to twenty-five years in prison. He walked free on 19 January 2019, having served eighteen years in international custody.

And so, when international visitors go to Murambi, one of six national genocide memorial sites, they may not realise how their own governments connived in the early release of a man who on 21 April 1994 handed out weapons to militia surrounding the technical college there, how having recruited and trained Interahamwe he directed the massacre of thousands of Tutsi families who had sought shelter. His orders were to get rid of 'this filth'. At Murambi, there were an estimated 50,000 people murdered.

After the genocide was over in November 1994 the Council, in accordance with its duty to punish the crime under the 1948 Genocide Convention, had carried the legal and financial burden of proving the guilt of the perpetrators. The Council had provided the means needed to defend the accused and had established a tribunal that found them guilty for their part in a campaign of extermination. It had established as a historic fact the 1994 genocide of the Tutsi.

Now, this same international judicial system, established to take the high-level perpetrators out of circulation, had created a judicial process that seemed specifically designed to set these perpetrators free at the first opportunity, ignoring the commitment under the Genocide Convention to properly punish the perpetrators of the crime.

The prisoners released were individuals who had relentlessly challenged the historical facts that formed the basis for their convictions and, with some success, had duped unwary journalists who seemed incapable of recognising their lies, fooled by their disinformation and fake news.

In setting them free, the Mechanism had enabled their ongoing campaign.[36]

The harm to survivors was incalculable. The early releases posed a direct threat to their rights and welfare, contributed to their suffering, demonstrated a callous indifference, and devalued the gravity of their experiences and memories. For them, genocide is a crime with no end.

Acknowledgements

Just before the completion of the manuscript, a letter came from the US Defence Intelligence Agency (DIA) in response to a Freedom of Information Act (FOIA) request submitted more than a year earlier. I had asked for the declassification of cables sent to Washington in April–July 1994 from US Defence Attaché offices in Paris and Brussels. They contained vital information about the Rwandan coup d'état on 6 April 1994 and how the murderous ideologues of Hutu Power began their extermination campaign. The response to my request from the chief of records management and information services, Brian L. Jenkins, was that the DIA held twenty-six documents of some 100 pages, and all would remain classified.

It is this culture of secrecy that ensures that twenty-five years afterwards information about the 1994 genocide of the Tutsi remains hidden in government archives. In the US documents that have been declassified there are numerous redactions. A scandal exists in France where successive governments have prevented access for historians and journalists to crucial military and political archives, including those of President François Mitterrand and the officials who worked in his unaccountable Africa Unit in the Élysée Palace. President Emmanuel Macron, faced with criticism in 2019, created a fifteen-member commission to visit relevant collections, offer a 'historian's critical view' and analyse the role of France. French academics signed a petition to protest the composition of the commission, which contained not one expert on the subject. The same problem exists in Canada, one of the best-informed governments about events in Rwanda in 1994. Yet in Canada government secrecy enabled officials to claim few had any idea what was happening. As the years went by, the blame slipped away from those whose decision-making had made a decisive difference. The longer these critical sources remain secret, the less likely that anyone will be called to account for a failure to heed warnings and respond appropriately as the massacres were getting under way.

Another consequence of excessive government secrecy is the opportunity it afforded the génocidaires. An information vacuum gave them free rein to spread lies and disinformation with a view to denying their crime. They deceived the Western press, promoting lies faster than the facts could debunk them – the subject of this book.

An honourable exception to government secrecy was the release by New Zealand of five volumes of declassified diplomatic cables donated to the Rwandan government. The Ministry of Foreign Affairs and Trade released official files from 31 March to 9 November 1994 in five volumes. In the late stages of writing this book, I met for the first time since 1994 the remarkable Felicity Wong, first secretary of the New Zealand mission to the UN, who has informed the entire course of my work.

While most governments were loath to share their secrets, at the UN Secretariat I was allowed access by Kofi Annan, then head of the UN Department of Peacekeeping, to the files of the UN Assistance Mission for Rwanda (UNAMIR). It was a privilege in 2014 to have been given by Lieutenant General Roméo Dallaire his own archive from Kigali – his diaries, cables and sitreps from October 1993, when he arrived in Rwanda until he left in August the following year.

I thank Fiona Terry, who was with Médecins Sans Frontières France in the refugee camps from September to December 1994. Terry kindly provided me with a collection of documents, the files of the Hutu Power government and military found in abandoned buses in a refugee camp in Zaire in 1996. Her experiences of the manipulation of aid for political and military ends led her to explore such dilemmas in depth and today Fiona leads research at the International Committee of the Red Cross to explore how to influence fighting forces to act with restraint.

The extraordinary access I obtained in Rwanda to the country's National Archives made a decisive difference to the last twenty-five years of research. It was a privilege to consult the collections that survived the three-month civil war in the city of Kigali. My thanks go to all Rwandans who over the years helped me – the officials, archivists, librarians, diplomats and military officers who were patient enough to put up with a constant quest for documents or a photocopier. For my friends who are survivors, and who trusted me with their memories, I am indebted to you for all you taught me.

Anyone who embarks on research into the circumstances of the 1994 genocide of the Tutsi will understand the debt we all owe to Jacques Morel for his dedicated research. I am grateful for advice from Jean-François Dupaquier and Jean-Pierre Chrétien, for their help and for receiving a copy of their 2002 expert report on Hutu Power hate speech and propaganda prepared for the International Criminal Tribunal for Rwanda and co-authored with Marcel Kabanda and Joseph Ngarambe.

Among the experts consulted and for professional help and guidance, I thank Professor Gregory S. Gordon, Richard Johnson and Assistant Professor Roland Moerland. I thank Mehdi Ba, Alain and Dafroza Gauthier, Yooreck Maczka, Everard O'Donnell, William Schabas, Rafiki Ubaldo and Jos van Oijen. I am indebted to a source in Brussels. I was lucky to have the wise counsel of Peter Greaves. I thank Peter Gillman who rescued this book at a critical stage, and I thank my editor, Leo Hollis, and the staff at Verso.

My nephew Michael Melvern, a skilled computer consultant, saved the manuscript at critical moments. He ensured documents were protected; his patient help came at the crucial moments. I thank loyal friends Deborah Burton, Nick Eveleigh, Julian Fraser, Leni Gillman, Doris Hollander, Cathy and Peter Nicholls, Bill and Jane Rees, Sue Snell and Sally Taylor.

My remarkable brother, Richard Melvern, was as heroic and steadfast as always. Without my husband, Phill Green, I might never have got this done, and he and our son, Laurence, showed extraordinary forbearance and good nature. Their support for my work was unyielding.

Thank you.

Linda Melvern
London 2019

Chronology

1885 The Berlin Conference decided that Ruanda-Urundi be designated a German protectorate.

1894 The first European arrived in Rwanda, a German, Count Gustav Adolf von Götzen.

1910 The frontiers of the Belgian Congo, British Uganda and German East Africa – including Ruanda-Urundi – were decided at a conference in Brussels.

1916 Belgian troops chased out the Germans and occupied both Ruanda and Urundi.

1923 Ruanda-Urundi designated a mandated territory of the League of Nations under the supervision of Belgium.

1931 King Musinga was deposed by the Belgian administration and replaced with one of his sons.

1933 The Belgian administrators organised a census and issued everyone an identity card with the classifications: Hutu, Tutsi or Twa.

1945 The transfer of the Belgian mandate to a UN Trust Territory.

1946 The first UN Trusteeship Council visiting mission travelled to Ruanda-Urundi and Tanganyika.

1957 Publication of the 'Hutu Manifesto'.

1959 *July*: King Mutara Rudahigwa died in suspicious circumstances.

August–September: Political parties were created along ethnic lines.

November: Attacks on Tutsi authorities and civilians; large numbers of Tutsi fled the country. Belgian military and civilian officials placed Rwanda under military rule.

1960   Rwanda's first municipal elections gave Hutu a large majority.

1961   *January*: The monarchy was formally abolished by a referendum and a republic proclaimed. More Tutsi fled in fear.

1962   Proclamation of the independence of Rwanda. Grégoire Kayibanda declared president.

1963   More armed attacks by Tutsi attempting an enforced return home.

1964   British philosopher Lord Bertrand Russell called the killing of Tutsi in Rwanda the most horrible extermination of a people since the extermination of the Jews.

1967   Renewed massacres of Tutsi. No arrests are made

1973   A purge of Tutsi from schools and the National University of Rwanda, Butare. More massacres of Tutsi take place. A coup d'état by Major Juvénal Habyarimana.

1975   Creation of the one-party Mouvement Révolutionnaire National pour le Développement (MRND). France and Rwanda signed a military assistance agreement.

1978   Habyarimana promulgated a new constitution.

1979   The Rwandan Alliance for National Unity (RANU) was created in Kenya.

1983   Re-election of President Juvénal Habyarimana with 99.98 per cent of the vote.

1986   The government in Kigali announced that Rwandan refugees would not be allowed home because the country was too small.

1990   *July*: Habyarimana conceded the principle of multiparty democracy.

September: Thirty-three Rwandan intellectuals published a letter to denounce the Hutu one-party system.

1 *October*: The Rwandan Patriotic Front (RPF) troops came across the northern border to enforce a return home of 1 million Rwandan refugees living in neighbouring countries. The civil war began.

1992 *February*: Massacres of Tutsi in Bugesera. Radio Rwanda was blamed for broadcasting incitement to murder.

Coalition pour la Défense de la République (CDR) and MRND militias built up by Hutu Power supporters.

10 March: Antonia Locatelli, an Italian nun, is murdered for speaking up against government-planned massacres in Bugesera.

April: Lewis Preston, president of the World Bank, warned Habyarimana he was aware of the 'militarisation' of Rwanda.

August: Formal opening of a peace conference in Arusha, Tanzania.

November: The planning for a new commercial radio station began.

1993 *January*: The composition of a broad-based Transitional Government was agreed at negotiations at Arusha.

More than 300 Tutsi killed in the northwest.

March: At the UN Security Council in New York, France suggested the creation of a UN peacekeeping mission for Rwanda.

April: UN Human Rights Commission Special Rapporteur on extrajudicial, summary or arbitrary executions Bacre Waly Ndiaye visited Rwanda and concluded the nature of the massacres of Tutsi meant that the Convention on the Prevention and Punishment of the Crime of Genocide, 1948, was applicable.

June: The Security Council adopted unanimously resolution 846 creating the United Nations Observer Mission Uganda–Rwanda (UNOMUR).

A Canadian brigadier general, Roméo A. Dallaire, was appointed commander of UNOMUR.

8 July: The first broadcasts of Radio-Télévision Libre des Mille Collines (RTLM) with a weak signal on 106 FM.

4 August: The Arusha Accords were signed between the Rwandan government and the RPF.

September: The secretary-general recommended to the Security Council that a peacekeeping force be provided for Rwanda without delay.

October: The UN Security Council passed resolution 872 creating the UN Assistance Mission for Rwanda (UNAMIR), which was to oversee the implementation of the Arusha Accords.

UNOMUR was integrated into UNAMIR.

December: UNAMIR peacekeepers were deployed. As part of the Arusha Accords a contingent of RPF troops arrived in Kigali.

In accordance with the Arusha Accords the French troops withdrew. An unknown number remained with the Detachement d'assistance militaire d'instruction.

1994 *January*: Rwanda took its seat as a non-permanent member of the Security Council.

The Security Council adopted resolution 893 approving deployment of a second infantry battalion to the demilitarised zone in northern Rwanda.

An informer told the UN of hidden weapons stocks and plans to kill Belgian peacekeepers. Militia were organising in military formation and their project was to kill Tutsi.

February: The minister of information complained that RTLM was broadcasting calls to racial hatred.

A moderate politician, Félicien Gatabazi of the PSD, was assassinated.

Martin Bucyana, the president of the CDR, was murdered.

March: The broadcasts of RTLM achieved countrywide reception for its racist incitement to murder.

5 April: The Security Council, with resolution 909, renewed the mandate for UNAMIR with the proviso that the peacekeepers would pull out entirely unless in six weeks the Arusha Accords were back on track.

6 April: President Habyarimana and President Ntaryamira of Burundi and a number of government officials returning from a regional summit in Dar es Salaam were killed in a missile attack as Habyarimana's plane came in to land in Kigali.

7 April: Systematic killing of Tutsi and opposition politicians began. Ten UN peacekeepers guarding the prime minister are murdered.

9 April: The evacuation of foreign nationals began.

12 April: French embassy in Kigali closed its doors at 9 a.m.

14 April: Belgium announced the withdrawal of its troops from UNAMIR.

21 April: The UN Security Council approved resolution 912 to withdraw the bulk of UNAMIR peacekeepers from Rwanda.

28 April: Oxfam issued a press release to all the foreign news desks on each British newspaper stating that the killing in Rwanda amounted to genocide. Minimal coverage.

29 April: An eight-hour debate in the Security Council about whether to use the word genocide in a Presidential Statement. The UK and the US resisted the use of the word.

22 May: The RPF took control of the airport and the Kanombe military camp and extended control over the north and eastern part of the country. The government fled south as the RPF advanced.

24 May: In Geneva the UN Commission on Human Rights held a special session to discuss human rights violations in Rwanda.

2 June: The RPF liberated the death camp in Kabgayi.

8 June: The Security Council adopted resolution 925, which extended the UNAMIR mandate until December 1994.

22 June: UN Security Council resolution 929 approved the French proposal to dispatch troops to Rwanda under a UN humanitarian mission.

18 July: RPF defeat of the remnants of Rwandan government troops and a unilateral ceasefire.

2 October: An interim report of the Security Council Commission of Experts concluded a genocide had been perpetrated against Tutsi.

8 November: The UN Security Council voted resolution 955 creating an International Criminal Tribunal for Rwanda (ICTR).

1995 January: ICTR produced a list of some 400 category-one suspects on the run.

27 February: The Security Council passed resolution 978 with a request to states to detain international fugitives.

1996 July: Fugitives met in a Nairobi hotel to decide a common defence strategy.

27 December: First genocide trials began in Rwandan courts hearing category-one genocide cases.

1997 January: First trial opened at the ICTR.

February: Report of the Office of Internal Oversight Services on the audit of the ICTR published.

18 July: Seven category-one fugitives are arrested in Nairobi, Kenya, with the prime minister of the Interim Government Jean Kambanda found in a converted garage.

1998   *January*: The publication of a series of articles by Patrick de Saint-Exupéry in *Le Figaro* on the role of the French authorities in the circumstances of the genocide.

3 March: The creation of an investigation known as a Mission of Information by the French National Assembly, an 'Inquiry on the Rwandan tragedy 1990–1994'.

27 March: The French judge Jean-Louis Bruguière began his inquiry into the assassination of Habyarimana.

July: The first conviction for genocide handed down in an ICTR courtroom when Jean-Paul Akayesu was sentenced to a life term.

2000   *May*: The first congress of the Forces Démocratiques pour la Libération du Rwanda (FDLR), the latest incarnation of Hutu Power's military wing.

October: The media trial began at the ICTR. Two defendants were found to be running their own websites promoting denial.

2001   The creation of the Collectif des Parties Civiles pour le Rwanda (CPCR), a pressure group created to 'provide moral and financial support for all those who bring legal cases against Rwandan genocide suspects, principally those on French soil'.

January: Rwanda passed an Organic Law which created the Gacaca courts, to put on trial low- and mid-level perpetrators. They were elected popular assemblies and comprised non-professional judges.

December: The Rwandan Ministry of Local Government produced a preliminary report based on a census and established there were 951,018 victims in the genocide of the Tutsi.

2002   *June*: The US Rewards for Justice programme launched to catch perpetrators indicted by the ICTR but still at large.

2004   *March*: *Le Monde* carried a front-page news story that the French judge Jean-Louis Bruguière had concluded that the RPF was responsible for the downing of the presidential jet on 6 April 1994.

7 April: At the tenth commemoration of the genocide President Paul Kagame denounced the determining role of France in the circumstances of the genocide

2005   *February*: *Hotel Rwanda*, a Hollywood film purporting to be based on a true story, released.

2006   *June*: The judges in an appeal decision at the ICTR (decision ICTR-98-44 Ar73) determined the genocide of the Tutsi an established fact of world history, constituting a matter of common knowledge.

July: The Gacaca trials began in Rwanda after a fifteen-month pilot period.

November: Bruguière published his full report blaming the RPF for downing the presidential jet and requesting nine international arrest warrants for senior members of the Rwandan government he held responsible.

December: Paul Rusesabagina awarded the Presidential Medal of Freedom by George W. Bush.

2007   The lawyer for the widow of the pilot of the presidential jet declared the Bruguière report was intended to whitewash those responsible in France. They had all been manipulated.

April: The Rwandan government named a commission to investigate the 6 April attack on the president's plane. It was named after its chairman Jean Mutsinzi, a former president of the Supreme Court in Rwanda.

2008   *April*: Paul Rusesabagina, the hero of *Hotel Rwanda*, appeared as a witness in a London courtroom to try to prevent the extradition to Rwanda of alleged génocidaires living in the UK.

2009   *April*: Kenneth Roth, executive director of Human Rights Watch (HRW), described the Gacaca courts as a form of repression.

October: Agathe Habyarimana was refused political asylum in France. The case remains on appeal.

14–16 November: A conference on the ICTR legacy from the 'defense perspective' was held in The Hague where it was argued the tribunal was a huge cover-up and ignored the 'complicity of the US and UK' in persecuting Hutu.

2010   *February*: President Sarkozy visited Kigali, the first official visit of a French president since Mitterrand in 1984. He pointed to grave mistakes and a failure to understand the genocidal intentions of those surrounding President Habyarimana.

May: Peter Erlinder, a US lawyer, arrested in Kigali for breaking Rwandan laws on genocide denial for stating publicly there was no planning, no genocide.

July: *The Politics of Genocide* by Edward Herman and David Peterson published, arguing that the Rwandan genocide never happened and the idea was an elaborate ruse by the US to gain a foothold in Africa.

2012 *June*: The official closure of the Gacaca courts during which 1 million suspects had been put on trial in community courts.

July: Judge Theodor Meron appointed president of MICT. He served until January 2019.

2014 *February*: France's first trial of an alleged génocidaire opened in Paris with Pascal Simbikangwa in the dock.

March: Simbikangwa sentenced to twenty-five years for his part in the genocide of the Tutsi.

2015 *July*: ITV News broadcast an interview with Jean Kambanda, who said he was innocent of all charges.

2017 *July*: UK High Court ruled that the five alleged génocidaires in the UK could not be returned to Rwanda.

2018 *June*: Valentine Rugwabiza, the Rwandan UN ambassador, complained to the UN Security Council that Judge Meron had used a secret and unaccountable process to allow génocidaires their freedom.

2019 *April*: President Emmanuel Macron announced a panel to study France's archives concerning Rwanda, with 15 members chosen by him.

Notes

1. Prime Suspects

1 Hutu Power was the name for the extremists' political grouping, first used in November 1993 at a political rally. The movement comprised the following political parties: Mouvement Révolutionnaire National pour le Développement (MRND), MDR Power faction, Coalition pour la Défense de la République (CDR) and senior military officers. Its voice was Radio-Télévision Libre des Mille Collines (RTLM). Hutu Power was also the name given to an ideology whose adherents were rabidly anti-Tutsi. Racist and nationalistic, its supporters were opposed to power sharing. Hutu Power sought the elimination of all Tutsi and all pro-democracy Hutu. The ideology of Hutu Power divided Rwandan society into three races – Hutu, Tutsi and Twa – each with distinct and different characteristics with the use of crude stereotyping. The ideology taught that Tutsi came from elsewhere in Africa. Rwanda 'belonged' to Hutu.

2 President Bill Clinton, speech in Kigali to survivors, 25 March 1998.

3 Gérard Prunier, *The Rwanda Crisis: History of a Genocide*, New York: Columbia University Press, 1997, 355.

4 Rwandan Ministry of Defence, 'Report on my journey to Cameroon', 14 March 1995. The following were identified as resident in Cameroon: Justin Mugenzi, Joseph Nzirorera, Pasteur Musabe and Ferdinand Nahimana (author's archive).

5 The names published in the newspaper are in US Embassy, Yaoundé, Cameroon, Cable to Secretary of State, Washington, DC (unclassified), Cable number 005956, 28 July 1995 (PTQ1589).

6 Mpiranya remains a fugitive and is believed to be in Zimbabwe as of 2018. In 2019 some reports placed him in South Africa.

7 Professor Gregory Gordon, 'On the Early Release of the "Rwandan Goebbels": American Free Speech Exceptionalism and the Ghost of the Nuremberg-Tokyo Commutations', Faculty Research Seminar, 31 January 2018.

8   Jean-Pierre Chrétien and Marcel Kabanda, *Rwanda, racisme et géno-
    cide: L'idéologie hamitique,* Paris: Belin, 2016; Ferdinand Nahimana,
    Le Rwanda. Émergence d'un état, Paris: L'Harmattan, 1993. The
    research of Nahimana was far from the sum total on ethnicity in post-
    independence Rwanda. For numerous and bitter academic arguments
    on this issue, see Johan Pottier, *Re-imagining Rwanda,* Cambridge:
    Cambridge University Press, 2002.

9   Colonel Théoneste Bagosora, 'L'assassinat du Président Habyarimana
    ou l'ultime opération du Tutsi pour sa reconquête du pouvoir par la
    force au Rwanda', unpublished (author's archive).

10 United States Department of State (9 August 1994), Cable number
    02676, 'International Criminal Tribunal for Rwanda'.

11 Email correspondence with Esther Mujawayo, 27 January 2014.

12 The members of the UN Security Council in 1994 were the US, UK,
    China, France and Russia (permanent members) and Czech Republic,
    Djibouti, New Zealand, Nigeria, Oman, Pakistan, Spain, Argentina,
    Brazil and Rwanda (two-year-term non-permanent members). For
    duty after failure see: 'The Long Road to Justice', *The Listener,* 21
    January 2016.

13 UN Security Council resolution 935, on 1 July 1994, mandated the
    creation of an impartial commission of experts to examine and analyse
    information concerning serious violations of international law, includ-
    ing genocide. The experts were Atsu Koffi Amega, a former president
    of the Supreme Court of Togo; Habi Dieng, a former attorney general
    of Guinea; and Salifou Fomba, a law professor in Mali who was a
    member of the UN International Law Commission. Interim Report of
    the Commission of Experts established in accordance with Security
    Council resolution 935 (S/1994/1125), 4 October 1994.

14 Final Report of the Commission of Experts established in accord-
    ance with Security Council resolution 935 (S/1994/1405), 9 December
    1994.

15 The mandate of the ICTR created by the Security Council under reso-
    lution 955 of 8 November 1994 was to bring justice for alleged human
    rights abuses of the Rwandan Patriotic Front, an issue discussed later
    in the book.

16 Colin Keating, 'An Insider's Account', in David Malone (ed.), *The
    UN Security Council from the Cold War to the Twenty-First Century,*
    Boulder, CO: Lynne Rienner, 2004.

17 Bill Berkeley, 'Judgment Day', *Washington Post,* 11 October 1998.

18 John Eriksson, Chapter 4: 'Rebuilding Post-Genocide Rwanda', *The
    International Response to Conflict and Genocide: Lessons from the
    Rwandan Experience,* 1996, 74.

19 Françoise Bouchet-Saulnier (Director of Legal Affairs, Médecins Sans
    Frontières), 'Justice dumb in the face of genocide', *Guardian,* 6 April
    1995.

20 Paul J. Magnarella, *Justice in Africa: Rwanda's Genocide, its Courts, and the UN Criminal Tribunal*, Ashgate, VT: Contemporary Perspectives on Developing Societies, 2000.

21 'Hutus pile on pressure', *Guardian*, 19 April 1995.

22 African Rights, *Rwanda: Death, Despair and Defiance*, London: African Rights, 1994.

23 UN Document, Security Council, 3504th meeting, 27 February 1995, S/PV.3504.

24 David Scheffer, *All the Missing Souls: A Personal History of the War Crimes Tribunals*, Princeton: Princeton University Press, 2012, 110. The aim of the US had been to authorise governments to arrest leading genocide suspects prior to their formal indictment and to coordinate efforts to investigate and track them down.

25 United States Department of State (12 July 1994), Cable number 184612, 'Consultations with France and Others on Rwanda War Crimes Issues'. See also: United States Department of State (23 July 1994), Cable number 197812, 'Rwanda: 22 July Security Council Meeting', United States Department of State (5 August 1994), Cable number 210227, 'Visit of A/S John Shattuck'.

26 Scheffer, *All the Missing Souls*, 61.

27 Frank Smyth, 'French money is behind the over arming of Rwanda', *New York Times*, 15 April 1994.

28 US declassified cable, State Department: Cable from Sec. State Washington to Embassy Yaoundé, 13 April 1995, PTQ3122. The four identified by the US authorities were Joseph Nzirorera, Justin Mugenzi, Ferdinand Nahimana and Pasteur Musabe.

29 They included Protais Mpiranya, commander of the Presidential Guard; military officers Lieutenant Colonel Leonard Nkundiye, Lieutenant Colonel Ephrem Setako and Major Augustin Barihenda; and politicians Joseph Nzirorera, Justin Mugenzi and Sylvain Mutabaruka.

30 The names given in a caption to the photograph in *Africa International*, 294, May 1996, are: André Ntagerura, Ferdinand Nahimana, Jean-Bosco Barayagwiza, Anatole Nsengiyumva, Théoneste Bagosora, Telesphore Bizimungu, Michel Bakazakundi, Augustin Ruzindana, Jean-Baptiste Butera, Pasteur Musabe, Laurent Semanza, Félicien Muberuka.

31 Jean-Marie Aboganena, 'Quelle diplomatie pour le Cameroun', *Africa International*, 294, May 1996.

32 Email correspondence with Lennart Aspegren, September 2018.

33 Magnarella, *Justice in Africa*.

34 The three others arrested in Cameroon with Nahimana and surrendered with him to the ICTR were: André Ntagerura, Colonel Anatole Nsengiyumva and Théoneste Bagosora. See ibid.

2. Propaganda Wars

1   The non-permanent members of the Council in April 1994 were New Zealand, Djibouti, the Czech Republic, Nigeria, Oman, Pakistan, Argentina, Brazil, Spain and Rwanda.

2   UNPROFOR also consists of 2,600 local civilian staff, 2,000 international staff, such as public affairs and information officers, 800 civilian police and 700 military observers. See 'Briefing Report to the Majority Leader, US Senate, Peace Operation, Update on the Situation in Former Yugoslavia', May 1995, US General Accounting Office.

3   UK FCO Cable, from Dar es Salaam, 21 February 1993.

4   Colin Keating, 'Rwanda: An Insider's Account', in David Malone (ed.), *The UN Security Council: From the Cold War to the Twenty-First Century*, Boulder, CO: Lynne Rienner Publishers, 2004, 504x.

5   USHMM – The Hague Institute for Global Justice Conference p. 224n4, 'International Decision-Making in the Age of Genocide: Rwanda 1990–1994', The Hague, 1–3 June 2014, Colin Keating.

6   Bacre Waly Ndiaye, Special Rapporteur for the UN Commission on Human Rights, visited Rwanda between 8 and 17 April 1993 to investigate human rights violations and 'arbitrary executions'.

7   Interview, Bacre Waly Ndiaye, UN Secretariat, New York, 10 October 2002.

8   Amnesty International, October 1990, May 1992; *Africa Watch*, February 1992, June 1993; International Commission of Inquiry, March 1993; UN Special Rapporteur, August 1993; and Human Rights Watch Arms Project, January 1994.

9   International Federation of Human Rights (FIDH), *Africa Watch*, InterAfrican Union of Human Rights, and International Centre for Human Rights and Democratic Development, Report of the International Commission of Investigation of Human Rights Violations in Rwanda since 1 October 1990 (7–21 January 1993).

10   CIA, 'Rwanda, Background to the crisis', Clinton Library, 9 April 1994, declassified in part.

11   USHMM – The Hague Institute for Global Justice Conference, transcript.

12   Colin Keating, 'Rwanda: An Insider's Account', in David Malone (ed.), *The UN Security Council: From the Cold War to the Twenty-First Century*, Boulder, CO: Lynne Rienner Publishers, 2004, 505.

13   Interview, Colin Keating, New York, 13 September 1994.

14   *Kangura*, 55, January 1994, Expert Report Media trial, Evidence number 26838.

15   There were eleven *préfectures*, each governed by a préfet (prefect). The *préfectures* were further subdivided into *communes* that were placed under the authority of *bourgmestres*.

16   The UN cables quoted are from the UNAMIR collection of Lieutenant General Roméo Dallaire (author's archive).

17 UNAMIR Force HQ, to Annan from Jacques-Roger Booh-Booh, SRSG, Kigali, MIR 723, 8 April 1994 (author's archive).
18 Assemblée Nationale, Mission d'Information Commune, *Enquête sur la tragédie rwandaise (1990–1994)*, Book III: *Auditions*, vol. 1, Paris, 296.
19 Lieutenant General Dallaire archive, UNAMIR Force HQ cable to Annan, UNATIONS, Daily sitrep, 10 April 1994.
20 Keating, 'Rwanda: An Insider's Account'.
21 New Zealand cable, New York to Wellington, 'Security Council: Rwanda', 27 July 1994.

3. The Ultimate Villain

1   ICTR, Bagosora et al., Testimony witness DAS, 7 November 2003.
2   ICTR, Transcript of sixty-hour interrogation of Jean Kambanda (author's archive).
3   Jean Hélène was murdered by a police officer in the Côte d'Ivoire on 21 October 2003 while working for RFI.
4   USHMM – The Hague Institute for Global Justice Conference, 'International Decision-Making in the Age of Genocide: Rwanda 1990–1994', The Hague, 1–3 June 2014, Jean-Philippe Ceppi.
5   Author interview, UNAMIR MILOB Major Jerzy Mączka, Oxford, October 2009.
6   Author interview, Philippe Gaillard, Lausanne, Switzerland, July 1997.
7   UN Doc. S/1994/531, 3 May 1994, Letter dated 13 April 1994 from the permanent representative of Rwanda to the UN, addressed to the president of the Security Council.
8   USHMM – The Hague Institute for Global Justice Conference, Prudence Bushnell, June 2014.
9   Interview, New York, First Secretary New Zealand Mission to the UN, Felicity Wong, 2 June 1994.
10 US Department of State, MGRWO1 Rwanda Monitory Group Secret, from 7 April 1994, 74, released in part.
11 Michael Barnett, *Eyewitness to a Genocide: The United Nations and Rwanda*, Ithaca: Cornell University Press, 2002, 76.
12 Security Council informal consultations, Contemporaneous account, 1 April–30 May 1994 (author's archive).
13 FOIA UK Doc., FCO UK mission to New York, Cable 1538, 30 April 1994, signed David Hannay.
14 Mission Permanente auprès des Nations Unies, New York. Monsieur le Ministre des Affaires Étrangères et de la Coopération, 6 June 1994, signed Jean-Damascène Bizimana, Ambassadeur (author's archive).
15 jacques.morel67.pagesperso-orange.fr/ccfo/crimcol/node46.html.
16 Jean-Marc Simon, 'Compte rendu de l'entretien avec le Ministre des

Affaires Étrangères', 27 April 1994, in Laure Coret and François-Xavier Verschave, *L'Horreur qui nous prend au visage*, Paris: Karthala, 2005, 494.

17 Ibid., 494.

18 New Zealand to Wellington, Security Council: Rwanda, 2 May 1994, Ministry of Foreign Affairs, Official Diplomatic Reporting, Volume 2, documents presented to Rwandan government, April 2019.

19 Déclaration de Son Excellence Mons. Jérôme Bicamumpaka, New York, May 1994 (author's archive).

20 Security Council informal consultations, Contemporaneous account, 1 April 1–30 May 1994 (author's archive).

21 UK Foreign and Commonwealth Office, unclassified, from the UK Mission New York to the FCO, 16 May 1994, released through FOIA to author, 2014.

22 US Department of State, 'Rwandan Radios', from INR/AA – Janean Mann to Ms A. Render, 3 May 1994, released in full.

23 Comité de Crise de la Communauté Rwandaise de Belgique, c/o Papias Ngaboyamahina, 'Déclaration du 7 avril' (author's archive).

24 Comité de Crise de la Communauté Rwandaise de Belgique, 7 April, Demande de retrait du contingent belge de la MINUAR, to UN SG (author's archive).

25 US Department of State, MGRWO1 Rwanda Monitory Group Secret, from 7 April 1994, released in part, 41.

26 République Rwandaise, Ministére des Affaires Étrangères, 'À l'attention des missions diplomatiques: Objet, Mise au point au sujet de la tragédie rwandaise', 15 April 1994 (author's archive).

27 Ambassade de la République Rwandaise, Mons. le Ministre, Objet, 'Entretien avec le Secrétaire Général du MINAFFET Belge', 29 April 1994, signed François Ngarukiyintwali (author's archive).

28 Ambassade de la République Rwandaise, Mons. le Ministre, Objet: 'Entretien avec le Secrétaire Général du MINAFFET Belge', 11 May 1994, signed François Ngarukiyintwali (author's archive).

29 Belgian Senate, Commission d'Enquête Parlementaire concernant les Événements du Rwanda, *Rapport,* Brussels: Sénat de Belgique, 6 December 1997.

30 US Department of State, unclassified, from Embassy Nairobi to Sec. State Washington, 8 April 1994, Nairobi 06321.

31 USHMM – The Hague Institute for Global Justice Conference, Lieutenant General Roméo Dallaire.

32 US Department of State Cable, Nairobi 06551, 12 April 1994.

33 US Department of State, Daily Activity Log, 8 April 1994, Cable number 092083, secret, released in full.

34 US Department of State, from Secretary of State Washington, State 139505, INR Assessments, 24 May 1994, declassified in part.

35 US Embassy Paris, to Secretary of State Washington, Paris 11541, signed Harriman, 28 April 1994, declassified in part.

36 US Embassy Paris, to Secretary of State Washington, Paris 11541, signed Harriman, 9 April 1994, declassified in part.

37 Defense Intelligence Report, Rwanda: The Rwandan Patriotic Front's Offensive (U) Key Judgements, secret, 9 May 1994, J2-210-94, declassified.

38 US Department of State, Declassified Information Memorandum, To M. Tarnoff from Toby T. Gati, Subject: 'Attempted Conflict Resolution in Rwanda and Burundi: what went wrong?', 27 May 1994.

39 US State Department, secret, from State to all African diplomatic posts, R 250700, May 1994.

40 Summary of testimony by Lieutenant General Roméo Dallaire and Major Beardsley, Evidence Analysis, Office of the Prosecutor, 16 December 2003 (author's archive).

4. Public Relations

1 Summary of testimony by Lieutenant General Roméo Dallaire and Major Beardsley, Evidence Analysis, Office of the Prosecutor, 16 December 2003 (author's archive).

2 Force Commander Archive, Original list with Interahamwe signatures (author's archive).

3 J. Morel and G. Kapler, 'Concordances humanitaires et génocidaires, Bernard Kouchner au Rwanda', 13 November 2006.

4 ICTR Prosecution Testimony, Lieutenant General Roméo Dallaire, Military One, 19 January 2004.

5 James Orbinski, *An Imperfect Offering: Dispatches from the Medical Front Line*, Toronto: Random House Canada, 2008, 201.

6 Laurence Binet, 'Genocide of Rwandan Tutsi', *MSF Speaking Out*, September 2003, 39.

7 Interview, Ambassador Colin Keating, New York, 4 June 1994.

8 Cable New York to Wellington. 'Security Council-Rwanda'. Ministry of Foreign Affairs, Official Diplomatic Reporting. 26 April 1994. Volume 5. Documents presented to Rwandan government April 2019.

9 USHMM – The Hague Institute for Global Justice Conference, 'International Decision-Making in the Age of Genocide: Rwanda 1990–1994', The Hague, 1–3 June 2014, Colin Keating.

10 UN Doc., 'Informal Consultations of non-paper', to Annan UNATIONS, from Dallaire, Outgoing Code Cable, MIR 952, 12 May 1994 (author's archive).

11 Binet, 'Genocide of Rwandan Tutsi', 53.

12 UN Doc., Force Commander's documents, to Annan from Dallaire, 20 July 1994.

13 Force Commander Archive, République Rwandaise, Ministère des Affaires Étrangères, Kigali, No. 168.03.00.CAB AP.

14 US Document, State Department, 'The French in Rwanda', Memorandum from Toby Gati to G. Wirth, 12 July 1994, declassified.

15 US Document, State Department, from Secretary of State Washington to US Mission New York, Telegram number: 167034, 22 June 1994, declassified.

16 UK FCO restricted, Subject: Rwanda: French initiative. Tel number 689, from Paris, 16 June 1994, declassified, FOI (author's archive).

17 New Zealand cable New York to Wellington, 17 July 1994.

18 New Zealand cable Ottawa to Washington, 21 July 1994.

19 FCO UN mission to London, 'Rwanda: French initiative', telegram number 2197, 21 June 1994, declassified.

20 FCO UN mission to London, 'Rwanda: French initiative', telegram number 2221, 23 June 1994, declassified.

21 Lieutenant General Roméo Dallaire, *Shake Hands with the Devil: The Failure of Humanity in Rwanda*, Toronto: Random House Canada, 2003, 425.

22 'Cholera in Goma, July 1994', *Bioforce Review Epidemiol Santé Publique*, 44: 4, August 1996, 358–63.

23 *The International Response to Conflict and Genocide: Lessons from the Rwanda Experience, Joint Evaluation of Emergency Assistance to Rwanda*, Copenhagen, March 1996, Vol. 3, 12. On 24 July, the UNHCR reported 2.1 million refugees and 1.4 million displaced within the French zone, and 1.2 million displaced in the rest of the country.

24 Binet, 'Genocide of Rwandan Tutsi'.

25 Jean-Francois Dupaquier, 'Seychelles: L'envers de la carte postale', *Karthala*, April 2019.

26 Philippe Dahinden, *Address given by Reporters without Borders before the United Nations Human Rights Commission Special Session on Rwanda*, 24 May 1994.

27 Jean-Marie Cavada, Jean-Pierre Bertrand and Sylvie Faiderbe, 'Rwanda: Autopsie d'un génocide', France 3, Production Theophraste, September 1994.

28 Brian Wood and Johan Peleman, Chapter 3: 'Brokering Arms for Genocide', *The Arms Fixers*, Washington, DC: NISAT, 1999.

29 Interviews with former Canadian army officer, 2019.

30 'Rapport de la réunion du Haut Commandement des Forces Armées Rwandaises et des membres des commissions tenue à Goma du 02 au 08 September 1994' (original given to author by Fiona Terry).

31 Fiona Terry, *Condemned to Repeat: The Paradox of Humanitarian Action*, Ithaca: Cornell University Press, 2002, 156.

32 Jérome Bicamumpaka, Rapport de Mission en France, Goma, 5 October 1994 (author's archive).

33 Bicamumpaka was arrested in Cameroon in 1999. He was put on trial on genocide charges at the ICTR and acquitted in 2011.

5. Crime Scene

1 Dr Gregory H. Stanton, 'Fixing the ICTR: conclusions of the AID/OTI team to Kigali and Arusha', November 1996 (author's archive).

2 UN Doc., Report of the Secretary-General on the Activities of the Office of Internal Oversight Services on the Audit and Investigation of the International Criminal Tribunal for Rwanda, A/51/789, General Assembly.

3 Carol Off, *The Lion, the Fox and the Eagle: A Story of Generals and Justice in Rwanda and Yugoslavia,* Toronto: Random House Canada, 2001.

4 John M. Goshko, 'Annan fires 2 top aides at the genocide tribunal', *Washington Post,* 28 February 1997.

5 UN Doc., Report of the Secretary-General on the Activities of the Office of Internal Oversight Services on the Audit and Investigation of the International Criminal Tribunal for Rwanda, A/51/789, General Assembly.

6 The UN Undersecretary-General for Legal Affairs was Hans Corell, 1994–2004.

7 Off, *The Lion, the Fox and the Eagle.*

8 Ibid.

9 M. Cherif Bassiouni, 'The Commission of Experts Established Pursuant to Security Council Resolution 780: Investigating Violations of International Humanitarian Law in the Former Yugoslavia', 5 CRIM, LF 279 (1994). M. Cherif Bassiouni was a professor of law; president, International Human Rights Law Institute, DePaul University; chairman, United Nations Security Council Commission Established Pursuant to Resolution 780 (1992) to Investigate Violations of International Humanitarian Law in the Former Yugoslavia.

10 M. Cherif Bassiouni, 'Appraising UN Justice-Related Fact-Finding Missions', *Journal of Law & Policy,* 5, 2001, 35.

11 Including from this author.

12 Nancy Amoury Combs, *Fact-Finding without Facts: The Uncertain Evidentiary Foundations of International Criminal Convictions,* Cambridge: Cambridge University Press, 2010, 167.

13 *The International Response to Conflict and Genocide: Lessons from the Rwanda Experience, Joint Evaluation of Emergency Assistance to Rwanda,* Copenhagen, March 1996.

14 The author consulted the SCR archive in Kigali, May–June 2011.

15 The agency changed its name to the Sûreté Nationale Rwandaise although the structure, methods and procedures stayed the same and remained in the control of the Belgian army intelligence officer responsible for its creation, Major Claude Turpin, replaced in 1963 by Bonaventure Ubalijoro.

16 Antoine Lema, *Africa Divided: The Creation of Ethnic Groups,* Lund: Lund University Press, 1993, 72.

17 Ibid., 72.

18 There were eleven *préfectures* in Rwanda. They were divided into 147 *communes* under the authority of a *bourgmestre,* appointed by the president. Each *commune* was subdivided into sectors and cells.

19 Raul Hilberg, *The Destruction of the European Jews*, New Haven: Yale University Press, 1961.

20 Author interview, Pierre Galand, 10 August 2018.

21 Commission of a Citizens' Inquiry into the Role of France during the Genocide of the Tutsi in 1994, Public session, 22–26 March 2004, Report, 'L'horreur qui nous prend au visage', Testimony Eric Gillet, 117. For twenty years, Birara has refused this author's numerous interview requests.

22 Colette Braeckman, 'À bout portant – Sur la situation actuelle du Rwanda et les perspectives d'avenir Jean Birara', *Le Soir*, 7 May 1994, 2.

23 Pierre Galand and Michel Chossudovsky, *L'Usage de la dette extérieure du Rwanda (1990/1994): La responsabilité des bailleurs de fonds*, Brussels and Ottawa, 1996.

24 'L'horreur qui nous prend au visage', 186. Testimony from Pierre Galand described countrywide arms distribution and mentioned the *préfecture* of Gitarama, with a population of 144,000 inhabitants, and 50,000 guns distributed.

25 ICTR-98-44, Amended Indictment.

26 'L'horreur qui nous prend au visage', Testimony Pierre Galand, 186.

27 'L'horreur qui nous prend au visage', Testimony Eric Gillet, 228.

28 IMF Rwanda, Briefing Paper – 1992 Article IV Consultation and Discussions on a Second Annual Arrangement, 14 May 1992, confidential (author's archive).

29 Rapport sur les financements du génocide au Rwanda: première expérience d'audit. Interview de Pierre Galand par Renaud Duterme, 29 Novembre 2016. For the interview and full report: www.cadtm.org/ Le Génocide (accessed 11 January 2018).

6. Denial

1 Rally for the Return of Refugees and Democracy in Rwanda, 3 April 1995.

2 Thierry Cruvellier, *Court of Remorse: Inside the International Criminal Tribunal for Rwanda*, Critical Human Rights, Madison: University of Wisconsin Press, 2006, 34.

3 Fiona Terry collection. Note au Chef d'État-Major FAR, de: Harelimana Célestin, pour Chef d'État-Major FAR, fait à Bulongo le 01.08.1996 (author's archive).

4 Michael Karnavas, 'The Quest for International Justice: National and International Efforts and Challenges', *The Champion*, May 1997.

5 Roland Moerland, *The Killing of Death: Denying the Genocide against the Tutsi*, Antwerp: Intersentia, 2016.

6 Case No. ICTR-96-4, Judgement 2 September 1998.

7 Cruvellier, *Court of Remorse*, 35.

8 Jean-François Dupaquier, *L'Agenda du génocide: Le témoinage de Richard Mugenzi ex-espion rwandais*, Paris: Karthala, 2010; *Encyclopaedia Britannica*, Biography, Rwandan Military Officer.

9 Testimony, Military One, 8 November 2005, 49.

10 ICTR Appeals Chamber, Théoneste Bagosora and Anatole Nsengiyumva v. the Prosecutor, Case No. ICTR-98-41-A_Dissenting view.

11 Bernard Lugan, *Le Génocide, l'église et la démocratie*, éd. du Rocher, 2004.

12 ICTR Bagosora et al., Transcript, 12 May 2005. See Bagosora et al., Judgement and Sentence, 534.

13 Peter Erlinder, The Rwanda Documents Project, Final Trial Brief Aloys Ntabakuze, Credibility of Defence Witnesses.

14 ICTR Judgement and Sentence, Bagosora et al., footnote 1627, 373.

15 Bagosora et al., Judgement and Sentence, 477.

16 Bagosora et al., Judgement and Sentence, 573.

17 See ICTR Prosecution cases against Édouard Karemera, Yussuf Munyakazi, Clement Kayishema, Obed Ruzindana, Eliézer Niyitegeka and Alfred Musema.

18 The first sentence of Article II of the 1948 Genocide Convention states acts of genocide must be committed with the intent to destroy a protected group.

19 The Prosecutor v. Théoneste Bagosora et al., Case No. ICTR-98-41-Judgement and Sentence 3, 18 December 2008.

20 The Tribunal's case law addressed the issue of conspiracy in eight cases: Kajelijeli, Kambanda, Musema, Nahimana et al., Niyitegeka, Ntagerura et al., Ntakirutimana and Seromba. Of the eight cases, a conspiracy was found by the Trial Chamber to exist in three of them: Kambanda, Nahimana et al. and Niyitegeka. Prime Minister Jean Kambanda pleaded guilty to conspiring with other ministers and officials in his government to commit genocide after 8 April 1994. The conspiracy conviction on Niyitegeka concerned a specific attack in the Bisesero region of Kibuye *préfecture* in June 1994 and was based on his participation and statements in several meetings in that region around the same time. In Nahimana et al., the Trial Chamber convicted the three accused 'for consciously interact[ing] with each other, using the institutions they controlled [Kangura, RTLM and the CDR party] to promote a joint agenda, which was the targeting of the Tutsi population for destruction'. However, the Appeals Chamber reversed the finding in Nahimana et al. because while the factual basis for the conviction was consistent with a joint agenda to commit genocide, it was not the only reasonable conclusion from the evidence. See page 42, Judgement and Sentence.

21 Thierry Cruvellier, 'ICTR Rwanda Genocide – no master plan', Radio Netherlands Worldwide, 19 December 2011, 151.

22 Ibid.

7. Monster Plot

1 Stephen W. Smith, 'Révélations sur l'attentat qui a déclenché le génocide rwandais', *Le Monde*, 10 March 2004.

2 Abdul Joshua Ruzibiza, *Rwanda: L'histoire secrète*, Editions du Panama, 2005.

3 francegenocidetutsi.org/OrdonnanceBruguiere.pdf. There is an English translation of this report from the International Criminal Tribunal for Rwanda: francegenocidetutsi.org/OrdonnanceBruguiereEng.pdf.

4 Jacques Morel and George Kapler, 'Analyse de l'ordonnance de soit-communiqué du juge Bruguière mettant en cause Paul Kagame pour l'attentat du 6 avril 1994 à Kigali', 12 January 2007.

5 Wikileaks, Classified Cable 1349 Rwanda: 'French Judge ends questioning of Rose', from Paris to Sec State, 11 October 2009.

6 Wikileaks cable, Secret, 07 Paris 322, 'Judge on France, Rwanda, Pakistan, and his political future', from Embassy Paris to Secretary of State Washington, signed Stapleton, 7 January 2007.

7 Morel and Kapler, 'Analyse de l'ordonnance'.

8 francegenocidetutsi.org/MemoHourigan.pdf.

9 Commission of a Citizens' Inquiry into the Role of France during the Genocide of the Tutsi in 1994, Report, 'L'horreur qui nous prend au visage', Testimony Colette Braeckman, 349.

10 Déclaration de Témoin, Abdul Ruzibiza, Investigators Hamidou Maiga and Mohamed Ali Lejmi, Redacted, 14, 17, 19 May 2002.

11 Letter to Le Chef d'État-Major de la Gendarmerie, from F.-X. Nsanzuwera, 29 March 1994 (author's archive).

12 UNAMIR CIVPOL from CPIO, H. J. Kranzl, Inspector to SRSG, 'Shooting of Minister of Public Works and Energy', 23 March 1994.

13 Interviews, 3–18 May 2014. Sources prefer to remain anonymous.

14 François-Xavier Nsanzuwera, 'Rapport d'expertise rédigé à la demande du tribunal pénal international sur le Rwanda: Procès contre Rutaqanda Georges, La criminalité des Interahamwe entre 1992 et avril 1994', Brussels, 21 June 1997.

15 Colette Braeckman, 'Le Rwanda le dos au mur', *Le Soir*, 23 February 1994.

16 Nsanzuwera, 'Rapport d'expertise'.

17 Assemblée Nationale, Mission d'Information Commune, *Enquête sur la tragédie rwandaise (1990–1994)*, 15 December 1998, Paris.

18 Ibid., Letter from Filip Reyntjens to Bernard Cazeneuve, 10 December 1998, Annexe 6, p. 251.

19 Morel and Kapler.

20 Alain Gabet and Sébastien Jahan, 'Quand la boussole perd le nord: 'Analyse de l'ordonnance' «Que sais-je ?» sur le génocide des Tutsi du Rwanda', *Cahiers d'Histoire. Revue d'Histoire Critique*, 139, 2018, 171–193.

21 The president of Burundi was Cyprien Ntaryamira.

22 Defence Academy of the UK, Cranfield University, Investigation into the Crash of Dassault Falcon 50. Contract Report by Mike C. Warden, Department of Applied Science, Defence Academy, Shrivenham, and W. Alan McClue, Fellow of Cranfield Forensic Institute, Annexes.

23 Republic of Rwanda, Committee of Experts Investigation of the 6 April 1994 Crash of President Habyarimana's Dassault Falcon 50 Aircraft, January 2010.

24 Report of Judge Marc Trévidic, Cour d'Appel de Paris, Paris, Tribunal de Grande Instance de Paris, Rapport d'expertise, Destruction en Vol du Falon 50, Kigali (Rwanda), 5 January 2012. The Commission of Experts comprised Claudine Oosterlinck, Daniel van Schendel, Jean Huon, Jean Sompayrac and Olivier Chavanis. The report is 314 pages long with twenty-four pages of conclusions numbered C1 to C24 and four annexes.

25 The interviews of Esther Mujawayo and Jean-François Dupaquier, 'Rapport Trévidic – Les Rwandais de France s'expriment', YouTube, 11 January 2012.

26 Esther Mujawayo, Souâd Belhaddad and Simone Veil, *Survivantes: Rwanda, dix ans après le génocide*, Aube: La Tour d'Aigues, 2004.

27 Stephen W. Smith, 'Rwanda in six scenes', *London Review of Books*, 17 March 2011.

28 Colette Braeckman, 'Ruzibiza était un temoin clé de l'attentat', *Le Soir*, 24 September 2010.

29 Letter from Emmanuel Ruzigana to Judge Bruguière, Oslo, 30 October 2006. See Morel and Kapler, 'Analyse de Cordennance', 6, note 23.

30 Jean-Philippe Ceppi, 'Les services secrets rwandais avaient leur central à Berne', *Le Quotidien*, 9 June 1994.

31 Commission Rogatoire Internationale siégeant au TPIR, Interrogatoire de M. Théoneste Bagosora, interrogé par le juge Jean-Louis Bruguière, le 18 mai 2000. Annexe 53 André Guichaoua: accessed on rwandadelaguerreaugenocide.univ-paris1.fr/wp-content/uploads/2010/01/Annexe_53.pdf.

32 Luc de Temmerman, 26 June 1994. Devant la Cour de Cassation, 2éme Chambre. Audience du 26 juin 1994. Attached Ex-Far equipment summary as of 6 April 1994 (author's archive).

33 ICTR-98-41Testimony, Théoneste Bagosora, 2 November 2005.

34 Author access to Kanombe camp and interviews, July 2012.

35 Grégoire de Saint Quentin has given the following statements: 26 May 1998 to the French Assembly Mission d'Information; on 8 June 2000 to the inquiry of Judge Jean-Louis Bruguière and on 7 December 2011 he sent a ten-page email to the Trévidic/Poux inquiry.

36   Bruguière report, 43.
37   Human Rights Watch Africa, *Rwanda: A New Catastrophe?*, London, December 1994.
38   UN Restricted, Daily Information Digest, Special Report Rwanda, DPKO-Situation Centre, CNR 530, 1 September 1994 (author's archive).
39   CIA, *Rwanda: Security Conditions at Kigali Airport: Capabilities and Intentions*, 13 July 1994, cia.gov/library/readingroom/docs/DOC_0000584721.pdf.
40   Gabet and Jahan, 'Quand la boussole perd le nord', 10.
41   René Lemarchand, 'Reconsidering France's role in the Rwandan genocide', Africasacountry.com, 13 June 2018.
42   Filip Reyntjens, *Le Génocide des Tutsi au Rwanda*, Paris: Que sais-je?, 2017.
43   Helen C. Epstein, *Another Fine Mess: America, Uganda, and the War on Terror*, Columbia Global Reports, 2017; Helen C. Epstein, 'America's hidden role in the Rwandan genocide', *Guardian*, 12 September 2017.

8. An Untold Story

1   Jean-François Dupaquier, *Politiques, militaires et mercenaires français au Rwanda: Chronique d'une désinformation*, Paris: Karthala, 2014, 161.
2   David Whitehouse, *In Search of Rwanda's Génocidaires: French Justice and the Lost Decades*, Niagara Falls, ON: Seraphim Editions, 2014, 261.
3   Ministére de Justice, intervention of Bruno Sturlese, 'La genèse des procès pour crime contre l'humanité: De l'affaire Barbie au génocide rwandais', *Table Ronde de l'Association Francaise pour l'Histoire et de la Justice* (AFHJ), 14 May 2014, mediateque.justice.gouv.fr.
4   Stéphane Audoin-Rouzeau, *Une initiation: Rwanda (1994–2016)*, Paris: Seuil, 2017. Audoin-Rouzeau is the research director at the École des Hautes Études en Sciences Sociales (EHESS) and the co-director of the Research Centre of the Museum of the Great War (Historial de la Grande Guerre), based in Péronne, in the Somme.
5   The White House, Statement of the Press Secretary, Office of the Press Secretary, for immediate release, 22 April 1994.
6   Testimony of Alison Des Forges to the House Committee on Foreign Affairs, subcommittee on Africa, 'The Crisis in Rwanda', 103rd Congress, 2nd Session, Hearings, 4 May 1994.
7   The Ligue pour la Défense des Droits de l'Homme et du Citoyen, the Fédération Internationale des Ligues des Droits de l'Homme (FIDH) and the Ligue Internationale contre le Racisme et l'Antisémitisme (LICRA).

8   *Rwanda, 20 ans après: L'histoire truquée,* film by Julien Teil and Paul-Éric Blanrue, Topdoc and Apocalypse France, 26 April 2014. See website: Conspiracy Watch.

9   Dupaquier, *Politiques,* 179.

10   CPCR website: Simbikangwa appeal, 9 November 2016.

11   Pierre Péan, *Noires fureurs, blancs menteurs: Rwanda 1990–1994,* Mille et Une Nuits, 2005.

12   *Rwanda, 20 ans après.*

13   Péan, *Noires fureurs,* 20.

14   Christian Davenport is professor at the Department of Political Science of the University of Michigan Institute for Social Research. Allan C. Stam is dean and professor at the Frank Batten School of Leadership and Public Policy at the University of Virginia.

15   Printed copy of email, Alison Des Forge to Barbara Mulvaney, ICTR Prosecutor, 22 December 2003 (author's archive).

16   Stam and Davenport, 6 October 2009, psmag.com/navigation/politics-and-law/what-really-happened-in-rwanda-3432, Kizito Michael George Library.

17   Christian Davenport and Allan C. Stam, 'What Really Happened in Rwanda?', *Miller-McCune,* 6 October 2009.

18   A conservative estimate in one study based on comparing local population data to the census data is that Tutsi were undercounted in the 1991 census by 40 per cent – see Marijke Verpoorten, 'The Death Toll of the Rwandan Genocide: A Detailed Analysis for Gikongoro Province', *Population,* 60:4, 2005, 331–367, available at cairn.info/revue-population-english-2005-4-page-331.htm.

19   UN Commission on Human Rights, Report on the Situation of Human Rights in Rwanda submitted by R. Degni-Ségui, Special Rapporteur of the Commission on Human Rights, 28 June 1994. The International Response to Conflict and Genocide: Lessons from the Rwanda Experience, Joint Emergency Assistance to Rwanda, Copenhagen, March 1996. Organisation of African Unity, Rwanda, The Preventable Genocide, Report of the International Panel of Eminent Personalities to Investigate the 1994 Genocide in Rwanda and the Surrounding Events, July 2000. Comprehensive Report on lessons learned from the United Nations Assistance Mission for Rwanda (UNAMIR), October 1993–April 1996, New York: United Nations, 1996.

20   Rwanda Ministry of Local Government, Preliminary Report, December 2001.

21   John Le Carré, *The Pigeon Tunnel: Stories from My Life,* New York: Viking, 2016.

22   The complaint to the BBC was joined by: Mehdi Ba, Bishop Ken Barham, Dr Margaret Brearley, Dr Gerald Caplan, Professor Frank Chalk, Jean-Pierre Chrétien, Senator Roméo Dallaire, Senator Alain Destexhe, Boubacar Boris Diop, Jean-François Dupaquier, Professor Margee Ensign, Dr Tim Gallimore, Alain Gauthier, Peter Greaves,

Fred Grunfeld, Dr Gabi Hesselbein, Dr Helen Hintjens, Dr Georgina Holmes, Nick Hughes, Dr Charles C. Jalloh, Marco Jowell, Richard Johnson, Eric Joyce MP, Ambassador Karel Kovanda, Françoise Lemagnen, Ambassador Stephen Lewis, W. Alan McClue, Linda Melvern, Dr Roland Moerland, George Monbiot, Jacques Morel, Barbara Mulvaney, Dr Jude Murison, Colonel Rich Orth (Ret), Professor James Putzel, Peter Raymont, Patrick de Saint-Exupéry, Jonathan Salt, Professor Josias Semujanga, Dr James Smith, Dr Cornelio Sommaruga, Keith Somerville, Professor Gregory H. Stanton, Rafiki Ubaldo, Dr Andrew Wallis, Lillian Wong.

23   The BBC trustees were: Rona Fairhead, chair, Sir Roger Carr, vice chair, Sonita Alleyne, Richard Eyre, Mark Damazer, Mark Florman, Bill Matthews (Scotland), Aiden McGinley (Northern Ireland), Elan Closs Stephens (Wales), Nicholas Prettejohn, Suzanna Taverne and Lord Williams of Baglan.

24   Roland Moerland, *The Killing of Death: Denying the Genocide against the Tutsi*, PhD Thesis, Maastricht University.

25   Ministère de la Justice, Cour d'Appel de Paris, Jean-Marc Hubert and Nathalie Poux, Réquisitoire Définitif aux fins de non-lieu, 11 October 2018.

26   Edward S. Herman and David Peterson in their book *The Politics of Genocide*, New York: Monthly Review Press, 2010. For brazen denial, see Moerland, *The Killing of Death*, 222.

27   Edward S. Herman and David Peterson, 'The Kagame-Power Lobby's Dishonest Attack on BBC Documentary on Rwanda', Pambazuka News.

28   Edward S. Herman and David Peterson, *Enduring Lies: The Rwandan Genocide in the Propaganda System, 20 Years Later*, Evergreen Park, IL: The Real News Books, 2014.

9. Decoding

1   Gérard Prunier, *The Rwanda Crisis 1959–1994: History of a Genocide*, London: Hurst and Company, 1995, 197.

2   African Rights, *Rwanda: Death, Despair and Defiance*, London: African Rights, 1995, 106.

3   Human Rights Watch/Fédération Internationale des Ligues des Droits de l'Homme, *Leave None to Tell the Story: Genocide in Rwanda*, 1999.

4   Human Rights Watch Africa, *Rwanda: A New Catastrophe?*, London, 1994, quoted in 'Comment se prépare la reconquête', *Le Monde Diplomatique*, March 1995.

5   Roland Moerland, *The Killing of Death: Denying the Genocide against the Tutsi*, Cambridge: Intersentia, 2016.

6   Ibid.

7   Hazel Cameron, *Britain's Hidden Role in the Rwandan Genocide: The Cat's Paw*, Oxford: Routledge, 2013.

8   Edward S. Herman and David Peterson, *The Politics of Genocide*, New York: Monthly Review Press, 2010.

9   Gerry Caplan, *Rwanda: The Preventable Genocide*, The Report of the International Panel of Eminent Personalities to Investigate the 1994 Genocide in Rwanda and the Surrounding Events were: Q. K. J. Masire, Botswana; Amadou Toumani Toure, Mali; Lisbet Palme, Sweden; Ellen Johnson- Sirleaf, Liberia; Hocine Djoudi, Algeria; Stephen Lewis, Canada; and P. N. Bhagwati, India.

10 Gerry Caplan, 'The Politics of Denialism: The Strange Case of Rwanda', 46, pambazuka.org/en/category/features/65265.

11 Daniela Kroslak, *The Role of France in the Rwandan Genocide*, London: Hurst and Company, 2007.

12 Agnès Callamard, 'French Policy in Rwanda', in Howard Adelman and Astri Suhrke (eds), *The Path of a Genocide: The Rwanda Crisis from Uganda to Zaire*, New Brunswick, NJ: Transaction, 1999, 168.

13 Asteris Huliaras, 'The "Anglo-Saxon Conspiracy": French Perceptions of the Great Lakes Crisis', *The Journal of Modern African Studies*, 36: 4, 1998, 594.

14 ICTR Document, Interview Notes of Colonel Bagosora with Kathi Austin from Human Rights Watch Arms Project, 15 February 1995 (author's archive).

15 Assemblée Nationale, Mission d'Information Commune, *Enquête sur la tragédie rwandaise (1990–1994), Audition Hermann Cohen*, 27 July 1998, Paris.

16 Ibid., Tome 1, *Rapport*, 359.

17 Barry Crawford, 'Rwanda: Myth and Reality', May 1997, retrieved from inshuti.org, 5 May 2004.

18 Chris McGreal, 'Genocide? What genocide?', *Guardian*, 3 March 2000.

19 Helen Hintjens, 'Explaining the 1994 Genocide in Rwanda', *Journal of Modern African Studies*, 37: 2, 1999, 241–286.

20 Rwanda: The Great Genocide Debate, conference papers and transcriptions, 27 July 1997 (author's archive).

21 Barrie Collins, *Rwanda 1994: The Myth of the Akazu Genocide Conspiracy and Its Consequences*, London: Palgrave Macmillan, 2014.

22 'La politique de la famille royale britannique', *Executive Intelligence Review*, 21: 43, 28 October 1994 (author's archive).

23 Keith Harmon Snow, 'The Rwanda Genocide Fabrications: Human Right Watch, Alison Des Forges & Disinformation on Central Africa', allthingspass.com, 6 April 2009. See also globalresearch.ca, taylor-report.com, sfbayview.com, zcommunications.org and black agendareport.com.

24 Keith Harmon Snow, 'The Grinding Machine: Terror and Genocide in Rwanda', allthingspass.com, 20 April 2007.

25 Edouard Kayihura and Kerry Zukus, *Inside the Hotel Rwanda: The Surprising Story and Why It Matters Today*, Dallas: Benbella Books, 2014. See also Alfred Ndahiro, *Hotel Rwanda, or the Tutsi Genocide as Seen by Hollywood*, Paris: L'Harmattan, 2008.

26 Alfred Ndahiro, *Impostor Made Hero in Hollywood*, 2009 manuscript, questionnaire results (author's archive).

27 SOS, 19 May 1994, Monsieur le Représentant de la CIRC, 21 May 1994 (author's archive).

28 Ancilla Mukangira, quoted in Ndahiro, *Impostor Made Hero*, 81.

29 Sabena, memo to Paul Rusesabagina from Michel Houtart, 18 May 1994 (author's archive).

30 Jonathan Beloff, 'Who is the real hero of *Hotel Rwanda*?', in Jean-Damascène Gasanabo, David J. Simon and Margee M. Ensign, *Confronting Genocide in Rwanda: Dehumanization, Denial and Strategies for Prevention*, Apidama Ediciones, 2015.

31 Taped interviews with Major Stefan Steć, London, April 2004.

32 Ibid.

33 Ibid.; see also Ndahiro, *Impostor Made Hero*, 59.

34 Alain Frilet, 'La France prise au piège de ses accords', *Libération*, 18 May 1994.

35 Jacques Morel, 'La France au coeur du génocide des Tutsi', *L'Esprit Frappeur*, 16:7.

36 Paul Rusesabagina with Tom Zoellner, *An Ordinary Man: The True Story Behind Hotel Rwanda*, New York: Bloomsbury, 2006.

37 Assemblée Nationale, Mission d'Information Commune, *Enquête sur la tragédie rwandaise (1990–1994)*, Tome III, *Auditions*, Vol. 1, 319.

38 Decision of the Westminster Magistrates' Court, Judgement, The Rwandan Government v. Vincent Bajinya, Charles Munyaneza, Celestin Ugirashebuja and Emmanuel Nteziryayo, 6 June 2008.

39 Ibid.

40 Ibid.

41 Jon Swain, 'Rwandan genocide suspect in Britain', *Sunday Times*, 29 January 2006.

42 African Rights, 'Charles Munyaneza. Evading Justice in Britain', *Witness to Genocide Series*, Issue 15, January 2006.

43 Trial, Profiles: trial-ch.org/en/resources/trial-watch/trial-watch, Emmanuel Nteziryayo.

44 Westminster Magistrates' Court, The Government of the Republic of Rwanda v. Vincent Brown (aka Vincent Bajinya), Charles Munyaneza, Emmanuel Nteziryayo, Célestin Ugirashebuja and Célestin Mutabaruka, Judgement, Deputy Senior District Judge Emma Arbuthnot, Deputy to the Chief Magistrate, 22 December 2015.

45 John Philpot, 'The ICTR – Justice Betrayed', September 1995, Africa Direct/philpot2.html (copy, author's archive).

46 johnphilpot.com.

47 Case No. ICTR-96-4, Judgement, 2 September 1998.

48 Case No. ICTR 94-4-T, Judgement and Sentence in the case of Jean-Paul Akayesu, 2 September 1998.

49 Situation of political prisoners of the ICTR in Mali and Benin [John Philpot-RPPSN, 08.09.2017] – L'HORA.

50 Law number 33 bis/2003: Repressing the crime of genocide, crimes against humanity and war crimes, Article 4.

51 Persecution not prosecution, retrieved from Cirque Minime/Paris Blog website: cirqueminime.blogspot.nl/2005/04/persecution-not-prosecution-by.html.

52 Letter, 'Rwandan "genocide"', *Guardian*, 15 June 2010.

53 Peter Erlinder, 'No Conspiracy, No Planning, No Genocide?', *Jurist Legal News and Research*, 24 December 2008.

54 Roland Moerland, *The Killing of Death: Denying the Genocide against the Tutsi*, Cambridge: Intersentia, 2016.

55 High Court of Justice, Queen's Bench Division, Case Nos.: CO/311/2016, CO/312/2016, CO/313/2016, CO/314/2016, CO/315/2016, 28 July 2017, Approved Judgement Lord Justice Irwin, Mr Justice Foskett, paragraph 20.

56 Anne-Marie Kundert, 'The Challenges of Extradition for International Crimes', Forum between Officers of the Prosecutors of the UN Ad Hoc Tribunals and National Prosecuting Authorities, 27 November 2008.

10. Infiltration

1 UNAMIR Outgoing Code Cable, 'Request for Protection for Informant', from Dallaire/UNAMIR/Kigali, to Annan, Attn. M-Gen Baril, 11 January 1994 (Dallaire Archive).

2 Rwanda was divided into ten *préfectures* comprising 146 *communes*. Each *commune* was organised into seven to ten *secteurs* and each of these divided into *cellules*.

3 Walter De Bock and Gert Van Langendonck, 'Legerstaf wist alles over nakende genocide Rwanda', *De Morgen*, 4 November 1995, 1.

4 ICTR Indictment, the prosecutor against Augustin Bizimungu, Augustin Ndindiliyimana, François-Xavier Nzuwonemeye and Innocent Sagahutu, Amended 25 September 2002, ICTR-00-56.

5 Christopher Black, 'View from Rwanda: The Dallaire Genocide Fax: A Fabrication', sandersresearch.com, 1 December 2005.

6 ICTR Ndindiliyimana et al., Witness T testimony, 24 May 2006.

7 To Force Commander from Deme, routing slip, handwritten note, 23 February 1994 (Dallaire Archive).

8 ICTR-00-5656 Prosecutor v. Augustin Ndindiliyimana, François-Xavier Nzuwonemeye, Innocent Sagahutu, Augustin Bizimungu. Testimony, Colonel Frank Claeys, 13 October 2005.

9   Christopher Black, 'View from Rwanda: The Dallaire Genocide Fax: A Fabrication', Sandersresearch.com, 1 December 2005. The story is reproduced in Hazel Cameron, *Britain's Hidden Role in the Rwandan Genocide: The Cat's Paw*, Oxford: Routledge, 2013.

10 Christopher Black, 'The Criminalization of International Justice', delivered at the 12th Rhodes Forum on 26 September 2014, The Slobodan Milošević Committee.

11 ICTR-98-41 Bagosora et al., Testimony of Colonel Frank Claeys, 7 April 2004.

12 ICTR-98-44, 23 November 2006, Karemera et al.

13 To Force Commander from Deme, routing slip, handwritten note, 23 February 1994 (Dallaire Archive).

14 Dallaire, *Shake Hands*, 143.

15 De Bock and Van Langendonck, 'Legerstaf wist alles over nakende genocide Rwanda'.

16 'Ghosts of Rwanda', Frontline PBS, 1 April 2004.

17 Interview with Iqbal Riza, The Hague, September 2014.

18 UNAMIR Outgoing Code Cable, 'Initiatives undertaken relating to latest security information', to Annan from Booh-Booh, 13 January 1994 (Dallaire Archive).

19 Roméo Dallaire, *Shake Hands with the Devil: The Failure of Humanity in Rwanda*, Toronto: Random House Canada, 2003.

20 UNAMIR Outgoing Code Cable, 'Further Information from Informant', from Dallaire/UNAMIR/Kigali, to Annan, Attn. M-Gen Baril, 12 January 1994 (Dallaire Archive).

21 Dirk Draulans, *Knack*, 20 December 2006.

22 The Proxy Lake, 'Rwanda: "Genocide of Tutsis", the Biggest Lie of the Century', theproxylake.com/2010/10/genocide-of-tutsis/3.

23 Letter addressed to Sara J. Bloomfield, 27 January 2014, signed by Dr Gregory Stanton, Professor Frank Chalk, Dr Gerry Caplan, Barbara Mulvaney, Stephen D. Smith, Dr James M. Smith, Professor Payam Akhavan, Esther Mujawayo, Linda Melvern, Ambassador Stephen Lewis, Major Brent Beardsley and Professor Margee Ensign.

24 André Guichaoua, *Rwanda: De la guerre au génocide*, Paris: Découverte, 2010, 228–9.

25 Hélène Dumas, 'Réflexion sur l'ouvrage d'André Guichaoua, *Rwanda: De la Guerre au Génocide*, Les politiques criminelles au Rwanda (1990–1994)', Paris: La Découverte, 2010.

26 Félicien Kabuga (fugitive) was a major financier of RTLM.

11. Identity

1   Joan Kakwenzire and Dixon Kamukama, 'The Development and Consolidation of Extremist Forces in Rwanda 1990–1994', in Howard

Adelman and Astri Suhrke (eds), *The Path of a Genocide*, Piscataway, NJ: Transaction Publishers, 1999.

2 Jean-Philippe Ceppi, *Le Nouveau Quotidien*, August 1994, 4.

3 Article 19, *Broadcasting Genocide: Censorship, Propaganda and State-Sponsored Violence in Rwanda, 1990–1994*, International Centre against Censorship, London, October 1996, 85–6.

4 There are currently four official languages in Rwanda: English, French, Kinyarwanda and Kiswahili.

5 ICTR-99-52 Summary Judgement, 3 December 2003.

6 Mary Kimani, 'RTLM: The Medium that Became a Tool for Mass Murder', in Allan Thompson (ed.), *The Media and the Rwandan Genocide*, Ottawa: International Development Research Centre, 2007, 110.

7 ICTR-96-11 Prosecutor v. Nahimana et al., Witness testimony, Matthias Ruzindana, 19 March 2002.

8 Noel Hitimana, RTLM, 3 April 1994.

9 Jean-Pierre Chrétien et al., *Rwanda: Les médias du génocide*, Paris: Karthala, 1995, 61.

10 Jean-Pierre Chrétien, *Le Défi de l'éthnisme*, Paris: Kasthala, 2012, 243.

11 Assemblée Nationale, Mission d'Information Commune, *Enquête sur la Tragédie Rwandaise (1990–1994)*, Vol. 1, 96.

12 Gérard Prunier, *The Rwanda Crisis: History of a Genocide*, London: Hurst and Company, 1995, 147.

13 Press release, 'Déclaration sur les massacres en cours de la population de la région du Bugesera', Kigali, 10 March 1992 (author's archive).

14 Bugesera comprised three *communes*: Kanzenze, Gashora and Ngenda, and it borders Burundi.

15 François-Xavier Nsanzuwera, *La Magistrature dans l'étau du pouvoir exécutif*, Kigali: CLADO, 1993.

16 ICTR expert report.

17 François-Xavier Nsanzuwera, *Rapport d'expertise rédigé à la demande du tribunal pénal international sur le Rwanda: Procès contre Rutaqanda Georges: La criminalité des Interahamwe entre 1992 et avril 1994*, Brussels, 21 June 1997.

18 Assemblée Nationale, Mission d'Information Commune, *Enquête sur la tragédie rwandaise (1990–1994)*, Vol. 1, 95.

19 J. J. Carney, *Rwanda Before the Genocide: Catholic Politics and Ethnic Discourse in the Late Colonial Era*, Oxford: Oxford University Press, 2013, 197.

20 Chrétien et al., *Rwanda: Les médias du génocide*, 51.

21 Hutu Power as a political grouping emerged in November 1993 and comprise MRND, MDR Power faction, CDR and senior military officers, with RTLM as its voice.

22 Deguine, 122.

23 Letter from Ambassade de France au Rwanda to Boniface Ngulinzira, Kigali, 14 March 1989 (author's archive).

24 Chrétien et al., *Rwanda: Les médias du génocide*, 51.

25 Deguine, 176.

26 Letter: Interahamwe MRND cell to the national secretary of the MRND Kigali, 5 May 1992. See expert report attachment, 26999.

27 L'indomptable Kinani, No. 1, May 1992, printing house proof, quoted in Chrétien et al., *Rwanda: Les médias du génocide*, 62.

28 ICTR Expert report 27069.

29 Ferdinand Nahimana, *Le Rwanda: Émergence d'un état*, Paris: L'Harmattan, 1993.

30 By 1921, the Force Publique Congolais had 650 men under arms in Ruanda-Urundi, with 230 in Kitega (Burundi), and the equivalent in Kigali, also seven officers from Europe, one officer for each unit. Overall command rested with a commander in Katanga.

31 Ferdinand Nahimana, 'Les principautés hutu du Rwanda septentrional', *La Civilisation ancienne des peuples des Grands Lacs*, Paris, 1981.

32 Dina Temple-Raston, *Justice on the Grass: Three Rwandan Journalists, Their Trial for War Crimes, and a Nation's Quest for Redemption*, New York: Simon and Schuster, 2005, 186.

33 There is no consensus among historians or anthropologists on the origins of the divisions of Hutu and Tutsi, so crucial to Rwanda's history. There is some evidence that the meanings attached to these categories changed significantly over time. The identities altered, and the meanings evolved differently in different places. There existed many criteria for the classification of Hutu and Tutsi, including birth, wealth in cattle, culture, place of origin, physical attributes and social and marriage ties. Hutu, Tutsi and Twa share the same language and culture. They lived together for centuries with no formal distinction and many Rwandans, not least southerners, have a 'mixed' background. The groups are not tribes. The groups are sometimes compared with castes including clans and extended families. See Chapter Two of *A People Betrayed*, 2009.

34 Gérard Prunier, *Rwanda: La crise rwandaise: Structures et déroulement*, July 1994, writenet.

35 Professor Gregory S. Gordon, *Atrocity Speech Law: Foundation, Fragmentation, Fruition*, Oxford: Oxford University Press, 2017.

36 Mary Kimani, 'RTLM: The Medium that Became a Tool for Mass Murder', in Allan Thompson (ed.), *The Media and the Rwandan Genocide*, Ottawa: International Development Research Centre, 2007, 110.

37 Charles Mironko, 'RTLM's Rhetoric of Ethnic Hatred in Rural Rwanda', in Thompson (ed.), *The Media*, 127.

38 Expert Report, Paris, 15 December 2001, by Jean-Pierre Chrétien with Jean-François Dupaquier, Marcel Kabanda and Joseph Ngarambe, Attachment to ICTR office memorandum, Disclosure of English translation, 15 February 2002 (author's archive). See also Chrétien et al., *Rwanda: Les médias du génocide*.

39 Jean-Pierre Chrétien and Marcel Kabanda, *Rwanda, racisme et génocide: L'idéologie hamitique*, Paris: Editions Belin, 2013.

40 Ibid.

41 ICRC, 'ICTR, The Media Case,' icrc.org.

42 ICTR Summary Judgement, Prosecutor v. Ferdinand Nahimana, Jean-Bosco Barayagwiza, Hassan Ngeze, Cast no ICTR-99-52, 3 December 2003.

43 Navi Pillay sat with Erik Møse of Norway and Asoka de Zoysa Gunawardana of Sri Lanka.

44 ICTR Media Trial Documentary, Parts 1–5, YouTube, accessed on 24 March 2017.

45 Dina Temple-Raston, *Justice on the Grass: Three Rwandan Journalists, Their Trial for War Crimes, and a Nation's Quest for Redemption*, New York: Simon and Schuster, 2005, 204.

46 Hervé Deguine, *Un idéologue dans le génocide rwandais: Enquête sur Ferdinand Nahimana*, Mille et Une Nuits, 2010, 122.

47 ICTR Media Trial Documentary, Parts 1–5, YouTube, accessed on 24 March 2017.

48 ICTR-99-52 Judgement and Sentence, 3 December 2003.

49 Barayagwiza died on 25 April 2010 in a hospital in Porto-Novo in Benin, where he was serving his sentence.

50 MIP Tome I, 141. In a 19 December 1990 diplomatic telegram, Ambassador Martres wrote: 'The latest issue of the paper *Kangura* of which I have reported in my TD 740 of December 17 has further accentuated the nervousness of the population within which the ideology of Hutu extremism gains ground with some, whereas it terrorises others'. *Id.* Tome II, 139.

51 Expert Report: P 27193, 27188 and 27816, ICTR document (author's archive).

52 ICTR Media Trial, Summary judgement and sentence, 21–22.

53 The financing of the ICTR is discussed in a later chapter.

54 Emily Wax, 'Journalists sentenced in Rwanda genocide', *Washington Post*, 3 December 2003.

55 Scott Straus, *The Order of Genocide: Race, Power and War in Rwanda*, Ithaca: Cornell University Press, 2006.

56 Ibid., 134–135.

57 See book review by David Backer, *The Order of Genocide: Race, Power and War in Rwanda*, by Scott Straus, in *Taiwan Journal of Democracy*, 4: 1, July 2008, 179–85.

58 Scott Straus, 'Studying Perpetrators: A Reflection', *Journal of Perpetrator Research*, 1:1, 2017, 28–38.

59 David Yanagizawa-Drott, *Propaganda and Conflict: Theory and Evidence from the Rwandan Genocide*, The Bureau for Research and Economic Analysis of Development, 2010, 27–28. To measure participation in the violence, the author used a nationwide village-level dataset on persons prosecuted for violent crimes committed during

the Rwandan genocide. The data came from the government agency National Service of Gacaca Jurisdictions. The prosecution data for each village came from local so-called Gacaca courts. This court system was set up in 2001 to process the hundreds of thousands of individuals accused of crimes committed during the genocide.

60 Frank G. Wisner, undersecretary of defence, Department of Defense, 'Memorandum for Deputy Assistant to the President for National Security Affairs, National Security Council', 5 May 1994, declassified 1-94/16544, Clinton Library.

61 New Zealand cables, from New York to Wellington, 'Security Council: Rwanda', 27 June 1994.

62 Force Commander Archive, Rwanda, 27 June, CNR 353, p 2.

12. Moral Equivalence

1 Conseil restreint du 13 avril 1994, Mitterrand archives, as cited in Jacques Morel, 'L'Inversion des rôles des tueurs et des victimse', in *Génocide des Tutsi du Rwanda: Un Négationnisme francais?*, Cités 57, 2014.

2 Philip Short, *Mitterrand: A Study in Ambiguity*, London: The Bodley Head, 2013.

3 Alain Juppé, 'Point de vue, "Intervenir au Rwanda"', *Libération*, 19 June 1994.

4 Gérard Prunier, *The Rwanda Crisis 1959–1994: History of a Genocide*, London Hurst, 1995, 339.

5 Roland Moerland, *The Killing of Death: Denying the Genocide against the Tutsi*, Cambridge: Intersentia, 2016, 167–171.

6 UN Security Council, 3377th meeting, 16 May 1994, S/PV.337.

7 Jos van Oijen, '*In Praise of Blood*: Sensational, but Does it Fit with Reality?', *ZAM Magazine*, 19 December 2019.

8 Mark Huband, 'Church of the Holy Slaughter', *Observer*, 6 June 1994.

9 Mark Doyle, 'Reporting the Genocide', in Allan Thompson (ed.), *The Media and the Rwandan Genocide*, London: Pluto Press, 2007.

10 Laurence Binet, 'Genocide of the Rwandan Tutsis', *MSF Speaking Out*, September 2003.

11 Larry Minear and Philippe Guillot, *Soldiers to the Rescue: Humanitarian Lessons from Rwanda*, Paris: Development Centre of the Organisation for Economic Cooperation and Development, 1996, 63.

12 John Eriksson et al., *The International Response to Conflict and Genocide*, Vol. 3, Paris: OECD, 96.

13 Fiona Terry, *Condemned to Repeat? The Paradox of Humanitarian Action*, Ithaca: Cornell University Press, 2002.

14 Amnesty International, *Rwanda and Burundi: The Return Home:*

Rumours and Realities, London, January 1996, cited in Fiona Terry, *Condemned to Repeat?*

15 African Rights, *Rwanda: Death, Despair, Defiance*, London, August 1995, 1084–1085.

16 The Gersony team of three people with anonymous Rwandan interpreters claimed to have visited nine UNHCR refugee camps and ninety-one locations in Rwanda, and interviewed more than 200 individuals. There were 14 *communes* in Rwanda.

17 US Department of State, 'Rwanda – Geneva Conventions', from Toby Gati to George Moose, 16 May 1994, declassified in part.

18 UNAMIR became UNAMIR II on 17 May 1994 under Security Council resolution 918.

19 UN Document, Outgoing Code-cable, The Gersony Report, Rwanda, to Annan, Goulding, from Shaharyar Khan, UNAMIR Kigali, 14 October 1994.

20 US State Department, Rwanda/Burundi Situation Report, 23 September 1994, declassified in full.

21 Interviews with Dr Phillip Drew, associate professor, Australian National University, College of Law, 2019.

22 US State Department, Country Director's evaluation of post reporting for Rwanda, from Ste to Kigali, State 307914, 16 November 1994.

23 Thomas P. Odom, *Journey into Darkness: Genocide in Rwanda*, College Station, TX: Texas A&M University Press, 2005.

24 US State Department, Kigali 02142, '11/10 Tour d'Horizon with French chargé', from Kigali to Secretary of State, Washington, 10 November 1994.

25 US State Department, 'UNHCR team finds evidence in Rwanda, from Christopher to US Embassy Kigali', State 254232, 20 September 1994, unclassified, released in full.

26 Interview, Oxford, 2013.

27 Human Rights Watch/Fédération Internationale des Ligues des Droits de l'Homme, *Leave None to Tell the Story: Genocide in Rwanda*, 1999.

28 Robin Philpot, *Rwanda and the New Scramble for Africa*, Montreal: Baraka Books, 2013.

29 Gerry Caplan, 'Rwanda's genocide: first the deed and then the denial', *The Globe and Mail*, 13 March 2007.

30 Conference, International Decision-Making in the Age of Genocide, 1–3 June 2014, Museum's Simon-Skjodt Centre for the Prevention of Genocide and The Hague Institute for Global Justice, in cooperation with the National Security Archive at George Washington University.

31 Filip Reyntjens, 'Les transitions politiques au Rwanda et Burundi', in *L'Afrique des Grands Lacs: Dix ans de transition conflictuelle*, Paris: L'Harmattan, 2006, 7.

32 Mahmood Mamdani, *When Victims Become Killers: Colonialism, Nativism, and the Genocide in Rwanda*, Princeton, NJ: Princeton University Press, 2001, 139.

33 Filip Reytnjens, *Trois décennies comme chercheur-acteur au Rwanda et au Burundi*, Paris: L'Harmattan, 2009, 45.

34 International Symposium, ICTR, 'Model or Counter Model for International Criminal Justice? The Perspective of the Stakeholders', Geneva, 3–5 July 2009.

35 See also William Schabas, *Unimaginable Atrocities: Justice, Politics, and Rights at the War Crimes Tribunals*, Oxford: Oxford University Press, 2012, 96.

36 Mark Doyle, 'Reporting the Genocide', in Allan Thompson (ed.), *The Media and the Rwandan Genocide*, London: Pluto Press, 2007.

37 Ibid.

38 Interviews with a survivor of Kabgayi at the commemoration of the liberation of the camp, 2 June 2014.

39 J. J. Carney, *Rwanda Before the Genocide: Catholic Politics and Ethnic Discourse in the Late Colonial Era*, Oxford: Oxford University Press, 2013, 2.

40 James Schofield, *Silent Over Africa: Stories of War and Genocide*, Sydney: HarperCollins, 1996, 158–159.

41 Scott Peterson, *Me Against My Brother*, London: Routledge, 2001, 277.

42 Lieutenant General Roméo Dallaire, *Shake Hands with the Devil: The Failure of Humanity in Rwanda*, Toronto: Random House Canada, 2003, 185.

43 Letter from HRW to Hassan Jallow, 13 August 2009.

44 International Symposium, ICTR.

45 Letter from Hassan Jallow to Kenneth Roth, 22 June 2009 (author's archive).

46 William Schabas, paper prepared for a conference on 1 July 2008. It is entitled 'Transfer and Extradition of Genocide Suspects to Rwanda'; quoted in 'In the High Court of Justice Divisional Court on appeal from the City of Westminster Magistrates' Court' (District Judge Evans), Lord Justice Laws and Lord Justice Sullivan. Between: Vincent Brown, aka Vincent Bajinya, Charles Munyaneza, Emmanuel Nteziryayo, Célestin Ugirashebuja, Appellants, and the Government of Rwanda. 8 April 2009.

47 Solange Nyiramwizce, 'The Travesty of Human Rights Watch on Rwanda (Richard Johnson)', medium.com, 21 July 2016.

48 Alex de Waal, 'Becoming Shameless: The Failure of Human Rights Organisations in Rwanda', *Times Literary Supplement*, 21 February 1997.

49 Anne-Marie Kundert, 'The Challenges of Extradition for International Crimes', Forum between Officers of the Prosecutors of the UN Ad Hoc Tribunals and National Prosecuting Authorities, 27 November 2008.

50 de Waal, 'Becoming Shameless'.

13. The Mechanism

1   MICT press office was unable to provide an exact date in spite of repeated requests.

2   ICTR-99-52, Prosecutor C. Ferdinand Nahimana, Jean-Bosco Barayagwiza and Hassan Ngeze, Judgement and Sentence, 3 December 2003.

3   MICT 13-37-ES1, Public Redacted Version of the 22 September 2016 decision for the early release of Ferdinand Nahimana, 0045/1.

4   They are: Jean-Paul Akayesu, Théoneste Bagosora, Sylvestre Gacumbitsi, Jean Kambanda, Jean de Dieu Kamuhanda, Mikaeli Muhimana, Yussuf Munyakazi, Alfred Musema, Hassan Ngeze, Eliézer Niyitegeka, Tharcisse Renzaho and Laurent Semanza.

5   This is specified in the agreement between the UN and the government of Mali dated 12 February 1999, which reads: 'Standard Minimum Rules for the Treatment of Prisoners approved by ECOSOC resolutions 663 C (XXIV) of 31 July 1957 and 2067 (LXII) of 13 May 1977, the Body of Principles for the Protection of all Persons under any Form of Detention or Imprisonment adopted by General Assembly resolution 43/173 of 9 December 1988, and the Basic Principles for the Treatment of Prisoners adopted by General Assembly resolution 45/111 of 14 December 1990'.

6   Judge Meron, Public redacted version of the 22 September 2016 decision of the president of the early release of Ferdinand Nahimana, MICT-13-37-ES.1.

7   The three lawyers are: Jean-Marie Biju-Duval, Diana Ellis QC and Joanna Evans.

8   Jessica M. Kelder, Barbora Holá and Joris van Wijk, 'Rehabilitation and Early Release of Perpetrators of International Crimes: A Case Study of the ICTY and ICTR', *International Criminal Law Review*, 14, 2014, 1177–1203.

9   'Men Behind Rwandan Genocide Languish in Mali Prison', Capital News FM, 6 April 2014, Bamako.

10   Ferdinand Nahimana, *Rwanda: Les virages ratés*, Éditions Source du Nil, 2007; Ferdinand Nahimava, *Le Combat pour la vérité*, Éditions Source du Nil, 2011.

11   Ferdinand Nahimana, 'Réponse de Ferdinand Nahimana à Jean-Baptiste Nkuliyingoma', *France-Rwanda Tribune*, 11 March 2012.

12   Robin Philpot, *Rwanda and the New Scramble for Africa: From Tragedy to Useful Imperial Fiction*, Montreal: Baraka Books, 2013.

13   For a detailed legal argument see Gregory S. Gordon, *Atrocity Speech Law: Foundation, Fragmentation, Fruition*, Oxford: Oxford University Press, 2017, 235.

14   ICTR-99-52-A, Prosecutor v. Ferdinand Nahimana, Jean-Bosco Barayagwiza, Hassan Ngeze.

15   Gordon, *Atrocity Speech*.

16 Bill Berkeley, 'Judgement Day', *Washington Post*, 11 October 1998.

17 ICTR, The Prosecutor v. Jean-Paul Akayesu, Case No. ICTR-96-4-I, Judgment, 2 September 1998, in particular paras 692 (re: crimes of humanity of rape and other inhuman acts), 731 (re: genocide) and 687 (re: torture).

18 Pamela Shipman and Lauren Rumble, 'Neglected Challenges: The Humanitarian Responsibility to Protect', in OCHA, *The Shame of War: Sexual Violence Against Women and Girls in Conflict*, Integrated Regional Information Networks (IRIN), 2007, 115.

19 Medina Haeri and Nadine Puechguirbal, 'From Helplessness to Agency: Examining the Plurality of Women's Experiences in Armed Conflict', *International Review of the Red Cross*, 92: 877, March 2010.

20 UN Security Council resolution 1966, 22 December 2010.

21 The speed with which the Security Council wanted to close the tribunals influenced the creation of the Mechanism. There were numerous delays in the completion deadlines set by the Security Council and so, in resolution 1966 – to put further pressure on the ICTR and the ICTY to finalise their work – it was decided the Mechanism would start its operations before the tribunals closed. As a result, the Arusha branch commenced functioning on 1 July 2012 and The Hague branch began its operations on 1 July 2013.

22 Roisin Mulgrew, 'Releasing International Prisoners', in Martine Herzog-Evans (ed.), *Offender Release and Supervision: The Role of Courts and the Use of Discretion*, Nijmegen: Wolf Legal Publishers, 2014, 21–51 (accessed from the University of Nottingham repository), eprints.nottingham.ac.uk/28959/4/Releasing%20International%20 Prisoners.pdf.

23 UN Security Council resolution 955, 8 November 1994.

24 'There shall only be pardon or commutation of sentence if the President of the International Tribunal for Rwanda, in consultation with the judges, so decides on the basis of the interests of justice and the general principles of law.'

25 See Mulgrew, 'Releasing International Prisoners', note 36, Rule 150 MICT RPE; para 7, MICT PDER.

26 Dr Roisin Mulgrew, assistant professor in law, Faculty of Social Sciences, Nottingham University.

27 Bisengimana, President's Decision, Public Redacted version, MICT-12-07, 11.12.12.

28 New Zealand from New York to Wellington, 'Security Council: The establishment of a criminal tribunal for Rwanda', 26 October 1994, Ministry of Foreign Affairs, Official Diplomatic Reporting, Volume 5, documents presented to Rwandan government, April 2019.

29 Chris McGreal, 'Rwanda appalled at chance of early release for genocide criminal', *Guardian*, 6 June 2018.

30 Jina Moore, 'Betraying justice for Rwanda's genocide survivors', *Nation*, 9 July 2018.

31 'Judge who freed 10 genocide convicts seeks new UN contract', *KT Press*, 29 January 2018.
32 UN Finance Committee figures.
33 The ten released were: Ferdinand Nahimana, Emmanuel Rukundo, Alphonse Nteziryayo, Gerard Ntakirutimana, Innocent Sagahutu, Paul Bisengimana, Omar Serushago, Tharcisse Muvunyi, Juvénal Rugambarara, Michel Bagaragaza.
34 UN Security Council, 8278 meeting, 6 June 2018, S/PV./8278.
35 The non-permanent Security Council members were Germany, Indonesia, South Africa, Domincan Republic, Belgium, Côte d'Ivoire, Equatorial Guinea, Kuwait, Peru and Poland.
36 UN Security Council, 8278 meeting, 6 June 2018, S/PV./8278.

Index